# ROCK STARS

DO THE DUMBEST THINGS™

# ROCK STARS

## DO THE DUMBEST THINGS™

**Margaret Moser** and **Bill Crawford**

RENAISSANCE BOOKS
*Los Angeles*

Dedicated to the
managers,
maids,
waiters,
janitors,
roadies,
lovers,
and all the others
who clean up
the stars' messes.

Library of Congress Cataloging-in-Publication Data

Moser, Margaret.
    Rock stars do the dumbest things / Margaret Moser & Bill Crawford.
       p.    cm.
    Includes index.
    ISBN 1-58063-023-5 (alk. paper)
    1. Rock musicians—Biography.  2. Rock music—Miscellanea.
I. Crawford, Bill, 1955– .  II. Title.
ML394.M.69  1998
781.66'092'2—dc21
  [B]                                   98-17774
                                             CIP
                                           MN

10 9 8 7 6 5 4

*Design by Lee Fukui*

Manufactured in the United States of America

Distributed by St. Martin's Press

First Edition

# CONTENTS

# ACKNOWLEDGMENTS

**Thanks to Team Dumb:** Michael Bertin, Christopher Gray, Ken Lieck, and Andy Langer. Special thanks to Andy McCord, John Taliaferro, Todd Wolfson, Howard Mandelbaum at Photofest, and Michael Shulman at Archive Photos/Film. And we couldn't have done it without our agent Jim Hornfisher and our editor James Robert Parish.

Bill Crawford would like to thank Diana, Amelia, Joe, Rebecca, Rob, and Rich for putting up with so much dumb stuff.

Margaret Moser would like to thank Louis Black, Nick Barbaro, and the *Austin Chronicle* staff for all their indulgences; E. A. Srere for moral support; all my WBS and AOL net-friends for their endless enthusiasm. Thanks most of all to Mom and Fred, my brothers Scott, Stephen, and Bill; and all the Moser clan for bearing with me through my dumbest acts.

# INTRODUCTION

**The secret is out:** Rock stars do the dumbest things. Okay, maybe it's no big secret. But it's still hard to believe that the rulers of rock have done such dumb stuff. Elton John's wooden pants. Aerosmith's cocaine makeup. Van Halen's "no brown M&M's" clause. Michael Jackson's sharply dressed chimp. Elvis Presley's drunk chimp. Led Zeppelin's taste for seafood-loving groupies. John Lennon and his Kotex toupee.

Wanton acts of wretched excess. Big time goof-ups. Radical bloopers. Mega-errors in judgment. *Webster's* dictionary defines *dumb* as "markedly lacking in intelligence." And there are few people on earth who have done more conspicuously unintelligent things than rock stars.

Why is it that rock stars are so prone to acts of public stupidity? Maybe it's the money. Maybe it's the drugs. Or maybe it's because there is no difference between fame and infamy in the world of rock. The bottom line is, dumb stunts make good publicity.

"Never underestimate the value of bad press," said Paul Westerberg of the Replacements. "In the end it's about the same as good press because it makes people talk about you."

*Rock Stars Do the Dumbest Things* is the world's first compendium of the dumbest things in rock. To find this information we sifted through hundreds of rock bios, rock zines, and online rock sites. Believe it or not, all the material in this book has appeared in other published sources—usually more than one. Our "job" has been merely to select and edit the dumbest of the dumb for your reading pleasure.

We are proud to have created one of the "dumbest" products in the history of publishing—the Spinal Tap of rock books. Crack open *Rock Stars Do the Dumbest Things!* Smell the print! Get to know what dumb really is! And, please, pass the secret along.

By the way, if you need to use any page of this book as toilet paper, go right ahead.

## KEY TO ENTRIES

We have included two different types of entries: one for musicians and one for rock bands. The entries are listed in alphabetical order according to the last name of a performer, or the first word of a band name. If you are looking for a particular name, check the index.

ix

**The entries for individuals include the following sections:**

## DUMBEST QUOTE

Lists the dumbest quote or quotes spoken by the rock star.

## FACTS OF LIFE (and Death)

**ORIGIN:** Gives the full name, place of birth, date of birth, and (where appropriate) the date, place, and cause of death of the rock star.

**FORMATIVE YEARS:** Describes formal and/or informal educational experiences which contributed to the development of the rock star.

**FAMILY PLANNING:** Lists spouses, dates of marriages and divorces, and, occasionally, other related factoids.

**ROMANTIC INTERESTS:** Lists girlfriends and/or boyfriends and/or quotations and/or other sexy stuff.

## SELECTED HITS (and Misses)

Lists selected products of the rock star including **SONGS** (with the year they became hits), **FILMS** (with their year of release), **TV SHOWS** (with the years of broadcast), and **STAGE PRODUCTIONS** (with the year of production). Occasionally, **ALBUMS** (with their year of release) are also listed. WARNING: THIS SECTION IS INTENDED TO PROVIDE A QUICK SNAPSHOT OF THE ROCK STAR'S CREATIVE OUTPUT. READERS WHO USE THIS LIST AS A COMPREHENSIVE DISCOGRAPHY, FILMOGRAPHY, OR ANY OTHER TYPE OF "OGRAPHY" DO SO AT THEIR OWN RISK.

## QUICKIE BIO

A brief biography of the rock star.

## _____ DOES THE DUMBEST THINGS

Lists the dumbest incidents in the career of the rock star. If an item is marked with an icon, i.e. 🎸 , the item is also included in one of the Dumbest Hits lists. Check out the Dumbest Hits lists at the back of the book to see how individual incidents rate with the dumbest things of all time.

**The entries for bands include the following sections:**

## DUMBEST QUOTE

Includes the dumbest quote (or quotes) uttered by a member (or members) of the band.

## FACTS OF LIFE (and Death)

**RINGLEADERS:** Lists members of the band who did the most dumb things. The list gives the full name, the place of birth, the date of birth, and (where applicable) the place, date, and cause of death of the band ringleaders. WARNING: THIS IS NOT A COMPLETE LIST OF ALL THE MUSICIANS WHO EVER PLAYED WITH THE BAND. IT ONLY LISTS THE MUSICIANS WHO PLAYED WITH THE BAND AND DID A BUNCH OF REALLY DUMB THINGS.

## SELECTED HITS (and Misses)

Lists selected products of the band including **SONGS** (with the year they became hits), **FILMS** (with their year of release), **TV SHOWS** (with the years of broadcast), and **STAGE PRODUCTIONS** (with the year of production). Occasionally, **ALBUMS** (with their year of release) are also listed. WARNING: THIS LIST IS INTENDED TO PROVIDE A QUICK SNAPSHOT OF THE BAND'S CREATIVE OUTPUT. THIS LIST IS NOT INTENDED TO BE A COMPREHENSIVE DISCOGRAPHY OR FILMOGRAPHY.

## QUICKIE BIO

A brief sketch of the band's history.

## ———— DOES THE DUMBEST THINGS

Lists the dumbest incidents in the career of the band. If an item is marked with an icon, i.e. 💰, the item is also included in one of the Dumbest Hits lists. Check out the Dumbest Hits lists at the back of the book to see how individual incidents rate with the dumbest things of all time.

Team Dumb has worked hard to provide the most accurate, up-to-date, and dumbest information available. All the quotes, dates, and anecdotes included in this book have appeared in other publications, or have been recounted by firsthand observers. If you want more details, check out the bibliography. If you notice any errors, please notify us immediately. E-mail your corrections to *screwups@dumbest.com.* Your efforts will be rewarded in heaven (or hell).

—Margaret Moser and Bill Crawford

PS. If we've overlooked some dumb stuff (and we know we have) let us know about it. Contact us on the Internet at *rockstars@dumbest.com.* Be sure you've got printed, taped, or eyewitness proof of your item.

# AC/DC

## FACTS OF LIFE (and Death)

**RINGLEADERS:** Angus Young (guitar)—born March 31, 1955, Glasgow, Scotland; Malcolm Young (guitar)—born January 6, 1963, Glasgow, Scotland; Bon Scott (vocals)—born Ronald Belford Scott, July 9, 1946, Angus, Scotland, died February 20, 1980; the coroner's report declared that Scott had "drunk himself to death"; Brian Johnson (vocals)—born October 5, 1947, Newcastle, England.

## SELECTED HITS (and Misses)

**SONGS:** "Big Balls" (1976), "Whole Lotta Rosie" (1977), "For Those About to Rock (We Salute You)" (1981), "Mistress for Christmas" (1990), "Got You By the Balls" (1990), "Moneytalks" (1981).

## QUICKIE BIO

When the Australian brothers Malcolm and Angus Young saw their brother George playing in his own rock band, they decided that they could do a lot better. So in 1973, the two teamed up to create AC/DC. Original vocalist David Evans was soon replaced by wildman Bon Scott, who drank himself to death in 1980 and was replaced by Brian Johnson. Though the band changed singers, AC/DC never changed its look or its music.

## AC/DC DOES THE DUMBEST THINGS

✪ Before putting together AC/DC, Malcolm Young played with the Velvet Underground. No, not *the* Velvet Underground. Young's bandmates were Australians who simply stole the name.

"Big Balls" was a hit song for AC/DC. Lucky for band member Brian Johnson (below), Angus Young (above) didn't have huge ones. [photo courtesy of Photofest]

★ When he first started performing, Angus Young wasn't sure what to wear onstage. First he tried a gorilla suit. Then he tried a Zorro outfit. His sister suggested that he wear an Australian schoolboy's outfit. It suited Angus perfectly.

★ The Young brothers claimed that when they named their band AC/DC, they didn't realize that the electrical term was also slang for bisexual. The ambiguous name worked in their favor, as the band was hired to play many gay-themed gigs when they were just starting out.

★ Despite its ambiguous name, AC/DC developed into a hard-core heterosexual act. Boob-loving fans were excited to learn that Malcolm worked as a sewing-machine maintenance mechanic in a bra factory.

★ After AC/DC hit the big time, a voluptuous (42-39-56) strong-armed singer brought Scott back to her place and mated with him. Allegedly,

Scott was her twenty-ninth sexual conquest that month. The band dedicated a song to the well-endowed temptress—"Whole Lotta Rosie."

★ After a show in San Antonio, Texas, an intoxicated Scott proved what kind of a man he was by drinking a whole bottle of "liquor" in one gulp. Unfortunately, the bottle he downed was a bottle of aftershave.

★ Angus Young liked to get physical onstage. "I've jumped off amps and fallen ass over tit," confessed Young. "Made a complete fool of myself." When he broke his fingers, he put splints on them and used them to play slide guitar.

★ American soldiers found a use for AC/DC music. During the 1989 invasion of Panama, U.S. troops blasted out "Highway to Hell" at top volume in order to drive strongman Manuel Noriega out of the Vatican Embassy. When Johnson heard that AC/DC music was being used for psychological torture, the singer shrugged, "I guess now we won't get to play for the Pope."

★ When one journalist complained that AC/DC had made ten records that all sounded the same, Angus was insulted. "He's a liar," fumed Young. "We've made eleven albums that all sound the same."

# AEROSMITH

## FACTS OF LIFE

**RINGLEADERS:** Steven Tyler (singer)—born Steven Tallarico, March 26, 1948, New York City, New York; Joe Perry (guitar)—born September 10, 1950, Lawrence, Massachusetts; Joey Kramer (drums)—born June 21, 1950, New York City, New York.

## SELECTED HITS (and Misses)

**SONGS:** "Dream On" (1973), "Sweet Emotion" (1975), "Walk This Way" (1975), "Big Ten Inch" (1975), "Lord of the Thighs" (1978), "Dude (Looks Like a Lady)" (1987), "Janie's Got a Gun" (1989), "Cryin'" (1993), "Pink" (1997).

**FILM:** *Sgt. Pepper's Lonely Hearts Club Band* (1978).

## QUICKIE BIO

You name it, Aerosmith ingested it. Band frontmen Joe Perry and Steven Tyler were dubbed the "Toxic Twins" for their love of excessive chemical intake. Formed in 1970 when they were kids from the Boston area with more ambition than talent, Aerosmith toured relentlessly until the fledgling band became one of the biggest rock acts in America. Later, drugs tore the band apart. However, cash brought it back together. In 1991, a clean and sober Aerosmith signed a reported $30 million deal with Sony. The "Toxic Twins" will be well into their fifties by the time the contract runs out. Time for a remake: "Walk This Way—With a Cane."

# AEROSMITH DOES THE
# DUMBEST THINGS

⭐ At a 1975 gig in Memphis, local cops made a move to bust Steve Tyler after he said the f-word onstage. Aerosmith's road manager convinced the law enforcers to hold off on the bust until after the gig. One of the roadies tipped Tyler off. Tyler told the lighting guy to black out all the lights the instant the show ended. At the program's finale, Tyler jumped off the stage and stumbled through the pitch black auditorium. The vigilant cops nevertheless nailed the fugitive rock star in the lobby.

⭐ For its first tour of Britain, Aerosmith rented a forty-five-seat private plane at a cost of 18,000 British pounds per day. At the time, the band was bringing in only about 2–3,000 pounds per show.

Aerosmith suffered further culture shock on opening night of its first Japanese tour. The band went berserk and completely destroyed the backstage area. Why? Because the Japanese promoter had placed turkey roll on the buffet table. "I explicitly said, 'No turkey roll,'" explained Tyler. What a turkey!

⭐ Tyler soon got so interested in drugs that he lost interest in turkey— and women. "I started getting so screwed up that getting f***ed-up was more important than getting f***ed," sighed Tyler. "Part of me is still bummed out that I didn't have all of the sex I could have had in the seventies."

⭐ In 1977, the band rented a convent in upstate New York and turned it into a recording studio. The chemically inclined Tyler enjoyed locking himself in the convent tower and shooting at the animals frisking on the sacred grounds below. At one point, Tyler passed out while leaning on his loaded gun.

⭐ The band liked to bring a chainsaw with them on tour so that they could chop up hotel rooms with greater efficiency. The musical group also traveled with extra-long extension cords. Why? So that the TVs they threw out of their hotel rooms would keep playing all the way down to the ground...or the pool.

⭐ At a stadium show in Toronto in the late 1970s the band members boarded limousines to travel the hundred yards from their dressing rooms to the stage. Talk about conserving energy!

⭐ Joe Perry believed in spending quality time with his wife. Before the band's first gig at New York's Madison Square Garden, Perry and the little woman acquired a stash of cocaine and partied until they passed out. At six P.M. the day of the show Perry was still in Boston, still passed out. His mother-in-law went to their house to see what was going on. When she found the inert couple, she started crying because she thought they were both dead.

Perry's wife, in fact, liked cocaine so much that she wore it as an eyeliner.

"I'll tell you what's fun," said a completely loaded Steve Tyler to a completely lucky reporter, "finding the right stewardess and turning her upside down in the back of the plane. Ever done it? You come so fast, it's the greatest."

⭐ After its "reunion" dinner—the first time the band had eaten together in five years, the group was hanging out at a friend's house. Someone put on "You See Me Crying" from their 1975 album *Toys in the Attic.* "Hey! That's great!" shouted Steve Tyler "We should cover this. Who is it?" "It's us, f***head," Perry replied. "Who the f*** do you think it is? It's that song you made us get a 109-piece orchestra for."

⭐ After partying for more than twenty years and being clean and sober for eleven months, Perry was asked, "How do you feel?" The toxic twin replied, "A little hungover."

# G.G. Allin

## FACTS OF LIFE (and Death)

**ORIGIN:** Born Jesus Christ Allin, August 29, 1956, New Hampshire, died June 28, 1993 in New York City of a heroin and cocaine overdose.

**FAMILY PLANNING:** Married his high school sweetheart but was soon living with a thirteen-year-old because, according to his brother, "G.G. liked 'em young."

**ROMANTIC INTERESTS:** "Sex is better with someone you hate, but I still prefer jerking off over any of it."

## SELECTED HITS (and Misses)

**SONGS:** "Suck My Ass It Smells" (1993).

**ALBUMS:** *Eat My F\*\*\** (1983), *You Give Love a Bad Name* (1987), *Brutality and Bloodshed for All* (1993).

**FILM:** *Hatred in the Nation* (1987).

## QUICKIE BIO

The self-proclaimed "most violent man in rock and roll," G.G. Allin was so vile that he makes Marilyn Manson look like a Sunday-school teacher. Allin was arrested more than four dozen times for everything from attempted murder to indecent exposure, and bragged of having warrants issued for him in more than seven states. During his short life, the New York City-based entertainer excreted onstage, rolled in it, ate it, and hurled it at the crowd. (He also engaged in every other offensive behavior his demented mind could imagine.) Allin boasted that for his final performance he was going to kill himself and take others with him. Instead, he died alone in his apartment. He wasn't found until the rigor mortis was so bad that his brother Merle "couldn't get his rings off."

## G.G. ALLIN DOES
## THE DUMBEST THINGS

⭐ The Allins were religious fanatics who raised their two sons in a log cabin without electricity, running water, or flush toilets. G.G. was named Jesus Christ Allin by his father; his mother changed it to Kevin Michael when he began school.

⭐ Allin was not as antisocial as he sounded. In fact, Allin tried to be penpals—with John F. Hinckley! Allin's attempt to buddy-up with the would-be presidential assassin aroused federal law enforcement interest. Hinckley did not respond, so Allin struck up correspondence with yet another infamous individual—serial killer John Wayne Gacy.

⭐ Before a gig at a New York City club, Allin entered the women's restroom and asked for a volunteer to urinate in his mouth. One recruit declined but gave him a sanitary product she had removed from herself. Said Allin, "I just ate it right in front of her, just swallowed the thing." Such incidents seem almost ordinary from the one who recalls, "One time someone threw a dead cat up onstage and I tried to [have sex with] it."

⭐ Allin was charged with felony assault in Ann Arbor, Michigan, when he slashed and burned a woman with cigarettes during a rather bizarre three-day stay at her place (at her invitation). He served eighteen months in prison but continued to give interviews by phone.

⭐ For what proved to be his last performance in June 1993, Allin sang a couple of songs, beat up some people, beat up himself, then stripped and walked out into the street followed by a group of fans. The charismatic leader climbed onto a bus, caused a riot, then explained to his "followers" that he was not the messiah, and to leave him alone. He overdosed a few hours later.

⭐ Allin was buried in a leather jacket and a jockstrap upon which was written the epitaph Eat Me.

🕯 At the open-coffin funeral, a microphone was placed in Allin's hand as well as a bottle of Jim Beam bourbon. His friends periodically removed the bottle and swigged from it, while putting pills into the corpse's mouth. Others pulled down the jockstrap, took pictures, waved around the body's arms, and drew on Allin's corpse with a felt-tipped pen.

# The Allman Brothers Band

## FACTS OF LIFE (and Death)

**RINGLEADERS:** Howard Duane Allman (guitar)—born November 20, 1946, Nashville, Tennessee, died October 29, 1971, after a motorcycle wreck in Macon, Georgia; Gregg Lenoir Allman (singer, keyboards)—born December 8, 1947, Nashville, Tennessee; Berry Oakley (bass)—born April 4, 1948, Chicago, Illinois, died November 11, 1972, after a motorcycle wreck in Macon, Georgia—three blocks from the site of Duane Allman's fatal wreck; Dickey Betts (guitar)—born December 12, 1943, West Palm Beach, Florida.

## SELECTED HITS (and Misses)

**SONGS:** "Statesboro Blues" (1971), "In Memory of Elizabeth Reed" (1971), "Whipping Post" (1971), "Melissa" (1972), "Ramblin' Man" (1973), "Straight from the Heart" (1981), "I'm No Angel" (Gregg Allman solo—1987).

**FILMS:** *Rush* (Gregg Allman—1991).

## QUICKIE BIO

Brothers Duane and Gregg Allman began playing together in the Allman Joys before forming the Allman Brothers Band in 1969 and moving to Macon, Georgia. The boys wallowed in blues, booze, drugs, babes, and busts. In other words—southern rock. Southern rock turned into southern wreck when Duane and drummer Berry Oakley died in separate motorcycle accidents in the early 1970s. The band was never the same. Especially after brother Gregg went gaga for Cher. Said Greg about his time with Cher, "I'm sure there have been stranger relationships." Oh, yeah?

## THE ALLMAN BROTHERS
## DO THE DUMBEST THINGS

★ To get little brother Gregg out of the draft, Duane threw a "foot-shootin' party." Gregg put on a moccasin, marked it with a bull's-eye, called an ambulance, and bang! A doctor, who noticed the bull's-eye, put a Band-Aid on the hole in Allman's foot and sent the draft dodger home.

★ Guitarist Dickey Betts emblazoned the back of his leather motorcycle jacket with the words "Eat S***." Observed a friend, "Dickey had to work on his attitude."

★ Betts got hungry one day, riding around on his motorcycle. He stopped along the road, jumped into a field, killed a cow, and started to butcher it. A passing cop walked up to the bloody Betts and arrested him.

★ A club owner in Buffalo, New York, was a little too crabby for the band's taste. When the band showed up fifteen minutes late for a gig, the club owner refused to pay them. Roadie Twiggs Lyndon didn't think that was nice. So he stabbed the man three times with a fishing knife. The club owner died. Lyndon was arrested for first-degree murder. And the drug-addled band went back on the road.

🚬 At Lyndon's murder trial, defense attorneys set out to prove that Lyndon had been temporarily insane when he did the stabbing. Lyndon's lawyers argued that touring with the Allman Brothers would drive anyone insane. To prove this, the lawyer called Oakley to the stand. During his testimony, the incoherent Oakley ran from the courtroom to the bathroom several times to throw up. "Did you take any dope last month?" the attorneys asked Oakley. "Uh-huh." "In the last week?" "Oh, yeah." "What about the last hour?" "You bet." Lyndon was found not guilty.

★ The Allman Brothers liked to party at home as well as on the road. One night, Betts trashed the Capricorn Records offices in Macon. Then he went to a downtown club, had a few drinks, and punched out one of his buddies. When another friend asked what was going on, Betts answered, "Just havin' a little fun."

✪ The Allman Brothers didn't have fun with photographers. When one tried to take a photo for the cover of their 1971 album *The Allman Brothers Band at Fillmore East*, the band members just glared. Then Duane ran over to meet a friend. He scored a bag of coke and came scooting back to pose. The band cracked up, and the photographer clicked away. In-the-know fans enjoyed pointing out Duane hiding dope in his hands on the album cover.

✿ One parachuting fan decided to make a big impression on the crowd of 600,000 who gathered to hear the Allman Brothers play at Watkins Glenn, New York, in 1973. The fan lit a stick of dynamite, jumped out of a plane, and threw the explosive. However, the fan forgot that dynamite and parachutists fall to earth at the same rate of speed. The dynamite exploded just as he pulled his ripcord, and blew him away.

✪ Gregg took his motorcycle into a Macon, Georgia, shop to get it fixed. When Gregg got there, he saw his mechanic, John Charles "Scooter" Herring, reeling around the room in a drug-induced daze. Gregg was concerned and asked the repairman what he had taken. Scooter said Demerol. "Hey man," said Gregg, "can you get me any?"

✪ Scooter got Gregg some Demerol—and a whole bunch of other stuff. Scooter even started working as Gregg's "dope holder and procurer and general valet." When the law came down on Gregg in 1975, Scooter was sure his boss would treat him right. Wrong! Gregg, the boss man, fingered Scooter, the bag man. Gregg got off the hook, while Scooter served time in jail.

✿ Gregg married Cher just a few months after testifying against Scooter. Cher broke up with the Allman brother after Gregg passed out face first into a plate of spaghetti at an Italian restaurant.

# The Beach Boys

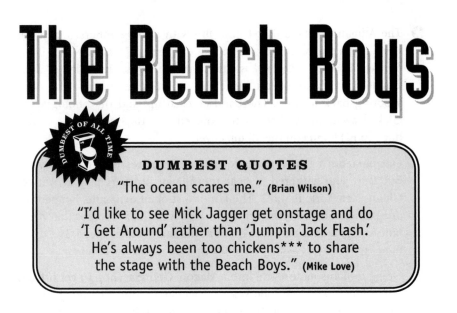

**DUMBEST QUOTES**

"The ocean scares me." (Brian Wilson)

"I'd like to see Mick Jagger get onstage and do 'I Get Around' rather than 'Jumpin Jack Flash.' He's always been too chickens*** to share the stage with the Beach Boys." (Mike Love)

## FACTS OF LIFE (and Death)

**RINGLEADERS:** Brian Wilson (bass, keyboards, vocals)—born June 20, 1942, Inglewood, California; Dennis Wilson (drums, vocals)—born December 4, 1944, Inglewood, California, died December 28, 1983 (drowned); Carl Wilson (guitar, vocal)—born December 21, 1946, Hawthorne, California, died February 7, 1998 in Los Angeles, California (cancer); Mike Love (vocals)—born March 15, 1941, Baldwin Hills, California; Al Jardine (guitar, vocals)—born September 3, 1942, Lima, Ohio.

## SELECTED HITS (and Misses)

**SONGS:** "Surfin' USA" (1963), "I Get Around" (1964), "Fun, Fun, Fun" (1964), "Good Vibrations" (1966), "Sail On Sailor" (1973), "Kokomo" (1989).

**FILM:** *Two-Lane Blacktop* (Dennis Wilson—1971).

**TV:** *The Beach Boys: It's OK* (special—1976), *Summer Dreams: The Story of the Beach Boys* (telefeature—1990).

## QUICKIE BIO

Managed by their father Murray Wilson, brothers Brian, Dennis, and Carl hooked up with cousin Mike Love and friend Al Jardine to form the Beach Boys. The nonsurfing band had their first breakthrough in 1961 with the single "Surfin.'" After a series of huge hits, the Southern California boys began to flake out. Brian suffered a nervous breakdown and retired

12

from touring in 1964. As their popularity waned, the band hit the Fourth of July nostalgia circuit. In 1989, the Beach Boys scored a number one hit with "Kokomo." It had been twenty-four years since their last top-of-the-chart hit—the longest such span in rock history. In the 1990s, the Beach Boys spent much of their time suing one another and their relatives. Brian took time out to boost the recording careers of his daughters Carnie and Wendy, while Carl and Mike Love opened rock-and-roll restaurants.

## THE BEACH BOYS
## DO THE DUMBEST THINGS

★ The first time the Beach Boys heard one of their songs played on the radio, guitarist Carl got so excited that he threw up.

★ During the band's first professional tour in 1962, Dennis painted his penis green, hung it out of his pants zipper, and walked down to the hotel lobby to get a Coke.

★ After playing on the first five Beach Boys albums, guitarist David Marks left the group in 1964. "I thought my new group [Dave and the Marks-men] would take right off," sighed the guitarist three decades later. Sorry, Dave.

★ After the 1966 album *Pet Sounds*, the chemically enhanced Brian got the itch to do a little redecorating. He insisted that his den, where his piano was located, be turned into a giant sandbox so that he could feel the sand under his feet as he wrote music.

★ Brian had a few other redecorating ideas. He decided to have a hole punched in the den wall for ventilation. Every now and then he knocked on the wall and his wife blew marijuana smoke through the hole and into Brian's mouth.

★ The follow-up album to *Pet Sounds* was first called *Dumb Angel*, then *Smile*. To record the album, Brian and a collaborator bought $2,000 worth of black hash, toked up, set their microphones about a foot from the ground, and lay down on the floor. They ultimately decided to stand back up to keep from falling asleep.

★ During a recording session for the album *Smile*, Brian brought a flaming bucket into the studio and insisted that everyone wear a red toy fire helmet—including the violin players and the engineers. The song he was recording? "Mrs. O'Leary's Cow," otherwise referred to as "Fire." Brian later tried to burn the tapes, but they wouldn't ignite.

✪ On a flight to Los Angeles, a stewardess offered Brian a dinner menu. Brian decided he wanted all of the entrees on the menu. The flight attendant tried to explain that that was not how things worked. Brian pitched a fit. The flight attendant finally relented and presented the chubby rocker with the entire menu.

Brian spent the years from 1971 to 1975 in bed.

✪ Eight months after emerging from his bed, Brian was lured by a TV producer to try surfing for the first time. The name of the resulting TV special? *The Beach Boys: It's OK.*

✪ The other Beach Boys were never really okay. Following the example of the Beatles, Love and the other band members became followers of transcendental meditation guru the Maharishi Mahesh Yogi. In May of 1968, the Beach Boys toured with the Maharishi. Each concert began with a lengthy, unintelligible lecture by the Hindu preacher. The tour was a financial disaster for the Beach Boys, but not for the holy man. "The Maharishi laughed," recalled the Beach Boys' road manager. "He laughed all the time. He got his money."

Dennis Wilson got interested in even more-suspicious gurus. During the summer of 1968, he hung out with Charles Manson and his "family." The charismatic Manson soaked the Beach Boy drummer for about $100,000. A year later, Manson and Family were involved in the brutal murders of actress Sharon Tate and others in Los Angeles. Dennis never testified at the high-profile Manson trial. "I don't talk about Manson," said the overfriendly Beach Boy. "I think he's a sick f***."

✪ Dennis was pretty sick himself. On July 28, 1983, at the age of thirty-eight, he wed Shawn Love. The doe-eyed teen was the illegitimate daughter of Dennis's first cousin and bandmate, Beach Boy Mike Love. Dennis, the band's only surfer, drowned a few months later.

# The Bee Gees

## FACTS OF LIFE

**RINGLEADERS:** Barry Gibb (vocals)—born September 1, 1946, Isle of Man, England; Robert and Maurice Gibb (vocals)—fraternal twins—born December 22, 1949, Isle of Man, England.

## SELECTED HITS (and Misses)

**SONGS:** "Battle of the Blue and Grey" (1963), "New York Mining Disaster 1941" (1967), "Massachusetts" (1967), "I've Gotta Get a Message to You" (1968), "Jive Talkin'" (1975), "Love So Right" (1976), "Stayin' Alive" (1977), "How Deep Is Your Love" (1977), "You Win Again" (1987), "One" (1989).

**FILMS:** *Saturday Night Fever* (soundtrack—1977), *Sgt. Pepper's Lonely Hearts Club Band* (1978).

**TV:** *Cucumber Castle* (1969).

## QUICKIE BIO

Born to British bandleader Hughie Gibb, the Bee Gees spent little time in school and a lot of time as a kiddie singing act on the Australian lounge circuit. The brothers hit it big after returning to England in the late 1960s, then dissolved into obscurity until the dawning of the disco era and the 1977 film musical *Saturday Night Fever*. The Bee Gees tried to match their feverish success in the 1980s. However, it took the 1990s disco revival to bring the Gibb brothers back into the limelight. In 1997, the Bee Gees announced the opening of *Saturday Night Live*, the musical, on the London stage. Zombie disco. It just won't die!

## THE BEE GEES DO THE
## DUMBEST THINGS

⭐ According to mother Barbara, "Robin was a firebug. He would light fires anywhere...." Robin set fire to golf courses and abandoned houses. Confessed the eldest Bee Gee, "I was a little swine actually."

⭐ "We broke the law about as much as you can," said Barry Gibb. The local British police knew only too well about the delinquent Bee Gees. "Look," said a policeman to the Bee Gees' father, "if you wanna avoid your kids going to reform school, emigrate to Australia." The family moved to Australia in 1958.

💰 The Bee Gees got so desperate to sell records, they actually gave members of their fan club the money to go out and buy them. Luckily, there were only six members.

⭐ The Bee Gees returned to England and auditioned for record executive Robert Stigwood in 1967. As the trio sang through a set that included "Puff the Magic Dragon," Stigwood walked out. Nevertheless, he later signed the band.

⭐ After the Bee Gees signed with Stigwood, they told their manager that they wanted to change the name of the band to Rupert's World. Stigwood gave the boys a strange look. The boys didn't understand why. As Gibb recalled, "It was like changing your name from Charlie S*** to Fred S***."

⭐ For their appearance on *The Simon Dee Show* in England in 1967, the Bee Gees donned cowboy hats and fur coats. They hoped to start a fashion trend. "Instead," recalled the brothers, "we were knocked for looking like baboons."

⭐ In 1967, the Bee Gees released a record to protest all the too-groovy hippie stuff going on in San Francisco. The name of the song—"Massachusetts."

⭐ In the late 1960s, riding his first wave of success, Maurice indulged in booze and cars. He especially enjoyed driving Rolls-Royces. One problem: he was so short, he had to sit on a phone book to see over the hood.

⭐ Barry got into girls. His standard pick-up line was that he had fallen in love and wanted to marry. He walked around with a pocket full of engagement rings to prove his passion. The technique got him into trouble. Especially when five or six of his fiancées gathered at the stage door.

⭐ Barry later appeared with the rest of the Bee Gees on a Howard Stern TV special and performed a song about losing one's penis. The song was dedicated to John Wayne Bobbitt, who was in the studio audience.

⭐ In 1986, Barry tried to go it alone with a concept album titled *We Are the Bunburys.* The album was about a family of cricket-playing rabbits.

"I was the piss artist, Barry was the pothead, and Robin was the pillhead," explained Maurice Gibb of the Bee Gees. [photo courtesy of Photofest]

# Chuck Berry

## FACTS OF LIFE

**ORIGIN:** Born Charles Edward Anderson Berry, October 18, 1926, St. Louis, Missouri (according to Chuck) or San Jose, California (according to others).

**FORMATIVE YEARS:** Degree from the Poro School of Beauty Culture.

**FAMILY PLANNING:** Married Themetta "Toddy" Suggs (beautician), October 28, 1948.

**ROMANTIC INTERESTS:** "I have always been subject to the sight of the female anatomy reaching my retina and taxing my tolerance."

## SELECTED HITS (and Misses)

**SONGS:** "Maybellene" (1955), "Roll Over Beethoven" (1956), "Sweet Little Sixteen" (1958), "Johnny B. Goode"(1958), "Run Rudolph Run" (1964), "My Ding-a-Ling" (1972).

**FILMS:** *Rock, Rock, Rock* (1956), *Mr. Rock and Roll* (1957), *Go, Johnny, Go!* (1959), *Chuck Berry! Hail! Hail! Rock 'n' Roll* (1987).

## QUICKIE BIO

After serving time in reform school, Chuck Berry started playing at the Crank Club in St. Louis and has cranked out rock and roll ever since. His onstage duck walk is as legendary as the words to his songs, which helped define rock and roll. Abused by the music biz, Berry learned to abuse others, including the many woman with whom he chose to party. Musicians and fans stayed loyal to one of the true legends of rock and roll—even after they saw his oh-so-naughty home movies.

## CHUCK BERRY DOES THE DUMBEST THINGS

★ While he was in grade school, Berry went out with a girl who was studying to be a nurse. According to Berry, the girl tricked him into being circumcised.

★ As a boy, Berry enjoyed shinnying up the legs of swing sets. "I was bestowed with a stimulation in my loins that surprised but pleased me," Berry confessed.

👓 Berry opened a restaurant called the Southern Air in Missouri. According to a former waitress, Berry wired the lavatory with a video camera and recorded some 200 women on the toilet, including three minors. The state attorney general filed charges against Berry, claiming that the tapes were made "for the purpose of the entertainment and gratification of the abnormal…sexual fetishes and sexual predilections of defendant Chuck Berry." The charges were later dropped, while Berry agreed to a cash settlement for those who claimed exposure to his potty cam.

📺 Some of Berry's video experiments received wide public exposure. One famous underground release showed Berry relieving himself on a young woman. When the woman asked Berry to kiss her, the rock star refused saying, "You smell like piss."

★ During a 1975 TV appearance on *The Sammy Davis, Jr. Show,* Berry walked out in front of the camera and picked up the diminutive Rat Packer. "Put me down!" Davis yelled. "Are you funny or something?" After releasing Davis, Berry took a seat next to Lucille Ball. He grabbed her hand and held on to it throughout the broadcast. Later, he asked forgiveness from Lucy's husband Desi Arnaz. Confessed Berry, "I love Lucy as well."

★ Berry created his own version of Disneyland outside of St. Louis. The forty-two-acre Berry Park featured a guitar-shaped swimming pool and other attractions, including Berry's girlfriends Fran, Candy, and Rachel. The park's real theme became obvious when police raided the place in 1990 and confiscated marijuana, hash, and pornography.

Since 1957, Berry has always toured solo, demanding that promoters supply him with a backup band. Things were rocking at Hollywood's Palladium in 1972, until the lead guitarist swapped with another guy. The new guitarist played so loud that Berry stopped in the middle of the song and asked the first guy to come back out. Later, Berry's girlfriend told him that the guitarist he had kicked off the stage was "that Rolling Stones guy," also known as Keith Richards. "Since then," confessed Berry, "I have never invited anyone off the stage without asking who it is."

"You can smell my fart," said Chuck Berry to a girl on one of his XXX home videos. Notice that Chuck liked to keep a video camera handy, even when traveling overseas. [photo courtesy of Photofest]

 Nine years later, Berry ran into Keith Richards at a New York City nightspot. Berry didn't recognize the Rolling Stone and punched him. In 1983, Berry dropped a lit match down Richards' shirt at the Los Angeles International Airport. According to Richards, "Every time him and me got in contact, whether it's intentional or not, I end up wounded."

 To make his life simpler, Berry has always called everyone Jack.

Berry complained when his record company recorded a 1972 performance in London. Berry stopped complaining when a song from the performance went on to become the biggest-selling hit of his career. The song was about a subject close to Berry's heart—"My Ding-a-Ling."

# Björk

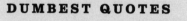

## FACTS OF LIFE

**ORIGIN:** Born Björk Gudmundsdottir, November 21, 1965, Reykjavik, Iceland.

**FORMATIVE YEARS:** Raised in an Icelandic hippie commune where her stepfather played in a band.

**FAMILY PLANNING:** "I'm actually married to myself." (Also married guitarist Thor Eldon Johnson in 1986; divorced in 1989.)

**ROMANTIC INTERESTS:** Björk describes herself as "outrageously greedy" when it comes to sex. To get rid of sexual frustration, she exercises and claims to masturbate every day. That is, when she's not busy with a boyfriend.

## SELECTED HITS (and Misses)

**SINGLES:** "Human Behavior" (1993), "Big Time Sensuality" (1994), "Violently Happy," (1994), "It's Oh So Quiet" (1995), "Joga" (1997), "All Neon Like" (1997).

## QUICKIE BIO

Who would have thought that frigid Iceland, of all places, would provide rock with one of its more colorful personalities? Ever since the Sugarcubes (formerly known as KUKL—Icelandic for "witch") appeared in the late 1980s with their quirky, cold, screechy pop-rock, their diminutive lead singer Björk has grabbed headlines. She became known internationally for her nuttiness as well as her vocal pipes. In the 1990s, Björk left her band and scaled the heights of art rock stardom. Known for eccentric interviews and temper tantrums, the "elfin chanteuse" confused many music industry honchos. But at least one fan thought Björk was to die for!

## BJÖRK DOES
## THE DUMBEST THINGS

✪ In 1986, Björk smashed the windows of a Reykjavik disco "because it was full of boring people."

✪ On the two-hundredth anniversary of the founding of Reykjavik, Björk and her fellow Sugarcubes broke into the government radio station and played songs they considered "realistic." Their realism earned them time in jail.

 When Björk was pregnant with her son Sindri, she shaved her eyebrows, bared her belly, and sang punk-rock songs on Icelandic TV. "That combination was evidently too much for some of the viewers," Björk explained. "A woman got a heart attack while watching the program, and she sued me."

Many people believed songs like "Human Behavior" contained lyrics sung in Icelandic. They were gibberish. "People think it's Icelandic," said Björk, "but it's actually whatever noise it feels naturally to sing."

✪ During interviews with the press, Björk had the annoying habit of touching herself continually. According to one writer, "It's as if she's just been given her body for the first time and is unsure whether or not it fits."

✪ Unlike Madonna, Björk is a party—rather than a material—girl. "I'm not very into drugs," confessed the Icelandic warbler. "I like my drinking too much." And what does Björk like to chug? "Vodka by the bottle, that's the kind of culture I come from. We don't sip a drink we f***ing drink it."

✪ Like Madonna, Björk developed a distinctive fashion sense. Björk sported geometric hairdos, platform shoes, and fake fur jackets. The thrift-shop space-case got caught in a fashion pinch before a mid-1990s concert in England. She put together a dress an hour before her performance, cutting out a pattern and sticking it together with tape. No wonder the British TV series *Spitting Image* featured a character called "Björk the dork."

An exterminator from Hollywood, Florida didn't think Björk was a dork. The obsessed fan mailed a book booby-trapped with sulfuric acid to Björk's London home. He then videotaped his own suicide while playing the Björk song "I Miss You."

# David Bowie

## FACTS OF LIFE

ORIGIN: Born David Robert Jones, January 8, 1947, London, England.

FORMATIVE YEARS: Dropped out of high school.

FAMILY PLANNING: Married Mary Angela (Angie) Barnett, March 19, 1970; divorced February 8, 1980; Married Iman Abdul Majid (model and actress), April 24, 1992.

ROMANTIC INTERESTS: "Sex suddenly became all-important to me," admitted Bowie. "It didn't really matter who or what it was with." Bowie's sexual fixations included: Lindsay Kemp (the male leader of a mime troop), Natasha Kornilof (the female set designer for the same mime troop), Hermione Farthingale (actress), Nita Bowes (who slept in the same bed with David and his wife Angie), Cherry Vanilla (one of the Andy Warhol crowd), Jayne (Wayne) County (rock star), Bebe Buell (mother of Liv Tyler), and Marianne Faithfull (singer, lover of Mick Jagger).

## SELECTED HITS (and Misses)

SONGS: "The Laughing Gnome" (1967), "Space Oddity" (1969), "The Jean Genie" (1972), "All the Young Dudes" (1975), "The Little Drummer Boy" (duet with Bing Crosby—1982), "Let's Dance" (1983), "Hello Spaceboy" (1995).

FILMS: *Ziggy Stardust—The Motion Picture* (1973), *The Man Who Fell to Earth* (1976), *Just a Gigolo* (1978), *Merry Christmas, Mr. Lawrence* (1983), *The Hunger*

23

(1983), *Absolute Beginners* (1986), *Labyrinth* (1986), *The Last Temptation of Christ* (1988), *The Linguini Incident* (1991), *Basquiat—Build a Fort, Set It On Fire* (1996).

**TV**: *Pin-Ups, The 1980 Floor Show* (1973—never aired).

### QUICKIE BIO

David Bowie started his career in the early 1960s as an earnest folkie, but didn't score a major hit until the early 1970s when he blossomed into a full-blown transsexual weirdo. Over the decades, Bowie morphed from Ziggy Stardust to Aladdin Sane to the fascist Thin White Duke to a hard-rockin' straight guy. Through it all, he managed to keep his mind (and his bank book) intact. In 1997, Bowie was heralded as Britain's richest pop star, worth $919 million. Who says it doesn't pay to wear spandex?

### DAVID BOWIE DOES
### THE DUMBEST THINGS

⭐ David Jones was never really satisfied with his name. Especially after future Monkee Davy Jones hit it big on the London stage. Young Jones first called himself Lou, then Calvin. Finally, in 1966, he changed his name to Bowie, after a famous Texan who carried a long knife.

⭐ As a young up-and-comer on the London scene of the 1960s, Bowie enjoyed running around his apartment naked. A friend recalled Bowie's equipment "swaying from side to side like a pendulum of a grandfather clock."

⭐ In the 1960s, Bowie was into mime, poetry, art, Buddhist incantations, and folk music. Recalled one friend, "David was something of a twerp in those days."

⭐ Bowie loved to tell people that he and his wife met because they were "f***ing the same bloke." The story was true. The "same bloke" was record executive Calvin Mark Lee.

⭐ Bowie proposed to his first wife Angie with the words "Can you handle the fact that I don't love you?"

⭐ One morning, Angie went up to the bedroom and found her husband naked in bed with Mick Jagger. "Do you want some coffee?" she asked Bowie and his Rolling Stone.

⭐ After a successful New York City gig, David disappeared into a closet with Mick Jagger and Bette Midler. Partygoers were surprised to

"You don't know what you're missing. I'm a pop star! I have a big cock!" explained David Bowie. The photo suggests otherwise. [photo courtesy of Archive Photos]

hear giggles, grunts, and groans coming from the closet. The trio emerged an hour later—refreshed and invigorated.

★ Bowie liked to pick up guys from gay clubs and bring them home to Angie, while Angie like to pick up girls from lesbian clubs and bring them home to Bowie. "We had to lock our bedroom doors," recalled the neighbors, "because in the middle of the night these people would come looking for fresh blood."

✎ In September 1973, a groupie climbed into Bowie's apartment. She went over to Bowie, knelt down and asked if she could kiss his foot. Bowie stretched out a leg and said, "You can kiss my boot." Angie called the police.

★ Bowie's favorite pick-up line was "The eyes are my soul and the face is my conscience." Observed one friend, "Anything to get a hand job."

🛏 Bowie eventually became blasé about copulation. "I would sit in a chair sometimes and talk to him while he was having sex," recalled Marilyn Monroe look-alike Cyrinda Foxe. "I'd watch television and sit in a chair, because he wanted someone to talk to."

★ Bowie first declared himself a homosexual in 1972. Then in the 1980s, he denied it. Finally, Bowie admitted to what he really was—a trisexual. Explained Bowie, "I'll try anything once."

# Boy George

## FACTS OF LIFE

**ORIGIN:** Born George Alan O'Dowd, June 14, 1961, Eltham, England.

**FORMATIVE YEARS:** Expelled from high school in 1976.

**FAMILY PLANNING:** Has described himself as "absolutely queer."

**ROMANTIC INTERESTS:** Lenny ("snogged him at a party"); Jeremy ("snogged him briefly over the punch bowl"); Gary ("he just lay there while I did all the work"); Wilf ("at first we did nothing but shag"); Tranny ("he would have survived alone on the amount of protein he was taking in"). In summary, Boy George observed, "Sex? I'd rather have a cup of tea."

## SELECTED HITS (and Misses)

**SONGS:** "Do You Really Want to Hurt Me" (1982), "Church of the Poisoned Mind" (1983), "I'll Tumble 4 Ya" (1983), "Karma Chameleon" (1983), "The Crying Game" (1992).

**TV:** *Face the Nation* (1984), *The A-Team* (cartoon series—1986).

## QUICKIE BIO

A club-hopping London gay blade, Boy George first modeled hair styles before teaming up with drummer Jon Moss to form Culture Club in 1981. Culture Club rocked the charts from 1982 to 1985, inspiring black-hatted, big-shirted, heavily made-up Boy George impersonators worldwide. The band

(and Boy George) fell apart in 1986. George later created the More Protein music label, joined the Hare Krishnas, and formed the band Jesus Loves You. In 1995, he published a trashy, tell-all autobiography. The title? *Take It Like a Man.*

## BOY GEORGE DOES
## THE DUMBEST THINGS

✪ George's passion for fashion got him into trouble early on. He began to rip off stores by sticking coat hangers into the letter box and pulling things like nylon shirts and plastic snakeskin belts out of the windows. The police eventually arrested him for shoplifting but dropped the charges when they discovered he was only fifteen.

✪ George enjoyed dressing up as Miss Boadicea. The costume included a silver lamé helmet with a mane of white plumage, a white toga, stiletto heels, and a Union Jack shield and trident. When Miss Boadicea appeared at the changing of the guard at Buckingham Palace, Japanese tourists eagerly clicked his picture.

🏁 George fought furiously with his Culture Club bandmate and lover Jon Moss. In 1983, the two began bickering on the tour bus. Jon pushed Boy. Boy kicked Jon and said, "Piss off, dwarf." Jon threw a punch at Boy, missed, hit the window, and broke his finger. The band told the press that Jon had fallen—and paid the bus driver 400 pounds to keep quiet.

✪ In 1984, George and the band were supposed to attend a function at a Hong Kong hotel. Jon said, "Come on, George, don't be such a slob." George again called Jon a dwarf and threw a Coca-Cola bottle at him. The bottle smacked Jon in the head and knocked him out cold. After a trip to the hospital, Jon and Boy made up and had "great sex."

🏺 Inspired by a trek to Egypt, George entered the stage for Culture Club's 1983 Christmas show through the head of a giant sphinx. On the first night, the sphinx wouldn't open. Boy George stood behind the head screaming and swearing. The stage crew pulled the head open and George appeared, skipping and smiling.

✪ George liked to hang out with socialite Cornelia Guest at New York's Palladium club in the 1980s. As they left the hot spot one evening, Boy picked up Cornelia and turned her upside down. The gathered paparazzi was astounded. Cornelia wasn't wearing any underwear. George teased, "Leave it to beaver. Leave it to beaver."

✪ George once admitted that he wanted to be "reincarnated as Matt Dillon's underwear."

⭐ George made a cameo appearance as a character in *The A-Team* action TV cartoon series. George earned $100,000 for saying immortal lines like, "Go for it, Hannibal," and "Totally awesome, Mr. T." The episode was called "Cowboy George."

⭐ At an anti-apartheid rally in 1986, drug-addled George appeared covered in flour and wearing a white jean jacket bearing the slogans "Heroin Free Zone" and "Suck My Nob." He left the stage yelling, "I'm a drag addict, not a drug addict," and promptly nodded off during a post-rally television interview.

⭐ "Madonna is a gay man trapped in a woman's body," George said. "Imagine having sex with George Michael," observed Boy, "it would be like having sex with a groundhog." George defended his critical comments of fellow singers by saying, "I am bitchy, but I'm not a bitch for the sake of being bitchy." So there!

# Bobby Brown

## FACTS OF LIFE

**ORIGIN:** Born Robert Baresford Brown, February 5, 1967, Boston, Massachusetts.

**FORMATIVE YEARS:** Dropped out of school to sing with a band.

**FAMILY PLANNING:** Married pop diva Whitney Houston, July 18, 1992.

**ROMANTIC INTERESTS:** Fathered three children by two different women before wedding Houston. Gentleman Bobby reportedly preferred blonds. He once bragged that he "had Madonna in the back of a limo."

## SELECTED HITS (and Misses)

**SONGS:** "Candy Girl" (with New Edition—1983), "Cool It Now" (with New Edition—1984), "Rock Wit' Cha" (1988), "My Prerogative" (1988), "Humpin' Around" (1992), "Hit Me Off" (1996), "Home Again" (with New Edition—1996).

## QUICKIE BIO

Bobby Brown shot to stardom as an original member of the New Edition, the wildly successful group modeled after the Jackson Five by industry kingmaker Maurice Starr. The New Edition brought contemporary soul back onto the charts with their pumpin' harmonies and show-stopping dance routines. After leaving the group in 1986, Brown embarked on an equally successful solo career. His home life wasn't quite so successful. Brown became as well known for his fights with his wife—the chart-topping singer Whitney Houston—as for his hits. "Nobody thought we'd get this far," said Brown. "but we did because our love is real." Surreal may be more like it.

# BOBBY BROWN DOES
# THE DUMBEST THINGS

⭐ After leaving New Edition, Brown proved that he could make records (and get into trouble) all on his own. During a concert in Columbus, Georgia, Brown invited a female fan to join him onstage. The two performed a dance that was so lewd it was deemed illegal. Brown was slapped with a $652 fine for "a sexually explicit performance harmful to minors."

⭐ In January 1990, Brown was awarded the Martin Luther King, Jr., Musical Achievement Award. Brown didn't care enough to attend the presentation ceremony. (Wife Whitney Houston also pulled a political boner when she showed up two hours late to a White House dinner honoring South African freedom fighter Nelson Mandela. When asked why she was so tardy, Whitney shrugged and said, "I just got off tour." She had—four days earlier.)

👓 In 1995, Brown was walking outside of a Disney World club in Orlando, Florida. A white man stared at him. The two argued. Brown claimed the white guy spit at him. Brown's bodyguard decked the offender, then Brown clobbered him with a bottle, nearly taking off his ear. The police arrived, arrested Brown, and threw him into a squad car. Brown peed on the seat, then carved a four letter word into the upholstery with a pen.

⭐ Whitney was no slouch herself when it came to finding trouble. In 1991, Whitney and her brother Michael got into a fight with three pushy autograph-seekers at a hotel bar in Kentucky. Guests at the hotel were shocked to see Whitney Houston throwing punches at her fans and screaming, "You're going to die, you stupid-a** bitch!

⭐ Whitney fought especially hard with her longtime friend and roommate Robyn Crawford. The two regularly flew into jealous rages. Said one observer, "I'm surprised those two haven't killed each other by now."

⭐ After singing the national anthem at the 1991 Super Bowl, Whitney started to flirt with rapper M.C. Hammer. Crawford got jealous and slapped Houston. Houston's mother (noted singer Cissy Houston) slugged Crawford in the face and screamed, "I'll kill you you stupid-a** bitch!"

⭐ Brown, Houston, and Crawford went shopping one time in New York City. Houston and Crawford tried on a bunch of men's clothes. Brown complained. Crawford got in his face. The two started punching at each other until Houston dragged Crawford away. According to Whitney, "Since I've been with him [Brown], I've gotten, you know, a little freer with my s***."

"I've got a good man. He takes care of me. I don't have to be scared of anything because I know he will kick every a\*\*," hissed Whitney Houston talking about her a\*\*-kicking husband, Bobby Brown. [photo courtesy of Darlene Hammond/ Archive Photos]

⭐ Brown went into rehab in 1995. He confessed that he abused Houston because she made him feel low "every time she went off with another woman." A few days after leaving rehab, Brown met with reporters at a Miami bar, ordered champagne, drank a couple of beers, and declared, "The bottle's out of my life for good." He later went back into rehab.

⭐ In 1996–1997, Brown set off on a reunion tour with his New Edition bandmates. Brown didn't show for several of the gigs. When he did appear, he treated his bandmates like backup singers, swore from the stage at opening act Keith Sweat, and then reportedly swapped punches with Sweat. When he showed up late for rehearsal, Brown pulled down his pants and shouted, "Kiss my a\*\*." Brown later declared that the reunion had been no fun. Now whose fault was that, Bobby?

⭐ Whitney had even less fun than Brown on that tour. While traveling by bus to Salt Lake City, Utah, Brown argued with Whitney, threw her off the bus, headed for the airport, and flew home alone to Los Angeles. "Ooooh he makes me so mad," said Houston about her frequent quarrels with Bobby. "He has a temper from hell, but I love him so."

⭐ In 1997, Brown and Houston partied together at a bar in Hawaii. Brown cursed patrons, dirty-danced with Houston on a pool table, and punched out a guy who brushed against Houston. The wild times started after Brown mixed a white powdery substance with his champagne. Some folks thought it was cocaine. Houston and Brown claimed it was whipped cream.

# James Brown

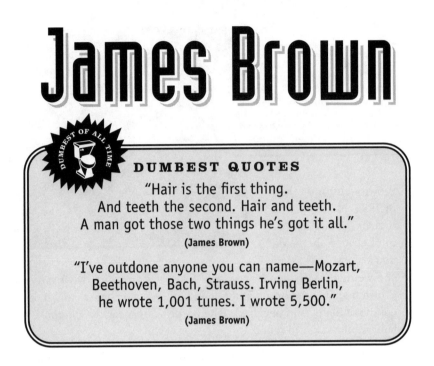

## DUMBEST QUOTES

"Hair is the first thing.
And teeth the second. Hair and teeth.
A man got those two things he's got it all."
**(James Brown)**

"I've outdone anyone you can name—Mozart,
Beethoven, Bach, Strauss. Irving Berlin,
he wrote 1,001 tunes. I wrote 5,500."
**(James Brown)**

## FACTS OF LIFE

**ORIGIN:** Born James Joe Brown, Jr., May 3, 1933 (or 1928), Barnwell, South Carolina.

**FORMATIVE YEARS:** Dropped out of seventh grade.

**FAMILY PLANNING:** Married Velma Warren, June 19, 1953; divorced; Married Deirdre, October 22, 1969; divorced; Married Adrienne "Alfie" Rodriguez, 1989; widowed January 6, 1996.

**ROMANTIC INTERESTS:** "I tended to go with whoever was my lead female singer on the show at the time."

## SELECTED HITS (and Misses)

**SONGS:** "Please, Please, Please" (1955), "Papa's Got a Brand New Bag" (1965), "I Got You (I Feel Good)" (1965), "Say It Loud—I'm Black and I'm Proud" (1968), "Get Up (I Feel Like Being a) Sex Machine" (1970), "Get on the Good Foot" (1972), "Living in America" (1985).

**FILMS:** *The Blues Brothers* (1980), *Doctor Detroit* (1983), *Rocky IV* (1985), *When We Were Kings* (1997), *Blues Brothers 2000* (1998).

## QUICKIE BIO

James Brown worked his way up from a buck-dancing shoeshine boy to Soul Brother Number One. Along the way, he created funk, spent time in jail, indulged in a ferocious drug habit, and amazed the world as "the Hardest Working Man in Show Business." Public Enemy, The Red Hot Chili Peppers, and every other funky musician has copped the style of the Godfather of Soul. Released from jail in 1991, the fifty-eight-year-old Brown announced to the world, "I feel good," launched a world tour, and cut the song "Macarena Funk on a Roll." OOOOoooooowwwwww!

## JAMES BROWN DOES
## THE DUMBEST THINGS

✪ As a fifteen-year-old, "Little Junior" Brown was arrested and served time for stealing clothes from parked cars. Claimed Brown, "They sent me to prison for being dumb."

✪ In 1959, the "Please, Please, Please" man bought a brand new red Cadillac for the band. Brown and his group, the Famous Flames, kept the windows rolled up in order to pretend that the Cadillac had air-conditioning. On one tour through the desert, Brown and the other musicians stopped their car at a gas station. They kept the windows rolled up while the attendant slowly serviced the vehicle. A little old lady in her car at the next pump watched Brown and the Flames as they smiled and sweated...and smiled and sweated...and smiled and sweated. Finally the little old lady jerked open the Cadillac door shouting, "Get out quick before you...die in there."

✪ In 1965, Brown's manager circulated the rumor that Mr. Dynamite was going to get a sex change operation in Europe in order to marry his bandmate Bobby Byrd.

✪ In the late 1960s, Brown was scheduled to perform on television with Aretha Franklin. He was so intimidated by the Detroit diva that he turned her stage monitors off during the performance. Aretha was furious. Brown and Aretha were supposed to end the show by singing a duet. Instead, Brown grabbed a startled Aretha and slow danced with her while the band vamped an instrumental version of "It's a Man's World."

✪ In the 1980s, Brown allegedly threw his wife Adrienne's fur coats out on the lawn and blasted them with a shotgun. Adrienne later set fire to all of her husband's clothes.

"Sometimes, you let the hair do the talking!" shouted James Brown—arrested eight times, convicted three times, total time spent in jail five years, four days. [photo courtesy of Photofest]

Brown's recurrent gun play got him into serious trouble in 1988. After allegedly shooting at the walls of his bedroom, Brown pulled out a shotgun at an insurance seminar in Augusta, Georgia, and threatened people because someone had used the bathroom in his trailer. Brown then jumped into his truck and led police on a high-speed chase through two states. Brown finally stopped when police blasted the tires out from under his bullet-riddled vehicle. Brown was arrested and served two years in a penitentiary.

Brown's wife Adrienne passed away in 1996 of "PCP intake and atherosclerotic heart disease." A year later, Mr. Dynamite proposed on the air to television talk-show host Rolonda Watts. Responded Rolonda, "We're going to continue this discussion on the phone later, James."

In early 1998, James Brown wound up in the hospital after taking a bunch of painkillers. Less than a week after leaving the hospital, the singer was arrested for possession of marijuana and unlawful use of a firearm. "I have bad eyes," said Brown to explain the marijuana. "I got to have protection," said Brown about his illegal use of firearms. "Thank God it's a free country."

# Butthole Surfers

**RINGLEADERS:** Gibby Haynes (singer)—born Gibson Haynes, circa 1963;
Paul Leary (guitar)—born circa 1958; King Coffey—born circa 1958.

## SELECTED HITS (and Misses)

**SONGS:** "Bar-B-Q Pope"(1983), "The Revenge of Anus Presley" (1983), "The
Shah Sleeps in Lee Harvey's Grave" (1983), "Eye of the Chicken" (1984), "I
Saw an X-Ray of a Girl Passing Gas" (1988), "No I'm Iron Man" (1990), "Who
Was in My Room Last Night?" (1993), "Jingle of a Dog's Collar" (1993), "My
Brother's Wife" (1993), "Ulcer Breakout" (1993), "The Lord is a Monkey"
(1994), "Pepper" (1996).

## QUICKIE BIO

Gibby Haynes and Paul Leary met each other while studying business at
Trinity University in San Antonio, Texas. The two got into business selling Lee Harvey Oswald pillowcases and T-shirts before launching the Butthole Surfers in 1981. For fifteen years, the Buttholes amazed alternative-rock
crowds with their live rock-and-roll freak shows. The band hit the big time
with the release of their 1996 album *Electriclarryland*. Singer Haynes credited
a cartoon for his band's breakthrough success. *"Beavis and Butthead* made

'butthole' a safe word for the United States to say," Haynes told MTV. "They brought buttholes out of the bathroom and onto the dinner table."

## THE BUTTHOLE SURFERS DO
## THE DUMBEST THINGS

✪ When the future Buttholes first started playing together, they used a *different* name for the band at every show. Group names included: the Dave Clark Five, the Dick Gas Five, Nine Foot Worm Makes Own Food, the Vodka Family Winstons, Abe Lincoln's Bush, the Inalienable Right to Eat Fred Astaire's Asshole, and the just plain Right to Eat Fred Astaire's Asshole.

✪ During their formative period, the Butthole Surfers enjoyed performing while medical-curiosity films played in the background. The films were so graphic (e.g., scenes of sex-change surgery) that some people in the audience barfed.

✪ Offstage, the Buttholes enjoyed even more bizarre cinematic horrors. One of their favorite films starred Mr. Donut, a performer who was able to perform party tricks with his rectum.

✪ To wake up the crowd, Haynes occasionally fired off a shotgun over the heads of his fans.

✪ In Corpus Christi, Texas, a fan threw a watch and hit Haynes on the hand. "We've already got your money," Haynes screamed. "I don't care if you buy our record, you white-trash, scumbag pieces of s***!" Later Haynes' assailant came backstage to say hello. Haynes promptly punched him out.

✪ When Gibby worked as a DJ on a radio station in Austin, Texas, he consistently referred to the station's playlist as "puke chunks."

✪ Haynes told reporters that he met movie star Ellen Barkin backstage after the Academy Awards. "Helen," Haynes said, getting her name wrong, "that is such a beautiful dress. My mom used to have a purse like that." Ellen pulled out the front of her dress and said, "Yeah, it's neat material." The Butthole looked down the movie star's dress and said, "Helen, man, I fully saw your v*****." Ellen giggled and said, "I hate that word."

✪ The Buttholes wanted to call their *Electriclarryland* album *Oklahoma!* They changed their minds when record-company executives pointed out that they would probably be sued by the estate of Broadway composers Richard Rodgers and Oscar Hammerstein II. The band even compromised with the artwork for the album's cover. They substituted the photo of a prairie dog for the image of a guy with a pencil jammed into his bleeding ear.

Haynes loved the press. Maybe a little too much. "Take off your clothes," he said to a female interviewer. "I'll take off my clothes too and we'll do the interview naked." The interviewer declined to strip. "Is *Independent Worm Saloon* going to make you guys famous?" she asked. Haynes replied, "I'd like to put my worm in your saloon."

# The Carpenters

---

**DUMBEST QUOTE**

"I got upset when this whole 'squeaky clean' thing was tagged onto us.... I have every Zappa and Mothers of Invention record!"

(Richard Carpenter)

---

## FACTS OF LIFE (and Death)

**RINGLEADERS:** Karen Carpenter (vocals, drums)—born Karen Anne Carpenter, March 2, 1950, New Haven, Connecticut, died February 1, 1983, from complications due to anorexia nervosa; Richard Carpenter (keyboards)—born Richard Lynn Carpenter, October 15, 1946, New Haven, Connecticut.

## SELECTED HITS (and Misses)

**SONGS:** "(They Long to Be) Close to You" (1970), "Rainy Days and Mondays" (1971), "Top of the World" (1973), "There's a Kind of Hush" (1976), "Calling Occupants of Interplanetary Craft (The Recognized Anthem of World Contact Day)" (1977), "Touch Me When We're Dancing" (1981).

**TV:** *Make Your Own Kind of Music* (series—1971), *The Karen Carpenter Story* (telefeature—1989).

## QUICKIE BIO

Brother and sister Richard and Karen Carpenter went directly from music college at California State University, Long Beach, to rock stardom. First billed as a novelty act in the late 1960s, the Carpenters created an easy-listening sound that critics hated and record buyers adored. By the end of the 1970s, Karen's eating disorder and Richard's reputed pill-popping had ground the Carpenters' creative output to a halt. The emergence of 1970s nostalgia brought the Carpenters' sound back into popularity in the 1990s. Perhaps the oddest tribute to the smooth-singing siblings was a film titled *Superstar.* The rockumentary used Barbie and Ken dolls to portray the history of the Carpenters.

## THE CARPENTERS DO
## THE DUMBEST THINGS

⭐ In 1966, Richard and Karen formed a trio and won a battle of the bands at the Hollywood Bowl. The trio sang the song "The Girl from Ipanema" accompanied by drums, piano, and a tuba. A visionary record executive tried to sell the trio as a "rock tuba" supergroup. There were no buyers.

⭐ After the tuba sound blew out, Richard formed a rock band with his drum-playing sister. The group scored a Los Angeles gig as the opening act for Steppenwolf. The Carpenters were supposed to play three nights, but were fired after the first night because the hip audience hated them. Richard and Karen just weren't born to be wild.

⭐ The Carpenters' big hit, "We've Only Just Begun," was originally written by Paul Williams and Roger Nichols as a jingle for a California bank. Recalled Nichols, "They [the Carpenters] had a frightening amount of musical talent drooling off them."

⭐ Water was drooling off the Carpenters when they posed for the cover of their album *Close to You.* For the shoot, Richard donned a cashmere coat and Karen wore a full-length gown. Brother and sister stood together on the Pacific Coast as salt water splashed all over them. Recalled Richard, "That album's still out there with that cover. And it still stinks!"

⭐ When Richard hired Maria Luisa Galeazzi to be the hair stylist for the Carpenters, he told her that going out with band members was strictly forbidden. Then Richard changed his mind, and made a pass at her. The two wound up dating. Maria called Richard "Electric Fingers."

⭐ Karen thought Richard's choice of women was "dumb."

🗣 One time, Karen and Richard got into a family fight right before taping a TV show. Karen complained about the material. Richard said she didn't know what she was talking about. Karen shot back, "So what am I— just the dumb singer?" Richard nodded, "Yeah, that's right."

⭐ Richard and Karen played for former president Richard Nixon at a White House dinner in 1973. When someone left the microphones open, the seated dignitaries were surprised to hear Richard ask, "Who's the babe with Kissinger?" The "babe" was actress Mamie Van Doren.

⭐ At the end of their 1974 British tour, Richard and Karen sent six record-company executives a velvet box. The VPs were shocked when they opened their gifts. Inside each box was a gold ring inscribed with the word *love* on one side and the word *f\*\*\** on the other. Oh, those wild and wacky Carpenters!

# Kurt Cobain

## FACTS OF LIFE (and Death)

**ORIGIN:** Born Kurt Donald Cobain, February 20, 1967 Hoquiam, Washington, died April 5, 1994, Seattle, Washington, of a self-inflicted gunshot wound.

**FORMATIVE YEARS:** Dropped out of high school.

**FAMILY PLANNING:** Married Courtney Love in Waikiki, Hawaii, February 24, 1992.

**ROMANTIC INTERESTS:** Traci Marander (writer), Mary Lou Lord (musician), Kathleen Hanna (musician).

## SELECTED HITS (and Misses)

**SONGS:** "Spank Thru" (1988), "Bleach" (1989), "Smells Like Teen Spirit" (1991), "Come as You Are" (1992), "Rape Me" (1993), "I Hate Myself and I Want to Die" (1993), "Dumb" (1993).

## QUICKIE BIO

Grumpmeister Kurt Cobain took punk into the 1990s with his own blend of loud bummer-rock. Cobain started playing music with high-school party pal Chris (Krist) Novoselic in 1987. They called their band Ed Ted and Fred and Fecal Matter before cutting their first Nirvana single in 1988. By 1992 Nirvana had moved to Seattle and launched the grunge-rock fad with the huge-selling album *Nevermind.* Plagued by mysterious stomach complaints, tortured by self-doubt, and married to Courtney Love, Cobain took his own life in 1994, leaving behind their young child, Frances Bean. After the suicide, a distraught Courtney addressed a gathering of 7,000 people in Seattle. Her epitaph for Cobain climaxed as she led the crowd in chanting the word "A**hole."

## KURT COBAIN DOES
## THE DUMBEST THINGS

★ In 1986, Cobain decided that he wanted to have pets. So he bought a half-dozen turtles and placed them in a bathtub in the middle of his living room. When the turtle poop began to smell too badly, Cobain and a friend drilled a drain hole in the middle of the floor.

★ Cobain had other pets including rats, cats, and rabbits. But his favorite pet was a plastic chimp, Chim-Chim from the TV series *Speed Racer.*

★ After a 1988 gig, Cobain and Novoselic were so fed-up with drummer Chad Channing that they destroyed his percussion kit.

★ The destruction routine got to be part of the Nirvana act. If it was a bad show, they'd smash their instruments because they were angry. If it was a good show, they'd bust their instruments because they were happy.

★ Nirvana destroyed brain cells as well as instruments. After one Florida gig, the band crashed at a fan's luxury condominium. They got drunk and took acid. Novoselic fried up some mayonnaise, then took off his clothes and walked naked around the parking lot screaming "Cast away your possessions like I have! You're not worth anything!"

★ At a rock festival in England in 1992, Kurt wore a hospital gown and rolled onto the stage in a wheelchair. "I have absolutely no respect for the English people," explained the Yankee rocker. "They make me sick."

★ In Germany, Cobain enjoyed watching videos of the movie *This Is Spinal Tap* (1984) and set fire to the curtains of his tour bus while giving an interview.

★ Cobain had great difficulty coping with success. At the 1992 MTV Video Awards, Cobain arranged for a Michael Jackson impersonator to go onstage for Nirvana and accept a trophy. The impersonator confused the audience thoroughly when he announced to the world that he was "the King of Grunge."

 While performing the song "Lithium" on the same MTV awards show, Novoselic threw his bass up in the air. It came down and hit him on the head, knocking him silly. Cobain, who hadn't seen the accident, screamed at Novoselic for losing the beat.

 Cobain proclaimed his love for Love on a British TV show by announcing, "Courtney Love is the best f*** in the world." Courtney took it as a compliment.

 After marrying Love, Cobain wandered around their Seattle home in his pajamas, repeating phrases and numbers to himself to get them off his mind.

 Kurt was not a housekeeper. There was old garbage and rotting food all over his Seattle digs. When the Cobains tried to hire some help, the maid walked into their house, then ran out screaming, "Satan lives here!"

 While Love was in labor in 1992 in one wing of Cedars-Sinai Medical Center in Los Angeles, Cobain was in rehab in another.

 As the labor got harder, Love shocked her caregivers by leaving the delivery room, walking over to Cobain's room and yelling, "You are not leaving me to do this by myself!" Kurt dutifully followed his wife back to the maternity sector. He then puked and passed out as the baby's head appeared. According to Love, "It was pretty weird."

 Fatherhood didn't make Cobain much happier. In 1993, he locked himself in the bathroom of his Seattle home and threatened to kill himself. Love called 911. When the police arrived, Cobain explained that he wasn't suicidal. He was just hiding from Love.

 Cobain's mother once said, "He's probably going to turn up dead and join that stupid club [the club of dead rock stars]." She was right.

 The 1998 documentary film *Kurt and Courtney* investigated the alleged possibility that Courtney was potentially involved in the "murder" of her husband, Kurt. When Courtney learned about the new movie, she threatened to sue the organizers of the 1998 Sundance Film Festival if they screened the picture. The film was withdrawn from the festival. Nevertheless, it became an underground hit, thanks to Courtney's negative publicity campaign.

# Alice Cooper

## FACTS OF LIFE

**ORIGIN:** Born Vincent Damon Furnier, February 4, 1948, Detroit, Michigan.

**FORMATIVE YEARS:** Dropped out of Glendale Community College.

**FAMILY PLANNING:** Married Sheryl in March 1976. Alice lives with Sheryl and their three kids in Phoenix, Arizona. Yes, the family goes by the name Cooper.

**ROMANTIC INTERESTS:** "I had affairs with a whole series of pastry. It was messy and expensive, but it was worth it."

## SELECTED HITS (and Misses)

**SONGS:** "Don't Blow Your Mind" (1965), "Swing Low, Sweet Cheerio" (1968), "School's Out" (1972), "Billion Dollar Babies" (1973), "No More Mr. Nice Guy" (1973), "Hey Stoopid" (1991).

**FILMS:** *Diary of a Mad Housewife* (1970), *Sextette* (1978), *Roadie* (1980), *Prince of Darkness* (1987), *The Decline of Western Civilization Part 2: The Metal Years* (1988), *Freddy's Dead: the Final Nightmare* (1991), *Wayne's World* (1992).

**TV:** *Hollywood Squares.*

## QUICKIE BIO

In the mid-1960s, teenage Vincent Furnier separated from his missionary father in Phoenix, Arizona, and set out to follow his own twisted mission in Los Angeles. Vincent sang with a bunch of noisemakers who wore black eye-makeup and called themselves Alice Cooper. Discovered (and hidden) by Frank Zappa, the hard-partying band spent years recreating Halloween on-

44

stage in concert halls across the world. Furnier split with his bandmates in 1974 and took the name Alice Cooper for himself. Since then, Cooper has thrived as rock's Elvira, the grandpa of gruesome glam, threatening live birdies onstage, and shooting smooth birdies on the golf course.

## ALICE COOPER DOES
## THE DUMBEST THINGS

⭐ As a youth, someone told Cooper that his erection should point straight down, not straight out. The frightened young Cooper tried desperately to reroute his wandering wee-wee. He even kept a string tied from the end of it to his knee until he found out that ninety degrees was, indeed, the correct angle.

⭐ As his band got comfortable on the tour plane after a gig, Cooper's tour manager would get on the intercom to announce a rundown of the previous evening's off-stage activities. "Last night there were four three-ways, three five-ways, six one-on-ones, and two one-ways with poor response." Recalled Cooper, "Nothing like ball scores to start off a flight and put a smile on your face."

⭐ After landing in London, one of Cooper's road crew wore a Cyclops costume through customs and used his backstage pass as a passport. The customs agents referred to him as "Mr. Clops" and welcomed him to England.

⭐ Alice once hid a used feminine sanitary napkin under the pillow of the woman who was then the band's manager/landlady. The lady hit the sack with a bass player who discovered the crusty item. The woman rushed downstairs to Cooper yelling, "How could you do this to me? We're supposed to be a family!"

⭐ At one point, a confused fan came up to Cooper and asked, "You're Tiny Tim, aren't you?" "Sure," Cooper lied. "How did you know I was Tiny Tim?" "Well," said the fan, "I recognized you. From your nose."

⭐ When Cooper and his band auditioned for master musician Frank Zappa, he put his hands over his ears and yelled, "All right, all right, I'll sign you! I'll sign you! Just stop playing!" He wanted them to become a comedy act called Alice Cookies.

⭐ Cooper invited a prospective manager to attend their new gig. Soon after the band started playing, the crowd of 3,000 left. The manager was impressed. "Do you know how hard it is to get three thousand people to do anything?" he said.

"I've never killed a chicken on stage. Well, not purposely anyway," mused Alice Cooper. [photo courtesy of Photofest]

 During a concert in Toronto, someone from the audience handed Cooper a live chicken. Cooper serenaded the chicken for a while, then threw it out into the audience, thinking the bird would fly. The chicken flopped down into the audience, which promptly ripped it apart.

⭐ As Cooper chopped and mashed a watermelon onstage, someone handed him a crutch. Cooper continued mashing with the crutch, then threw the disgusting mess out into the audience followed by a mass of feathers. Thought Cooper, "This group of dummies just sat there." Later Cooper learned that the first five rows of the audience were filled with disabled fans. They couldn't move.

⭐ Cooper liked to appear onstage wearing a pet boa constrictor around his neck. He was rehearsing in his hotel room with a boa named Eva Marie Snake. Eva started to constrict around Cooper's neck and he couldn't get her to stop. Cooper's bodyguard tried to help, but the snake continued to squeeze. The bodyguard finally pulled out his pocket-knife and cut off the snake's head.

⭐ Cooper once threw a press party at a zoo in London. But it was the people, not the animals, who acted like, well, animals. While one human couple coupled behind the baboon cage, the amply-endowed rivals Sheila and Stacia stripped, then fought with each other. "Get out of here!" yelled Sheila, "Put your clothes back on! This is my gig!" Five people (not the strippers) were arrested for indecent exposure at the event.

 One night, Cooper decided to pull a prank on his bodyguard by pretending to mate with his television set. Cooper turned the set's volume up. With his pants down to his ankles, Cooper pretended to hump, his back to the hotel-room door. Cooper heard the door open and expected to see his bodyguard. Instead, he was greeted by a maid and the hotel detective.

 In 1988, the safety rope broke while Cooper was rehearsing his onstage hanging routine. Cooper would have hung himself if a roadie had not cut him down.

Fourteen years earlier, a group of Canadian teenagers weren't so lucky. Inspired by Cooper's stage act, the kids threw a hanging party. One of the young fans died in the process.

 The rise of creep rocker Marilyn Manson irritated bitter old Cooper. "Um, let me see. A guy with a girl's name and makeup and does theatrics. I wonder where I've heard that before?" spat the grandfatherly rock ghoul. "It's just shocking...."

# Jayne [Wayne] County

## FACTS OF LIFE

**ORIGIN:** Born Wayne Rogers, 1947, Dallas, Georgia.

**FORMATIVE YEARS:** Wore pink Mary Quant lipstick to his/her high school graduation.

**FAMILY PLANNING:** None.

**ROMANTIC INTERESTS:** Gender-bending adventures with many individuals including David Bowie, although County claimed "Bowie doesn't kiss as well as me."

## SELECTED HITS (and Misses)

**SONGS:** "(If You Don't Want to F*** Me, Baby) F*** Off" (1978), "Toilet Love" (1978), "Texas Chainsaw Manicurist" (1995).

**FILMS:** *The Punk Rock Movie* (1978), *Sid and Nancy* (1986), *Wigstock: The Movie* (1995).

**STAGE:** *Femme Fatale* (1968); *World—Birth of a Nation* (1969); *Pork* (1971).

## QUICKIE BIO

When Andy Warhol's glitzy 1960s New York scene died, few of its once-glamorous faces survived. But there, sashaying bravely on into 1970s punk was Jayne County, rock and roll's most disgusting transsexual (who never had the final sex-change operation). As a misplaced Georgia youth, the ambitious performer hopped on a bus and found kindred spirits in the crossover world of the New York City underground. S/he took the name of Iggy Pop's home, Wayne County, traveled to England, and got into the punk scene before taking the name Jayne in 1979. S/he continued to push the envelope of rock-and-roll sexuality by releasing albums and touring into the 1990s. The title of County's 1995 autobiography said it all: *Man Enough to Be a Woman.*

## JAYNE (WAYNE) COUNTY DOES THE DUMBEST THINGS

★ When Mrs. Rogers saw her teenage son dressing up like Cleopatra, she tried to bring her child back down to earth. "The Bible says it's wrong for a woman to wear makeup," said the Georgia housewife to the future Jayne County, "so it must be wrong for a man."

★ To support his flamboyant lifestyle in New York, County took a job at the American Foundation for the Blind. Unfortunately, s/he was tripping on acid much of the time. According to County, people would "order a cane and end up with a Braille bingo game."

★ County performed in a theatrical piece titled *World: The Birth of a Nation.* The show featured an actor dressed like John Wayne giving birth to a baby—from his rear.

★ During his/her years in the entertainment biz, County got close to many stars. Rod Stewart visited his/her hotel room. John Lennon bumped into County in a men's room. Bianca Jagger snubbed County at a gathering with Andy Warhol. And Jim Morrison refused to have his picture taken with the cross-dressing crooner. Sniffed County, "Mr. Macho Morrison, who used to take his dick out on airplanes and wave it at the stewardesses."

★ Others had a more violently negative reaction to County. During a performance in New York, a former pro-wrestler heckled County about his/her sexual orientation. County slammed the wrestler in the head with his/her microphone stand. The wrestler went to the hospital. County went to jail.

★ County's band once toured with the Police. County shared a dressing room with Sting. County contends that Sting flashed him/her on occasion, but admits that s/he embellished the story when s/he sold it to the British tabloids.

 County was romantically involved with David Bowie in the 1970s, but the two had a bitter breakup. "My advice to anyone who wants to get near David Bowie," warned County, "is to wear lots of garlic around your neck."

★ Johnny Rotten of the Sex Pistols told the press that County was the only woman he'd ever consider marrying. When the two met, Rotten yelled, "I hear you've got tits!" and grabbed County's chest. County grabbed Rotten's jewels.

★ At a 1996 Valentine's Day gig in Los Angeles, County donned a dress made of plastic bags, a wig filled with trash, and attacked the audience with a plunger while singing the song "Toilet Love."

# David Crosby

## FACTS OF LIFE

ORIGIN: Born David Van Cortlandt Crosby, August 14, 1941, Los Angeles, California.

FORMATIVE YEARS: Suspended from Santa Barbara City College after being arrested for burglary.

FAMILY PLANNING: Had a child with Debbi Donovan; Married Jan Dance, May 16, 1987.

ROMANTIC INTERESTS: "It's no good asking about details about the largest pile of bodies and who did what and with which and to whom. That's irrelevant...."

## SELECTED HITS (and Misses)

SONGS: "Mr. Tambourine Man" (with the Byrds—1965), "So You Want to Be a Rock-and-Roll Star" (with the Byrds—1969), "Marrakesh Express" (with Crosby, Stills and Nash—1969), "Suite: Judy Blue Eyes" (with Crosby, Stills and Nash—1969), "Teach Your Children" (with Crosby, Stills, Nash and Young—1970), "Hero" (1993).

## QUICKIE BIO

The portly, harmonizing David Crosby chased women and drugs into the booming 1960s Southern California folk-rock scene. A founding member of the Byrds, Crosby sported green leather capes and earned a reputation as the "bad Byrd." After contributing to the success of the Jefferson Airplane and other music groups, he settled down to record with friends Graham Nash and Stephen Stills. Crosby, Stills and Nash (later joined by Neil Young) played their first live gig at Woodstock and spent the next thirty years singing about it. Crosby's appetite for drugs led to numerous arrests and jail time. Crosby's conviction was eventually overturned, allowing him to take his proper place in the pantheon of wheezing rock geezers.

## DAVID CROSBY DOES
## THE DUMBEST THINGS

- As a young folk singer, Crosby was so obsessed with sex his friends called him "Old Tripod."

- When Crosby, Stephen Stills, and Graham Nash first began singing together, they were known as the Frozen Noses—for their unique harmonies and their drug habits.

- The band's sex life was as intertwined as its harmonies. Crosby slept with singer-songwriter Joni Mitchell and introduced her to Graham Nash. Nash slept with Joni, then dropped her for singer Rita Coolidge, who was going out with Stephen Stills. "Nowhere in my experience," said Stills, who got dumped by Rita, "had I ever seen anyone go about snaking a buddy's girl with so little discretion."

- In 1977, Crosby, Stills and Nash performed for former president Jimmy Carter at the White House. When the band was left alone for a few minutes in the Oval Office, they lit up a joint.

- Crosby wrote the song "Triad" about a guy who liked to mate with two women at the same time. According to one of Crosby's girlfriends, the triad concept wasn't that interesting. Said the girlfriend, "It basically came down to 'Whose turn is it?'"

- Crosby was as crazy about drugs as he was about three-way sex. At one point, he refused to perform at Carnegie Hall in New York City unless his Los Angeles-based manager David Geffen (who later became a recording-industry mogul) brought him some dope. The loyal Geffen tried, but got busted at the airport. When the dopeless manager finally arrived in Manhattan, Crosby screamed, "I'm gonna f***ing kill you!" Geffen stopped managing bands. Then he dated Cher.

- Crosby snorted so much cocaine, he wore a hole through the septum in his nose. "That was me," remembered Crosby, "'Ol' Crusting and Bleeding.'"

- Crosby then started freebasing—or smoking—cocaine. He recalled, "I set myself on fire, ignited the whole front of me at one point."

When he wasn't on fire, Crosby had trouble staying awake. While eating at a restaurant with Cass Elliot of the Mamas and the Papas, Crosby passed out face-first into a big plate of spaghetti. Cass left without paying the bill.

Onboard an airplane ready to fly from St. Louis to Denver, Crosby's roadie asked the flight attendant to bring Crosby's bag from the cargo hold. The roadie told the flight attendant that Crosby's "medication" was in the bag. Unfortunately, the hostess noticed that Crosby's luggage also contained a .22 Magnum, cocaine, hashish, marijuana, and heroin residue. Crosby's roadie and the latter's girlfriend were arrested for federal air piracy and marched off the plane, while Crosby stared out the window at the runway.

Crosby sold all his possessions to get drugs. He got a great deal on his dark blue Mercedes sedan. He exchanged it to one dealer for an ounce of cocaine and $4,000. The dealer gave him the cocaine, drove the car to a neighbor's house, overdosed on heroin and died. Someone drove the car back to Crosby's house.

Crosby sold the same Mercedes to another drug dealer who drove it until it blew up. The Mercedes wound up parked in Crosby's driveway. Crosby managed to sell the wrecked Mercedes several more times before the dumb dealers finally caught on.

In 1981, Grace Slick, Graham Nash, and a bunch of other rock stars went to Crosby's house to urge him to stop his drug use. In the middle of their intervention, "I did exactly the wrong thing," Crosby later confessed. "I snuck off into the bathroom and tried to smoke some more freebase."

# John Denver

## FACTS OF LIFE (and Death)

**ORIGIN:** Born Henry John Deutschendorf, Jr., December 31, 1943, Roswell, New Mexico, died October 12, 1997 when the small aircraft he was piloting crashed into Monterey Bay, California.

**FORMATIVE YEARS:** Dropped out of Texas Tech University in Lubbock, Texas.

**FAMILY PLANNING:** Married Ann Martell, June 9, 1967, divorced June 9, 1982; Married Cassandra Delaney (eighteen years his junior), August 12, 1988; divorced 1993.

**ROMANTIC INTERESTS:** "If they were available and a little challenging in their availability, and soft and warm, that spelled romance for me."

## SELECTED HITS (and Misses)

**SONGS:** "The Ballad of Spiro Agnew" (1969), "Leaving on a Jet Plane" (1969), "Take Me Home, Country Roads" (1971), "Rocky Mountain High" (1972), "Annie's Song" (1974), "Sunshine on My Shoulders" (1974), "Thank God I'm a Country Boy" (1975), "Calypso" (1975), "Windsong" (1975), "Please Daddy (Don't Get Drunk This Christmas)" (1975), "Shanghai Breezes" (1982).

**FILMS:** *Oh, God!* (1977), *Walking Thunder* (1993).

**TV:** *Foxfire* (telefeature—1987).

## QUICKIE BIO

A clean-cut folkie from the Midwest, John Denver adopted his surname to appeal to a whole generation of listeners who were high—and not just on the scenery. By 1975, Denver was the country's biggest-selling recording artist. "If you give Elvis the fifties and the Beatles the sixties," said an entertainment executive, "I think you got to give John Denver the seventies." But not the eighties. By that time, Denver's records had stopped selling and his spacey, enviro-spiritualism left many of his Aspen neighbors quaking. Busted twice in the mid-1990s for drunk driving, Denver almost came face-to-face with rock writer Hunter S. Thompson who was called to sit on Denver's jury. Denver's death in 1997 cut short the legal proceedings, as well as a career that was destined for an eventual comeback high. His autobiography, *Take Me Home* was published in 1994.

## JOHN DENVER DOES THE DUMBEST THINGS

⭐ After he saw the Rolling Stones perform in Long Beach, California, Denver confessed, "I didn't get Mick Jagger or his onstage gyrations. It just did not compute for me."

⭐ In 1965, Denver walked around the streets of New York in sandals. He approached a good-looking woman and asked, "Are you a model?" She looked at him and said, "No, I'm full-scale."

⭐ One night, after Denver and his wife Annie made love, Annie complained of chest pains. They went to a doctor who told Annie that Denver had broken one of her ribs. "I had become ardent," he explained, "but I was still dumb about ordinary life."

⭐ In 1972, Denver took some acid and drove around on a motorcycle. Then he wrote the song "Rocky Mountain High." Denver exclaimed, "What a far-out experience that was."

⭐ Denver thought saying "far out" was really far out. "The first time I appeared as guest host of *The Tonight Show*, I must have said 'far out' fifty times," Denver explained, "I would say 'far out' without even thinking. It was like a nervous tic...."

💰 In the 1970s, Denver teamed up with EST founder Werner Erhard. Denver, Erhard, and others initiated "the Hunger Project" which set up meetings (for whatever goal) with people such as Dick Gregory, Harry Chapin, Shirley MacLaine, John Glenn, John Warner, Burt Lance, Chip Carter, and Bob Dole. They spent thousands of dollars and released a study of their findings but never gave any money or food to hungry people.

- Denver was a pilot with a passion for space. He lobbied hard to fly on the U.S. space shuttle *Challenger* in 1986, but was turned down. The Russians then offered to let him fly on their space shuttle for $10 million. DJs across the United States started a collection to buy Denver a one-way ticket.

- A reporter in Australia asked Denver, "Do you smoke hash?" Denver replied, "Every chance I get." When his remark hit the headlines, the singer flushed his stash down the toilet. He later observed, "It was the wrong thing to say."

- Denver founded an environmental-research organization called Windstar. He put his first wife Ann Martell on the board. Then he put Martell's analyst on the board. The organization almost fell apart when Denver got sick of Martell's cooking and recommended that the board attend lectures on macrobiotic cuisine.

- When Martell had some trees near their Aspen house cut down, the singer went ballistic. He started choking her. Then he apologized, grabbed a chainsaw, and chopped up the kitchen table. Denver then tried to chop up his wife's bed, but the sheets jammed the saw and it stopped running.

- Before his second divorce, Denver consulted a shaman in Santa Fe, New Mexico. He recalled, "The shaman found three pieces of me that had been missing."

- In the fall of 1993, after the final hearing in his second divorce, Denver got drunk, got into his car, and got arrested for driving under the influence. One year later, the same thing happened again. Sighed Denver, "I must say there is a great tolerance in Aspen for the kind of fool I've been."

"If they were available and a little challenging in their availability, and soft and warm, that spelled romance for me," sighed John Denver
[photo courtesy of Photofest]

# Depeche Mode

## FACTS OF LIFE

**RINGLEADERS:** Vince Clarke (vocals, guitar)—born July 3, 1960, Basildon, England; David Gahan (vocals)—born May 9, 1962, Epping, England; Martin Gore (synthesizer)—born July 23, 1961, Basildon, England; Andrew "Fletch" Fletcher (synthesizer)—born July 8, 1960, Nottingham, England; Alan Wilder (synthesizer)—born June 1, 1959, London, England.

## SELECTED HITS (and Misses)

**SONGS:** "Just Can't Get Enough" (1981), "See You" (1982), "Everything Counts" (1983), "Strangelove" (1988), "Personal Jesus" (1989), "Enjoy the Silence" (1990), "I Feel You" (1993).

## QUICKIE BIO

Window-decorating student David Gahan teamed up with school chums Vince Clarke, Andrew Fletcher, and Martin Gore in 1980 to create Depeche Mode, one of the most durable of the 1980s synth-pop bands. They released a blizzard of singles before hitting it big on the concert circuit (minus Clarke, who refused to tour). "I think most of the people who bought our records have never been to a gig in their lives," shrugged Fletch, "and will never go to one." The onstage lineup changed as Gahan split and Fletch became business manager. But no one in the dance-crazed audience seemed to care. We're talking synthesizers here, folks. Guys onstage behind black boxes.

## DEPECHE MODE DOES
## THE DUMBEST THINGS

⭐ The band took its names from words Gahan discovered flicking through a French magazine. Depeche Mode means "fast fashion." French detractors of the band liked to call the English rock stars Depede Mode. Translation? "Dirty pedophiles."

⭐ It took Depeche Mode awhile to get the hang of their high-tech musical equipment. During an early performance, one of the band members got so frustrated, he walked to the side of the stage and kicked the plug board, plunging the group into total darkness. The blackout got the biggest applause of the night.

⭐ For their third album, *Construction Time Again* (1983), Depeche Mode relied heavily on a Synclavier. Unfortunately, no one in the band knew how to operate the instrument. Explained Gore, "The manual's very thick."

⭐ Depeche Mode used electronic wizardry to achieve amazing effects. "We've sampled a pygmy doing his wail," said group member Alan Wilder, "but we've turned that into something that sounds nothing like a pygmy."

 During one performance, the special effects screwed up and Depeche Mode had to play with half the stage hidden behind a curtain. "When you're on the road," sighed Wilder, "there are so many things that remind you of Spinal Tap."

⭐ "It's great fun!" said Gahan, describing dancing onstage. "You get to grab your dick in front of twenty thousand people and they all scream!" Others described Gahan's dance moves as the missing link between Michael Jackson and Howard the Duck.

⭐ One night, a group of thugs followed Clarke home from a gig. Vince got nervous. He wondered whether he should run or fight. Just as Vince started to bolt, the thugs began singing the first verse of the song "New Life." A relieved Vince confessed, "And even I had to wonder, What did it mean?"

⭐ German rockers didn't think too much of the synth-poppers. When the German band KMFDM asked fans to add words to the band's initials, the fans responded, "Kill Motherf***ing Depeche Mode."

⭐ At one point, Gore arrived at an international airport sporting a bleached-blond shock of hair, black nail polish, and a black leather skirt. A customs official asked him to step aside, then ushered the musician toward a set of cubicles for searching. "Just one thing, though," the customs agent asked. "Would you prefer we used the men's cubicle? Or the women's?"

⭐ In 1990, Depeche Mode appeared at a Los Angeles record store to promote the release of their album *Violator*. When a huge crowd also showed up, the band members looked at each other and agreed, "We gotta get outta here!" Depeche Mode snuck out the back door and the event was canceled. The crowd exploded. One hundred fifty police officers in full riot gear finally stopped the violence. "As bad and dangerous as the situation was," said Wilder, "it was good PR."

⭐ Axl Rose confided he was a big fan of Depeche Mode. As such, he invited the band to a Beverly Hills barbecue, where he proceeded to shoot a pig. Depeche Mode was shocked. The strict vegetarians sent out a press release saying that the band members "do not wish to associate themselves with anyone who goes 'round shooting pigs for fun."

# Neil Diamond

## FACTS OF LIFE

**ORIGIN:** Born January 24, 1941, Brooklyn, New York.

**FORMATIVE YEARS:** Studied at New York University on a fencing scholarship but dropped out.

**FAMILY PLANNING:** Married Jaye Posner (secretary), December 1961; divorced 1969; Nine days later married Marcia Kay Murphey (production assistant).

**ROMANTIC INTERESTS:** "We have some of the most beautiful women in the world," Diamond commented about America, "and some of the most beautiful problems in the world."

## SELECTED HITS (and Misses)

**SONGS:** "Cherry, Cherry" (1966), "You Got to Me" (1966), "Kentucky Woman" (1967), "Brother Love's Traveling Salvation Show" (1969), "Holly Holy" (1969), "Cracklin' Rosie" (1970), "Crunchy Granola Suite" (1971), "I Am…I Said" (1971), "Song Sung Blue" (1972), "Longfellow Serenade" (1974), "You Don't Bring Me Flowers" (with Barbra Streisand—1978), "Hello Again" (1981), "Heartlight" (1982).

**FILMS:** *Jonathan Livingston Seagull* (soundtrack—1973), *The Jazz Singer* (1980).

## QUICKIE BIO

Neil Diamond was the swashbuckler of Brooklyn, a high-school fencing champion who crooned his way into the hearts of middle-aged women all across the world. Diamond left his college studies in the early 1960s to start writing songs. Although his first writing partner described him as "obnoxious," Diamond struck gold when he penned the Monkees' big hit "I'm a Believer." "What am I, one of the Monkees?" Diamond later complained. In the 1970s, Diamond made believers out of record executives with his own hit songs—and flop films. Observed the self-enamored Diamond, "I don't think I'll be a phenomenon until I'm dead."

## NEIL DIAMOND DOES
## THE DUMBEST THINGS

⭐ One of Diamond's first songwriting assignments was to create a follow-up tune for Pat Boone's hit "Speedy Gonzales." At work with his creative partners, Neil was inspired. "We're a bunch of lonely guys sitting around here looking like a bunch of idiots," he said. "Let's write a song called 'Ten Lonely Guys.'"

⭐ Diamond's first album was *The Feel of Neil Diamond*. Nobody got the feeling. The 1966 disc bombed. His 1968 album *Velvet Gloves and Spit* fared even worse.

⭐ During a performance at a New York City club, someone in the audience set off a stink bomb. Diamond suspected that the culprits were associated with his former record label. Their name? Bang Records. Diamond started carrying a pistol to protect himself from Bang.

⭐ In the summer of 1968, Diamond announced the creation of an organization called Performers Against Drugs. That same year, he penned an anti-marijuana ditty called "The Pot Smoker's Song" and declared, "It has no more effect on me than a good screwdriver."

⭐ Eight years later, police searched Diamond's home and busted him for possession of pot. After the arrest, Diamond presented the cops with autographed albums.

⭐ By 1970, Diamond was dissatisfied with his television persona. "Saw myself on TV the other night and barfed all over my German shepherd," he wrote to a friend.

✈ For one tour, Diamond and his band traveled in separate limousines. Cruising down the road, the boys presented their boss with a "pressed ham," a naked butt pressed against the back window of the limousine. Diamond returned the gesture.

⭐ After failing a screen test for the lead in a film biography about comic Lenny Bruce, Diamond wrote the song "I Am...I Said." In the tune, Neil compares his life to that of a frog.

⭐ After a London gig, Diamond heard some familiar music. "Oh, they're playing 'Song Sung Blue,'" remarked Diamond, referring to his hit song. "No," said a friend. "They're playing Mozart." Diamond had apparently forgotten that he had "lifted" the tune from Mozart's Piano Concerto no. 21.

⭐ Diamond wrote the songs and music for the film *Jonathan Livingston Seagull,* based on the best-selling book about a New Age bird. A guy from Diamond's band called it "Jonathan Livingston Seaturkey." *Time* magazine called it "Bird Droppings."

⭐ Diamond walked around Australia wearing a T-shirt that said, "I'm not Neil Diamond—I just look like him."

⭐ Diamond constantly bit his nails. He didn't want anybody to know, so he had his personal manicurist flown in from Los Angeles for repair work before every show.

⭐ In concert, Diamond egged on the crowd to request the same song over and over again. During one performance, Diamond sang his hit "Forever in Blue Jeans" six times in a row, while wearing sharply creased slacks.

⭐ While starring in the 1980 movie *The Jazz Singer,* Diamond tried to get psyched for an emotional scene. "Play me something that will make me very angry," he said to a soundstage technician. The man played something, and Diamond went berserk, smashing equipment and furniture. What did the technician play? A song by Barry Manilow.

⭐ Diamond collaborated for many years with guitarist Robbie Robertson of The Band. In 1976, Robertson invited Diamond and Bob Dylan to perform at *The Last Waltz,* The Band's final concert, which was documented by Martin Scorsese. Diamond sang first, went back-stage, and smugly said to Dylan, "You'll have to be pretty good to follow me." Dylan snapped back, "What do I have to do, go onstage and fall asleep?"

# Bob Dylan

## FACTS OF LIFE

ORIGIN: Born Robert Allen Zimmerman, May 24, 1941, Duluth, Minnesota.

FORMATIVE YEARS: Dropped out of the University of Minnesota.

FAMILY PLANNING: Married Sara Lowndes, November 22, 1965; divorced December 1977.

ROMANTIC INTERESTS: Bonnie Beecher (supposedly "the girl from the North Country"); a sixty-year-old woman in a bar who had filed down her teeth; Suze Rotolo (the girl on the cover of the album *The Freewheelin' Bob Dylan*); Joan Baez (singer—allegedly the "Miss Lonely" of "Like a Rolling Stone"); Farida McFree (the babysitter for his kids); Sally Kirkland (actress). According to one of Dylan's friends, "There are a lot of different women he sees....But they all tend to have one thing in common. They're invariably all very weird or very intense."

## SELECTED HITS (and Misses)

SONGS: "Talkin' Hava Nagila Blues" (1961), "Blowin' in the Wind" (1963), "Motorpsycho Nitemare" (1964), "Like a Rolling Stone" (1965), "Just Like a Woman" (1966), "Lay Lady Lay" (1969), "Tangled Up in Blue" (1976), "Highlands" (1997).

**FILMS:** *Don't Look Back* (1967), *Pat Garrett and Billy the Kid* (1973), *Renaldo and Clara* (1978), *Hearts of Fire* (1987).

**TV:** *Eat This Document* (produced in 1965, aired in 1979).

## QUICKIE BIO

Bob Dylan is the Energizer Bunny of rock. He keeps going and going and going and going....From his early days as rockin' piano player Elston Gunn, to his folkie years in New York and Boston, to his controversial electric renaissance at the 1965 Newport Folk Festival, to his born-again (and again) spirituality, to his collaborations with everyone from Keith Richards to George Harrison, Dylan has succeeded in creating great music and great copy. In 1997, the aging rocker played for Pope John Paul II. The reason? So the pope could learn about the music of young people. Dylan, the man who wrote the song "Forever Young," was fifty-six at the time.

## BOB DYLAN DOES
## THE DUMBEST THINGS

⭐ In 1960, Dylan spent time in Colorado, playing folk music at a strip club called the Gilded Garter. "One night I was ready to strip myself," he later confessed. Instead, he borrowed twenty dollars from the cash register and split.

⭐ In August 1962, Bob Zimmerman legally changed his name to Bob Dylan. Later the fuzzy-folk poet declared, "I've done more for Dylan Thomas than he's ever done for me."

⭐ In 1963, Dylan went to a folk club in London. He stood at the back of the establishment yelling, "What's going on? Where's the drinks? How do you get a drink in here?" The balladeer onstage shot back, "I don't know if you realize it but we allow the performers to perform, during which time the audience keeps quiet." "I don't f***ing have to keep quiet!" screamed the Yankee. "I'm Bob Dylan!"

⭐ In December 1963, the Emergency Civil Liberties Committee presented Dylan with an award for his contribution to the civil rights struggle. Dylan attended the awards dinner but got so drunk he had to go puke. When he finally made it back to the podium to accept the trophy, the righteous folk singer shocked the crowd by saying that he saw something of Lee Harvey Oswald (the alleged assassin of former President John F. Kennedy) in himself. Dylan was booed off the stage. Later he reflected, "I don't even know what politics are, to tell you the truth."

"God is a woman...you take it from there," preached Bob Dylan, who performed for the Pope in 1997. [photo courtesy of Reuters/Paolo Cocco/Archive Photos]

⭐ On a tour of England in the 1960s with his girlfriend singer Joan Baez, Dylan became distracted by a woman named Dana Gillespie. "He was fairly blatant about it," said Gillespie. "And made some remark about my forty-four-inch bust."

⭐ Dylan later invited Joan Baez to appear in his 1978 feature film *Renaldo and Clara*. "I wondered what I was doing in this monumentally silly project," confessed Baez, who played a Mexican whore in the pretentious 292-minute movie, "and if Dylan was taking it seriously."

⭐ For his TV special *Eat This Document*, Dylan had himself filmed as he attempted to buy the girlfriend of a young Swedish fan. Dylan later described the special as "miles and miles of garbage."

⭐ In 1977, Dylan's wife Sara Lowndes came down to breakfast to find Dylan sitting with their children and a woman named Malka. Dylan reportedly hit Lowndes in the face and asked her to leave.

One of Dylan's biggest fans was A.J. Weberman. Weberman loved Dylan so much that he regularly sifted through the poet's garbage. One day, when Weberman went to get a soda at a New York City corner store, he was attacked by a man who seemed strangely familiar. Weberman thought, *Could Bob Dylan be punching me out? My idol, the guy that wrote all that great poetry?* It was indeed Dylan, who kept slugging Weberman until some hippies broke up the fight.

✪ While recording with Ron Wood at a Los Angeles studio complete with private sleeping rooms, Dylan decided to take a break. "He made off with my sheets and pillows and everything," explained Wood. "And Bob had made off with this girl, but she was in a plaster cast—her arms and legs in a plaster!… It was like *Invasion of the Zombies.*"

✪ Dylan became a born-again Christian in 1978 and was baptized in Tarzana, California. But no matter how much he preached, Dylan couldn't convince his producer Jerry Wexler to join the flock. "Bob," explained Wexler, "You're dealing with a sixty-two-year-old confirmed Jewish atheist. I'm hopeless. Let's just make an album."

✪ In 1982, Dylan traveled to Israel to attend his son's bar mitzvah. "As far as we're concerned," said one rabbi, "he was a confused Jew."

Dylan performed at *Live Aid* in 1985 with Rolling Stones guitarists Keith Richards and Ron Wood. The chain-smoking drunk trio played acoustic guitars which no one could hear while Dylan sang lyrics that no one could understand. Their performance was recognized as the low point of the yuppie fund-raising event. Sighed Ron Wood, "We came off looking like real idiots."

✪ During the recording sessions for the 1989 Traveling Wilburys album with George Harrison, Dylan got inspired. "Let's do one like [The Artist Formerly Known as] Prince!" he said. Then he started banging away on his guitar and singing, "Love your sexy body…."

# The Eagles

## FACTS OF LIFE

**RINGLEADERS:** Glenn Frey (guitar, piano, vocals)—born November 6, 1948, Detroit, Michigan; Don Henley (drummer, vocals)—born July 22, 1947, Gilmer, Texas; Bernie Leadon (guitar, vocals)—born July 19, 1947, Minneapolis, Minnesota; Don Felder (guitar)—born September 21, 1947, Topanga, California; Randy Meisner (bass, vocals)—born May 8, 1946, Scottsbluff, Nebraska.

## SELECTED HITS (and Misses)

**SONGS:** "Take It Easy" (1972), "Tequila Sunrise" (1973), "Already Gone" (1974), "Lyin' Eyes" (1975), "Hotel California" (1976), "The Greeks Don't Want No Freaks" (1979), "Get Over It"(1994).

**TV:** *South of Sunset* (Glenn Frey—1993).

## QUICKIE BIO

The Eagles started flapping their wings in 1971 when Glenn Frey, Don Henley, Bernie Leadon, and Randy Meisner quit Linda Ronstadt's band to do their own Southern California folk-rock thing. With help from manager David Geffen the band started recording—and fighting. The Eagles flew through the 1970s on a string of hits and mounds of cocaine. "Led Zeppelin might argue with us," said Glenn Frey, "but I think we had the greatest traveling party of the 1970s." The party ended in 1982 when the band split up. The bitter ex-Eagles said that they wouldn't play together again "until hell freezes over." In 1994, the band launched the *Hell Freezes Over* Eagles reunion tour, proving that time (*and* money) heal all wounds.

# THE EAGLES DO
# THE DUMBEST THINGS

✪ As a kid growing up in Michigan, Glenn Frey loved rock and roll and women—in that order. "Glenn," said his mother, "if your guitar had tits and an ass, you'd never date another girl."

✪ Of his youth, Henley recalled, "I made good grades, but I also got drunk and threw up every day."

✪ The Eagles played their first gigs in Colorado using the name Teen King and the Emergencies. "They were playing rock and roll," remembered record producer Glyn Johns, "but sort of badly."

✪ The band was not satisfied with Johns's work either. While recording their second album (*Desperado*, 1973) in London, drummer Henley walked up to Johns and asked, "Can you make me sound like John Bonham [Led Zeppelin's drummer]?" Johns sighed, "You don't play like John Bonham."

✪ In the mid-1970s, Henley had a passionate affair with Stevie Nicks of the band Fleetwood Mac. "To the best of my knowledge, she became pregnant by me," recalled Henley. "Then she had an abortion." According to Henley, "We still remain good friends."

✪ Guitarist Leadon went out with Patti Davis (Reagan), the daughter of former president Ronald Reagan, in the 1970s. Leadon convinced the band to include one of her songs ("I Give You Peace") on the album *One of These Nights*. The band was furious when Davis bragged to reporters, "I write songs for the Eagles."

✪ In 1975, Leadon flipped out at a hotel bar. He walked over to Frey, dumped a beer over his head, and quit the band.

✪ The recording of the album *The Long Run* (1979) took so long, industry executives called it *The Long One*. "You're dealing with people who have so much money that there is no financial spur," complained one executive. "We even sent them a rhyming dictionary."

👓 In 1980, Henley ordered some takeout hookers delivered to his door. One of the girls gobbled up a bunch of Quaaludes, smoked dope, snorted coke, and passed out. Henley freaked and called the fire department. The firemen arrived, took one look at the scene, and called the police. The law determined that the naked party girl was only sixteen. They busted Henley. "We were having a farewell to the Eagles," Henley later explained. "I was stupid."

- Later Henley decided the press was stupid for paying so much attention to the arrest and wrote the song "Dirty Laundry."

- Henley apparently had a lot of dirty laundry to hide. According to one lady of the night, Henley invited three girls over to his groovy pad one evening. "Bend over, all three of you. Over here on the couch," said the Eagle. The girls obeyed. "We gave great reaction performances as he swung his bat into each and every one of us, one after another, after another," recalled the bored hooker. For Henley's amusement she cried out, "Oh Don, you're the king," "Take me baby, it feels so good," and "Check me into the Hotel California, sweet thing."

- The first incarnation of the Eagles performed for the last time at a political fundraiser for then California senator Alan Cranston. Before the end of the show, Felder and Frey almost came to blows. "We were singing 'Best of My Love,'" recalled Frey. "But inside, both of us were thinking, 'As soon as this is over, I'm gonna kill you.'"

- After the Eagles split up, Frey tried to make it as an actor. He starred in a 1993 TV series called *South of Sunset*. When Frey saw the pilot for the program, he complained, "This is the most gutless, tasteless, chickens*** movie I've ever seen." Viewers agreed. The CBS network series was canceled after the pilot aired.

- The Eagles filed a lawsuit against eagles in 1988. In the lawsuit, the Eagles claimed that the National Foundation to Protect America's Eagles had infringed on the rock band's name and image by taking the Internet address *eagles.org*, and by using the phone number 1-800-2-Eagles. Before the lawsuit, Eagle Don Henley had adopted one of the eagles saved by the offending organization.

# Perry Farrell

## FACTS OF LIFE

**ORIGIN:** Born Simon Bernstein, March 29, 1959, New York City, New York.

**FORMATIVE YEARS:** Designed jewelry with his father and used to carry pockets full of diamonds.

**FAMILY PLANNING:** "Married" girlfriend Casey Niccoli in a scene from the film *Gift*, then broke up with her and paid $75,000 in palimony.

**ROMANTIC INTERESTS:** "I've gone through a whoring stage. That's fine, it's good to learn what it's like to be a whore."

## SELECTED HITS (and Misses)

**SONGS:** "Jane Says" (1987), "Whores" (1987), "Ocean Size" (1988), "Three Days" (1990), "Been Caught Stealing" (1990), "Pets" (1993).

**FILM:** *Gift* (1993).

## QUICKIE BIO

New York City-born, Los Angeles-raised Simon Bernstein is the P.T. Barnum of alternative rock, a musical showman with political flair who pushes the envelope of good taste all the way to the bank. Perry Farrell achieved his first success with the band Jane's Addiction in the late 1980s. He achieved even more success when he turned the band's 1991 farewell tour into a traveling rock-and-roll medicine show called Lollapalooza. When Lollapalooza faded, Farrell came back with a band called Porno for Pyros and, yes, a 1997 Jane's Addiction comeback tour.

## PERRY FARRELL DOES
## THE DUMBEST THINGS

⭐ Simon Bernstein adopted the stage name Perry Farrell because it sounded like "peripheral."

⭐ Farrell started in the music biz with the band Psi Com. For the cover of the first Psi Com album, Farrell chose the image of "an emaciated woman lying dead in the streets of Africa or Afghanistan." Affectionately, Psi Com nicknamed the corpse "the dancing anorexic."

⭐ Farrell created a myth about the metamorphosis of Psi Com to Jane's Addiction. According to Farrell, Psi Com's original drummer "had a business smuggling canaries into the country from Tahiti. He would drug them and then swallow them. He overdosed on the canaries and died on the plane."

⭐ After touring in a van with Jane's Addiction, Farrell claimed that he could identify the other band members by the smell of their farts.

⭐ During a Jane's Addiction music-industry showcase in New York City, Farrell dedicated a song to "the fat record-company executives with hairy bellies that f*** little boys."

⭐ When top execs in Los Angeles gathered to hear Farrell announce a major record deal, the bouncy performer jumped on a table and screamed, "F*** you, a**holes! We're gonna make our own record!"

⭐ Farrell decided to dress up like a clown one night in Florida. "Look!" shouted a group of Cubans, pointing to Farrell, "It's Boy George!" Farrell turned around and screamed, "Suck my dick!" A small-scale riot followed. "When the cops showed up, I was standing over my [hurt] friend in a clown suit going, 'Help him! Help him!" recalled Farrell. "It was the worst!"

⭐ British mag *Raw* called Farrell's show "fascinating without being particularly entertaining." The Brits were particularly interested in watching Farrell "root around in his trousers for his willy."

⭐ In October 1991, just after the ending of the first Lollapalooza tour (and the first farewell Jane's Addiction tour), Farrell was arrested when a

maid found syringes, white powder, and crack pipes in his Santa Monica hotel room. Farrell told the press that he needed some time off, so "I got myself a drug addiction and booked myself into a hospital instead."

⭐ At the inaugural performance of Farrell's band Porno for Pyros, he reminded the audience, "This year's an election year. Don't forget to vote—but more importantly, keep on f***ing."

⭐ Farrell and the boys from Porno for Pyros were in the studio recording when the L.A. riots broke out. Farrell decided to go out into the streets and check things out. He described the scene as "adorable."

⭐ Porno for Pyros shows featured Janet Louise, "the only six-foot-two hermaphrodite with a twelve-inch penis." During the song "Cursed Male," Farrell sprayed the crowd from a giant dildo. During the song "Cursed Female," two women mated onstage. Fire-eaters, gymnasts, body piercing, and clowns added to the sideshow effect.

⭐ Farrell's 1993 movie *Gift* features his former girlfriend Casey Niccoli shooting up heroin and "dying" of an overdose. Farrell has sex with her corpse, then decorates it with flowers. "Name something degrading," bragged Farrell, "and I've done it."

# Fleetwood Mac

## FACTS OF LIFE

**RINGLEADERS:** Mick Fleetwood (drums)—born June 24, 1947, Redruth, Cornwall, England; John McVie (bass)—born November 26, 1945, London, England; Peter Green (guitar, vocals)—born Peter Greenbaum, October 9, 1946, London, England; Stevie Nicks (vocals)—born Stephanie Nicks, May 26, 1948, Phoenix, Arizona; Lindsey Buckingham (guitar, vocals)—born October 3, 1947, Palo Alto, California.

## SELECTED HITS (and Misses)

**SONGS:** "Black Magic Woman" (1968), "Albatross" (1969), "Over My Head" (1975), "Rhiannon (Will You Ever Win)" (1975), "Go Your Own Way"(1977), "Don't Stop" (1977), "Tusk" (1979), "Hold Me" (1982), "Big Love" (1987), "Little Lies" (1987).

## QUICKIE BIO

Drummer Mick Fleetwood has led the band Fleetwood Mac through thirty years of blues, divorce, and multimillion-dollar debauchery. Guitar wizard Peter Green named the band in 1967 by combining the monikers of drummer Fleetwood and bass player McVie. Fleetwood Mac evolved from a hard-partying blues band in the 1960s to the 1970s ultra-pop group with the addition of songwriter Christine Perfect (who married John McVie), Stevie Nicks, and her boyfriend Lindsey Buckingham. In 1993, the band's song "Don't Stop" was picked as President Bill Clinton's campaign theme. After an inaugural-party performance, the band denied rumors that they were getting back together. That is until 1997, when they launched a reunion tour to celebrate the twentieth anniversary of their album *Rumours*.

## FLEETWOOD MAC DOES
## THE DUMBEST THINGS

⭐ According to Mick Fleetwood, the band was "really into this phallic trip." During each Fleetwood Mac show in the late 1960s, a roadie marched onstage carrying a big platter bearing a sixteen-inch pink rubber dildo named Harold. The roadie took Harold and attached it to the inside of Mick Fleetwood's bass drum. Harold spent the entire gig quivering and vibrating at the ladies in the audience.

⭐ In the late 1960s, Fleetwood took two wooden balls from a pub's toilet chain and wore them hanging on his belt. For his drum solo, Fleetwood began to step out in front of his drum kit and dance around playing his balls. To this day, he never plays without them.

⭐ In 1976, Mick broke up with his wife, the former Jenny Boyd. She took his house keys, which had a set of tiny silver balls attached to them. According to Fleetwood, "When I had to ask for my balls back, that was the point when it hit me that we weren't together anymore, and it was my own stupid fault."

⭐ In later years, Fleetwood named the album *Tusk* (1979) in honor of male genitalia. Stevie Nicks was so disgusted she threatened to quit the band—but didn't.

⭐ Long after breaking up with Jenny Boyd, Fleetwood fell in love with a girl he met on the telephone. He was convinced she was a beautiful, wealthy American aristocrat, complete with a black maid. For eight months he tried desperately to meet her. He even hired a private detective to find out who she actually was. When Fleetwood saw the detective's snapshots, he fell out of love with the girl and referred to her as "the Blob"

⭐ Playing guitar for Fleetwood Mac drove musicians crazy. Guitarist Peter Green cried while watching the TV news, wore white robes onstage, and fought to give all the band's money away to charity. When the band's manager tried to give Green a royalty check, Green attacked him with an air rifle and was sent to a mental hospital.

⭐ Guitarist Jeremy Spencer traveled with a tiny Bible sewn into the lining of his overcoat, filled condoms with milk, and hung them from the pegs

"It *can't* be *all* about cocaine," said Stevie Nicks. [photo courtesy of Fotos International/Archive Photos]

of his guitar. "I'll be right back," he told the band as he left their hotel in Hawaii. He never returned. Instead he changed his name to Jonathan and joined a religious group known as the Children of God.

⭐ Guitarist Danny Kirwan got very stressed out five minutes before a show in 1972. Kirwan vanished into a bathroom, bashed his head against the wall, smashed his guitar and said, "I'm not going on." Danny watched the gig from the soundboard and was later admitted to a mental institution.

⭐ While recording the album *Rumours* (1977), Fleetwood Mac snorted so much coke that they wanted to give their dealer credit on the album. The dealer was killed before the album came out, solving the dilemma.

⭐ Stevie Nicks snorted so much coke during this period that she was rumored to have hired a special assistant to help administer the drug up her butt.

During the *Rumours* recording sessions, the coked-out band spent four days trying to tune a piano, then brought in nine different pianos, then decided not to use a piano at all.

⭐ For the tour to support the *Rumours* album, the band spent thousands of dollars on a giant inflatable penguin, which they only inflated once.

⭐ Nicks and Lindsey Buckingham joined Fleetwood Mac as a couple in 1974. Two years later, Lindsey officially broke up with Nicks and wrote the song "Go Your Own Way." Nicks later compared Buckingham to the Ayatollah Khomeini.

⭐ Buckingham got his revenge in Australia in 1980. He flapped his arms around onstage mocking Nicks's swishy style. During the song "Rhiannon," Buckingham played a completely different song, laughed like a maniac, and began kicking at Nicks onstage.

 At a band meeting in 1987, Nicks yelled at Buckingham, "Hey, man, you'll never be in love with anyone but yourself." Buckingham grabbed Nicks, slapped her and shouted, "Get that woman out of my life—that schizophrenic bitch!" Buckingham decided to let Nicks back into his life for the 1997 Fleetwood Mac reunion tour.

💰 In 1997, Fleetwood estimated that he had spent a staggering total of $8 million on cocaine.

# Bob Geldof

## FACTS OF LIFE

**ORIGIN:** Born Robert Frederick Zenon Geldof, October 5, 1954, Dublin, Ireland.

**FORMATIVE YEARS:** Failed his exams at Blackrock College, Dublin. He later referred to the Irish college as "a toilet."

**FAMILY PLANNING:** Married Paula Yates (talk-show host), July 1986; divorced 1996.

**ROMANTIC INTERESTS:** Geldof confessed that he had an affair with "the niece of an extremely famous and preposterously wealthy American. She was very ugly and gave me the clap."

## SELECTED HITS (and Misses)

**SONGS:** "Looking After No. 1" (1977), "Rat Trap" (1978), "I Don't Like Mondays" (1979), "I Never Loved Eva Braun" (1979), "Do They Know It's Christmas?" (with Band Aid—1984).

**FILM:** *The Wall* (1982).

## QUICKIE BIO

Irish-born rock writer Bob Geldof traded his pencil for a microphone in 1975 and formed the Boomtown Rats. Though the rats enjoyed some success, Geldof found himself running short of inspiration and money by the mid-1980s. After seeing a TV report about the Ethiopian famine, Geldof decided to create the Jerry Lewis Telethon of rock. He organized Band Aid in 1984 and Live Aid in 1985. Though it's doubtful how much good the aid thing did for the people in Africa, it did a lot of good for David Bowie, Mick Jagger, Elton John, and other aging rock stars, including Bob Geldof. In 1986, he wrote his well-received autobiography, *Is That It?*, the same year he was knighted for his humanitarian activities. According to Sir Bob, "Music can't change the world."

## BOB GELDOF DOES
## THE DUMBEST THINGS

✪ A young Geldof asked a teenage friend to put the barrel of a cocked machine gun into his mouth until it touched the back of his throat. Geldof found the experience of sucking on a machine gun barrel "strangely calming."

✪ Geldof once lost a job at a photo-processing plant because he smoked joints in the darkroom and ruined a batch of film.

✪ As a struggling musician, Geldof's favorite pastime was to catch mice inside a shoebox. Geldof rattled the box to stun the rodents, then hurled them out the window and watched them splat on the ground.

✪ To promote the single "Tonic for the Troops," Geldof and his band-mates sent DJs a dead rat preserved in formaldehyde with the message "The Rats Are Coming." The promotion killed the record stone dead.

Geldof was inspired when he heard about a San Diego schoolgirl named Brenda Spencer. Spencer launched a sniper attack on her sub-urban neighborhood which left two men dead and eight children wounded. Spencer explained to reporters that she had committed the murders because she hated Mondays. In celebration of Spencer's "accomplishment," Geldof penned the hit song "I Don't Like Mondays."

✪ In his early years, Geldof expressed disdain for do-gooders. He described Pink Floyd's lyrics as "social-conscience-stricken-millionaire leftism."

✪ Geldof decided that millionaire leftism was fine, as long as it paid. The Irish rat agreed to play the role of "Pink" in the Pink Floyd movie *The Wall* because, in his words, "the money was good."

✪ The money wasn't good enough to silence Geldof. The surly actor told reporters that the story of *The Wall* was "a load of bollocks."

⭐ While filming *The Wall*, Geldof was supposed to perform a flying sequence wearing Superman's padded body mold. Geldof was too scrawny for Superman's costume. Instead, he wore Supergirl's outfit.

⭐ After raising millions of dollars for African relief, Geldof decided he'd better think about what to do with the money. He traveled to Africa and met with dignitaries such as Captain Thomas Sankara, a revolutionary leader in Burkina Faso. "I play the guitar," said the African leader to the Irish rocker. "I am thinking of forming a band." "But do you torture people?" asked Geldof. "I'm coming to that," said the African rock-star wannabe. "I'm coming to that."

⭐ Geldof couldn't save Africa. And he couldn't save his family. After divorcing Paula Yates, Sir Bob got into a nasty custody battle over their three children (Fifi Trixibelle, Peaches, and Pixie) and Heavenly Hiraani Tiger Lily, the child Yates had with her boyfriend, rock star Michael Hutchence of INXS. After Hutchence committed suicide by hanging in 1997, a drunken Yates dumped champagne over a flight attendant and blamed Geldof. "They call him Saint Bob," Yates said. "But that's a joke. It makes me sick."

# The Grateful Dead

## FACTS OF LIFE (and Death)

RINGLEADERS: Jerry Garcia (guitar, vocals)—born Jerome John Garcia, August 1, 1942, San Francisco, California, died August 9, 1995, Forest Knolls, California, of a heart attack while in a drug rehabilitation clinic; Phil Lesh (bass)—born Philip Chapman, March 15, 1940, Berkeley, California; Bob Weir (guitar, vocals)—born Robert Hall October 6, 1947, San Francisco, California; Pigpen (vocals, harmonica)—born Rod McKernan, September 8, 1945, San Bruno, California, died March 8, 1973, Corte Madera, California, of gastrointestinal hemorrhage and cirrhosis of the liver.

## SELECTED HITS (and Misses)

SONGS: "China Cat Sunflower" (1969), "Dark Star" (1969), "New Speedway Boogie" (1970), "Truckin" (1972), "Estimated Prophet" (1977), "Touch of Grey" (1987).

FILMS: *The Grateful Dead* (1977), *Tie-Died: Rock 'n' Roll's Most Deadicated Fans* (1995).

## QUICKIE BIO

San Francisco-area musicians Jerry Garcia, Pigpen, Phil Lesh, and Bob Weir were sitting around smoking DMT when they opened the dictionary and discovered the words *grateful dead* in reference to an Egyptian prayer. The Dead became the house band at the notorious "acid tests," big public parties that celebrated the powers of LSD, which was then legal. Said "Captain Trips" Garcia: "The Acid Test was the prototype for our whole basic trip." Building on a drug-friendly, bootleg-friendly attitude, the Dead became one of the world's most popular touring attractions. The trip came to a sad end with Garcia's death in 1995. In 1997, promoters announced plans to build a $10 million museum to recreate the Dead experience. Who needs $10 million? Flashbacks are free, man.

## THE GRATEFUL DEAD DO
## THE DUMBEST THINGS

✪ Owsley Stanley III, known as the Bear, was the chemist who created much of the LSD for the San Francisco-area acid tests. "His mind was completely shot," explained Garcia. "He thought they'd come and taken it from him." Later Garcia and the band hired Stanley to be their soundman.

✪ In spring of 1966, the band moved to Rancho Olompali off California's Highway 101. A sign out front said, "No Trespassing—Violators Will Be Experimented Upon."

✪ Grateful Dead lyricist Robert Hunter explained how he came up with the words for "China Cat Sunflower": "I had a cat sitting on my belly...and I followed this cat out to—I believe it was Neptune—and there were rainbows across Neptune, and cats marching across this rainbow....I wrote part of it in Mexico and part of it on Neptune."

✪ Garcia had munched on some of Stanley's best before he took the stage at the famous Woodstock concert of 1969. "I saw blue balls of electricity bouncing across the stage and leaping onto my guitar when I touched the strings," recalled Garcia. Behind him, freaked-out stage roadies yelled, "The stage is collapsing! The stage is collapsing!" Garcia called the band's performance "just plumb atrocious." However, Captain Trips did appear in the documentary film of the acclaimed festival (*Woodstock,* 1970) holding a joint and saying, "Marijuana, exhibit A."

✪ In 1969, the Grateful Dead were booked to play with the Rolling Stones at the Altamont Speedway just outside of San Francisco. First, the Dead suggested that the Stones hire the Hell's Angels to provide security for the concert. Then, the Dead decided not to play the gig. However, they did write a song about the deadly show: "New Speedway Boogie."

 In the 1970s, the band added their only female member, Donna Godchaux. There was only one small problem with Godchaux, the wife of their heroin-addicted piano player. According to Garcia, "She had a hard time singing in key onstage."

 In 1985, Garcia was busted for freebasing cocaine in the front seat of his parked BMW. The next year, Captain Trips lapsed into a diabetic coma. When Garcia came to, he looked around and tried to remember how to talk. His first words? "I'm not Beethoven."

 In 1991, Weir and the group's drummer Mickey Hart held a press conference to introduce two new breakfast cereals—Rainforest Crisp and Rainforest Granola. Weir claimed that the cereals would make "eating breakfast an environmentally responsible act."

 One day a guy came to Hart carrying his brother's skull. The guy explained that he wanted to give the skull to Hart, because his brother had been a major Grateful Dead fan. Hart took the skull, put it on his recording console and thought, "This is *really* a Deadhead!"

A group of Deadheads referred to as "the Spinners" began to worship Garcia as God. Asked if he minded, Garcia shrugged, "Well, I'll put up with it until they come for me with the cross and the nails."

 After Garcia's death, his first wife and his second wife got into a nasty court battle over his sizable estate. When bass player Lesh was called to the stand, he claimed that he had spent the last thirty years in "one big, smoky haze."

# Guns N' Roses

## FACTS OF LIFE

**RINGLEADERS:** Axl Rose (vocals)—born William Bailey, February 6, 1962, Lafayette, Indiana; Slash (guitar)—born Saul Hudson, July 23, 1965, Stoke-on-Trent, England; Izzy Stradlin (guitar)—born Jeffrey Isbell, April 8, 1962, Lafayette, Indiana.

## SELECTED HITS (and Misses)

**SONGS:** "Mr. Brownstone" (1987), "Welcome to the Jungle" (1988), "Sweet Child O' Mine" (1988), "One in a Million" (1988), "Patience" (1989), "November Rain," (1991), "Back Off Bitch" (1991).

## QUICKIE BIO

Few bands went farther out of their way to define 1980s excess than Guns N' Roses. When record-company executives discovered the group in Los Angeles in 1986, Rose and Company were living together and rehearsing in the squalor of a small one-bedroom apartment. "I'd f*** girls just so I could stay at their place," bragged guitarist Slash. The surprising success of their 1987 debut album *Appetite for Destruction* and their 1991 double-CD set (sold separately, however) titled *Use Your Illusion I* and *II* changed the band's lifestyle, but not their attitude. In 1996, Izzy Stradlin and Slash left the band, leaving Axl Rose to rely on his own illusions to come up with a new Guns N' Roses hit.

## GUNS N' ROSES DO
## THE DUMBEST THINGS

 As a teenager, Bill Bailey (who later changed his name to W. Axl Rose) was jailed more than twenty times by the local Indiana police. Rose's last arrest occurred after a joyride with a girlfriend in a "borrowed" car. Rose was busted for grand theft auto, contributing to the delinquency of a minor, and statutory rape. "After they filed the charges, I went over to her house and we had a party," recalled the unrepentant Rose. "Then I left town."

✪ Back in Indiana for a 1991 show, Rose compared his home state to Auschwitz.

✪ In 1985, Rose and his bandmates moved into a dinky Los Angeles apartment. To cook dinner, the band members set fire to a set of drumsticks and roasted hamburgers over the flames.

✪ "Dancing with Mr. Brownstone," a line from a song on *Appetite for Destruction,* became a slang term for heroin use. Stradlin, who cowrote the song ("Mr. Brownstone"), dismissed it as something he created "in about five minutes, while I was cooking something up."

On an earlier tour, Stradlin grew frustrated with the long lines for the airplane lavatory. So he relieved himself in the kitchen area. Stradlin's pee earned him a fine and a new nickname—"Whizzy."

✪ Worried about his reputation in 1988, Rose asked his road manager if he had truly become a prima donna. "Of course not," said the road manager, "you've always been a prick."

Rose got into a fight with rock performer Courtney Love backstage at the MTV Video Music Awards in 1992. Rose turned to Love's musician husband Kurt Cobain and said, "Shut your bitch up or I'm taking you down to the pavement." Love later said that Rose "should be exterminated."

✪ In 1988, the band interrupted its American tour to appear in front of 92,000 people at an outdoor festival in England. Rose reportedly ended the set by telling the crowd, "Don't kill yourselves." Unfortunately, two fans already had killed themselves, by slam-dancing a wee bit too hard.

✪ Touring Germany later that year, Stradlin confronted the drummer of another Los Angeles-based hard-rock act, Faster Pussycat. Stradlin bound the rival rocker with duct tape and tossed him into an elevator.

✪ Drinking in a Chicago (Illinois) hotel bar, Rose punched a businessman for calling him a "Bon Jovi look-alike." Rose went directly to jail.

✪ Rose's road manager bailed him out, then returned to the hotel bar to find Slash passed out drunk. The exhausted manager hoisted Slash over his shoulder and started to carry him to his room. On the way upstairs, Slash peed all over him.

 In Phoenix, Arizona, Slash flipped out on cocaine, destroyed a hotel room, then ran naked through a hotel lobby. Later he began promoting his favorite brand of alcohol—Black Death vodka.

 "I probably give the impression of being a real a\*\*hole most of the time," said Slash, who later hired a guard to carry him around when he passed out drunk. "But I'm really not that bad."

 Slash believed that Mick Jagger wasn't bad enough. Slash told the press that the Rolling Stones' supersinger "should have died after *Some Girls* [1978], when he was still cool."

 Slash has an extensive and expensive collection of rare snakes, including a "rear-fanged" mangrove and several boas, anacondas, Indian pythons, and Burmese pythons. "I think they're gorgeous," he boasted of his pet reptiles. "I'm one of those people who can get into their personalities."

"I'm pro-heterosexual. I can't get enough of women. I have sex as often as possible." (Axl Rose) [courtesy of Reuters/Stephen Jaffe/Archive Photos]

# George Harrison

## FACTS OF LIFE

**ORIGIN:** Born February 25, 1943, Liverpool, England.

**FORMATIVE YEARS:** Studied at Liverpool Institute.

**FAMILY PLANNING:** Married model Patti Boyd, January 21, 1966; divorced June 9, 1977; Married Olivia Trinidad Arias, September 2, 1978.

**ROMANTIC INTERESTS:** For a time, Harrison abstained from sex at the urging of his Hindu guru. Then he had an affair with Ringo Starr's wife Maureen Cox.

## SELECTED HITS (and Misses)

**SONGS:** "Something" (with the Beatles—1969),"My Sweet Lord" (1971), "Bangla-Desh" (1971), "Give Me Love (Give Me Peace on Earth)" (1973), "Dark Horse" (1975), "Crackerbox Palace" (1977), "All Those Years Ago" (1981), "Got My Mind Set on You" (1988), "When We Were Fab"(1988).

**FILMS:** *Wonderwall* (soundtrack—1966), *Monty Python's Life of Brian* (producer—1979), *Bullshot!* (producer—1982), *Water* (producer—1985), *Shanghai Surprise* (producer—1986); plus his movie collaborations with the other Beatles: *Help!* (1965), *The Magical Mystery Tour* (1967), *Yellow Submarine* (animated—1968), *Let It Be* (1970), *The Compleat Beatles* (1982).

# QUICKIE BIO

John Lennon didn't care much for George Harrison when the two first met in Liverpool in 1957. "He used to follow me around like a bloody kid," complained Lennon, who eventually let Harrison join the Quarrymen. When the Quarrymen became known worldwide as the Beatles, Harrison became known as the quiet one. He was also the most spiritual, the Beatle who stuck with the music and religion of India. After the Beatles' break up, the chanting Harrison set out on his own creative path. Among other things, the reclusive rock star organized a 1971 fund-raising concert for victims of war in Bangladesh, lost his wife Patti Boyd to Eric Clapton, formed his own record label and his own film production company, joined Bob Dylan in the short-lived supergroup the Traveling Wilburys, guested on *The Simpsons* TV cartoon series, and supported the work of his musical guru Ravi Shankar. "I don't have much to say," said Harrison upon his 1988 induction into the Rock and Roll Hall of Fame, "'cause I'm the quiet one."

## GEORGE HARRISON DOES THE DUMBEST THINGS

⭐ George Harrison, John Lennon, and their wives stopped by their dentist's house for coffee one day in 1965. After drinking their beverages, the dentist informed the Beatles that their coffee had been spiked with LSD. It was the Beatles' first trip. "Let's get out of here," said Harrison. "Perhaps he's trying for an orgy."

⭐ In 1966, Harrison read about cosmic communication. He climbed a mountain hoping to receive a message from God. The hopeful Beatle waited and waited. However, the only message he received was, "Climb back down the mountain."

⭐ In 1967, Harrison traveled to San Francisco with wife Patti. Their mission: to discover what the hippie thing was all about. The couple dropped some LSD and started walking through Golden Gate Park. Things stopped being cosmic when a group of fans recognized Harrison, shoved a guitar at him, and forced him to play. Harrison tried to strum "Baby, You're a Rich Man," but he couldn't remember the words. The Beatle and wife dashed to their nearby limousine to escape the wrath of the disappointed crowd. Bummer!

⭐ Patti Boyd introduced the Beatles to the teachings of the Hindu guru Maharishi Mahesh Yogi. In 1968, Harrison and Lennon led the Beatles, some of the girls, and others to Rishikesh, India, to study Transcendental Meditation at the Maharishi's ashram. The meditation trip went sour when the Maharishi made a pass at Mia Farrow. When the Beatles caught onto what was happening, they bolted.

Harrison later became captivated by A.C. Bhaktivedanta Swami Prabhupada, founder of the International Society for Krishna Consciousness. The swami's teaching was simple. Chant the words "Hare Krishna" a lot. Taking the advice to heart, Harrison drove from France to Portugal and chanted "Hare Krishna" for twenty-three hours. At the end of the drive, Harrison claimed that he had followed no road directions but had been guided to his destination transcendentally.

⭐ On another occasion, Harrison was traveling on a large commercial aircraft. When the plane passed through a storm, the guitarist pressed his feet into the seat in front of him and started yelling "Hare Krishna." Safe on the ground the chanting Beatle stated, "I know for me the difference between making it and not making it was chanting the mantra."

⭐ Harrison liked the "Hare Krishna" mantra so well, he thought it would make a hit record. The Beatle took some devotees into the Abbey Road recording studios in 1969 and cut the song "Hare Krishna Mantra." The song was a hit, but not as big as Harrison had anticipated. "You thought 'Hard Day's Night' was big," said Harrison to Paul McCartney. "Wait till this hits....It'll be number one in thirty countries." Not quite.

⭐ Harrison was playing a ukulele at a party, when a beautiful girl came up to him. "Come on upstairs with me luv," said the Hindu Beatle, "and give me a blow job." The girl followed Harrison upstairs. "The entire time I sucked him off," she later recalled, "he kept playing that damned ukulele." When Harrison reached orgasm, he ended the song with a big strum, then started playing another tune.

⭐ Harrison asked Bob Dylan to sing one of his biggest hits during the 1971 fund-raising concert for war victims in Bangladesh. When Harrison asked, "Do you think you could sing "'Blowin' in the Wind'?" Dylan responded, "Are you gonna sing 'I Wanna Hold Your Hand'?"

⭐ During his 1974 *George Harrison and Friends* tour, Harrison attempted to dish out a dose of consciousness. Mixing his makers, Harrison chanted, "Om Christ," and told his audience, "If we all chant together purely for one minute, we'll blow the roof off this place." No structural damage was done to any venue on the tour.

⭐ In 1992, Harrison helped the Maharishi get into politics. The former Beatle helped the Maharishi organize the Natural Law Party and field more than 200 candidates to run for the British Parliament. Harrison even tried to get Ringo Starr and Paul McCartney to run. The former Beatles refused, and all of the Maharishi's other candidates were defeated.

 Harrison stepped back from the music scene in the 1970s and became a film producer. However, the Beatle found out that movie luminaries could be just as nasty as rock stars. Harrison pumped about $15 million into the 1986 feature *Shanghai Surprise* which starred Sean Penn and his then wife Madonna. After the film flopped, Harrison sighed, "Penn is a pain in the ass." And of Madonna he said, "All of [her] aloofness and star stuff...it's just bulls***."

 Harrison didn't think much of younger pop stars either. In 1997, the quiet Beatle told the press that the music of the band Oasis was "rubbish." Oasis singer Liam Gallagher lashed out during a TV program, "I still love George Harrison as a songwriter in the Beatles, but as a person I think he's a f***ing nipple....And if you're watching, NIPPLE!" Harrison had no comment.

# Ice-T

## FACTS OF LIFE

**ORIGIN:** Born Tracy Morrow, February 16, 1959, Newark, New Jersey.

**FORMATIVE YEARS:** While in high school, hung out with the street gang the Crips in Los Angeles, dealing drugs, pimping, thieving, and trying to break into showbiz.

**FAMILY PLANNING:** Legally single, but calls a woman named Darlene his wife.

**ROMANTIC INTERESTS:** "The key to my eroticism is submission.... Sexual slavery is the ultimate."

## SELECTED HITS (and Misses)

**SONGS:** "Colors" (1987), "Freedom of Speech (Just Watch What You Say)" (1989), "New Jack Hustler" (1991), "Cop Killer" (1992), "Mama's Gotta Die Tonight" (1992), "99 Problems (and a Bitch Ain't One)" (1993).

**FILMS:** *Breakin'* (1984), *Rappin'* (1985), *New Jack City* (1991), *Ricochet* (1991), *Trespass* (1992), *Who's the Man?* (1993), *Surviving the Game* (1994), *Tank Girl* (1994), *Johnny Mnemonic* (1995).

**TV:** *Players* (series—1997).

## QUICKIE BIO

After releasing five hardcore rap albums, Ice-T obtained full outlaw status when former president George Bush, Dan Quayle, former New York governor Mario Cuomo, Charlton Heston, Oliver North, and a cast of millions condemned him for "Cop Killer," a track on his 1992 album *Body Count*. The song celebrated a character who bragged that he was "about to dust some cops off." The protest sent record sales into the stratosphere and made Ice-T a household name. By 1997, Ice-T had transformed himself from an outlaw to the Mr. T of rap, providing color commentary on issues of the day and starring in the TV series *Players*.

## ICE-T DOES
## THE DUMBEST THINGS

⭐ As a thief, Ice-T had it down. The typical Ice-T jewelry heist? "I'd be like, 'Yes, my father is working down the street, he's a developer, and he and Mom are having their twenty-fifth wedding anniversary. I'm interested in looking at that Rolex.' I knew how to give them that corny Bryant Gumbel shit."

⭐ After Ice-T bought a house in Los Angeles, several magazines ran features on his surprising interior-decorating skills. Where did he pick up talent? "Yo, I done broke into enough houses to know what kind of s*** I wanted when I got a f***in' house," he says.

⭐ For his role in the mid-1980s film *Breakin'*, Ice-T was offered $500 a day. Whined the gangsta rapper, "I spend that on sneakers, man."

⭐ Ice-T admitted that he slept with women on the road, but claimed that he didn't have an "open relationship" with his "wife" Darlene. "An open relationship is when girls come over to your house to pick you up," said Ice. "I ain't got it like that. I still gotta do my sneaking around." *That's* why he needed $500 sneakers.

⭐ In his autobiography, *The Ice Opinion* (1984), Ice-T told young males looking for women to "Wash your ass. Do some sit-ups." Ice's advice for getting laid: "Lie. Lie. Lie. Lie."

⭐ Ice-T believed that without the male sex-drive the economy would crash. "All we would do is lie around and eat and fart and get fat," said the gangsta economist.

⭐ Ice-T said the plan for his album *Body Count*, featuring an all-black-hardcore punk band of the same name, was simple: "*Body Count*, in a

way, should be slightly ignorant—meaning it can't be too intelligent. I want it to be very raw, and sometimes just stupid."

 "KKK Bitch," a song from the 1992 *Body Count* album, was a romantic fantasy about group sex with Tipper Gore's nieces.

 Ice-T once compared the song "Cop Killer" to the national anthem, saying, "'The Star-Spangled Banner' is about a shootout with the police....Paul Revere was running around saying, 'The redcoats is coming,' so he was basically saying, 'Here come the pigs, and a f***up is going down.'"

 When a fan asked Ice-T "What do you do when you're just hanging out?" the TV gangsta replied, "Usually put it back in and zip up my pants."

 During a performance of the song "Evil Dick" in 1993, Ice-T pretended to have sex with the floor while furiously stroking a huge imaginary penis. One writer commented that Ice-T's performance was "as historically powerful as anything in our culture right now."

 In 1993, Ice-T, the defender of free speech, outlined his position on the press: "You know what I do with reporters now?" he asked. "I let 'em know, 'If you write some s*** and I see you, I'm beatin' your f***in' ass.'"

 Although he protested police brutality, Ice-T didn't believe in protesting other things. The rapper shouted at crowds, "Everybody with AIDS be quiet."

 For the album *Home Invasion* (1993), Ice-T considered using an all-black cover and calling the release the *Black Album.*

 Ice-T's role model? Cher! Sighed Ice-T, "She can do [the 1983 movie] *Silkwood* and come off very conservative, then be butt-naked on a battleship the next week."

# Michael Jackson

## DUMBEST QUOTES

"We can fly, you know. We just don't know how to think the right thoughts and levitate ourselves off the ground." (Michael Jackson)

"I've only read two books in my life: the Bible and Peter Pan." (Michael Jackson)

"I'm not calling myself Jesus but I'm comparing the stress and pressure to Jesus." (Michael Jackson)

## FACTS OF LIFE

**ORIGIN:** Born Michael Joseph Jackson, August 29, 1958, Gary, Indiana.

**FORMATIVE YEARS:** Attended elementary school in Los Angeles. According to his teacher, "Occasionally he would disappear and turn up on television."

**FAMILY PLANNING:** Married Lisa Marie Presley, May 26, 1994; divorced January 18, 1996; Married Debbie Rowe (doctor's assistant) November 14, 1996.

**ROMANTIC INTERESTS:** Tatum O'Neal (actress), Diana Ross (musician), Brooke Shields (actress).

## SELECTED HITS (and Misses)

**SONGS:** "Ben" (1972), "Don't Stop (Till You Get Enough)" (1979), "Billie Jean" (1982), "Beat It" (1982), "Thriller" (1982), "I Just Can't Stop Loving You" (1987), "Bad" (1987), "Black or White" (1991), "In the Closet" (1992), "Will

You Be There" (1993), "Scream" (with Janet Jackson—1995), "You Are Not Alone" (1995).

**FILMS:** *The Wiz* (1978), *Thriller* (1984), *Captain Eo* (1985).

**TV:** *The Jackson 5ive* (cartoon series,1971–73), *The Jacksons* (variety series, 1976–77).

## QUICKIE BIO

The self-proclaimed "King of Pop" is perhaps also the reigning Emperor of Weird. His 1982 album *Thriller* did break almost every sales record imaginable, moving forty million copies worldwide, reaching number one in every Western country, spawning seven American Top Ten singles, and earning a dozen Grammy nominations. In recent years, however, his eccentricities have overshadowed his talents. Chief among them are Michael Jackson's alterations to his body (as obvious as they are numerous) and a variety of pesky allegations and full-blown lawsuits concerning paternity, child molestation, and other stuff. On May 26, 1994, Jackson wed Lisa Marie Presley, daughter of Elvis Presley. Less than two years later, the princess filed for divorce from the man who would be king. In November 1996, Jackson announced that Debbie Rowe (an assistant to his dermatologist) was carrying his baby and that he had married her. Then Jackson started hanging around again with ex-wife Presley while arranging to build an amusement park in Poland, and hinting that wife Debbie was pregnant yet again. Jackson's very loyal friend Elizabeth Taylor has called Michael "the least weird man I've ever known." When actress Brooke Shields heard that, she burst out laughing.

## MICHAEL JACKSON DOES
## THE DUMBEST THINGS

⭐ In 1977, Jackson had lunch with a reporter at a posh French restaurant in Manhattan. Wacko Jacko stuck his napkin in his T-shirt and began eating his Caesar salad with his hands. When a serving of quiche arrived, Jackson jabbed his fingers into it, began eating it off his hands, and said, "It's just like ham and eggs!"

⭐ After Jackson's first rhinoplasty in May of 1979, he took home a keepsake—a small glass vial containing a purplish slice of his own nose cartilage. All in all, Jackson has had at least six nose jobs, several face lifts, fat suctioned from his cheeks, bone grafted onto his cheekbones, a "forehead lift" to raise his eyebrows, and several eye jobs.

⭐ In addition to his own body parts, Jackson kept a brain in a jar in his room. He also enjoys watching surgical procedures, particularly brain surgery. One surgeon was surprised at Jackson's reaction to a particularly gruesome operation. "He was smiling through the whole thing."

⭐ While working on his solo album *Off the Wall* (1979), Jackson stopped bathing or changing his clothes. Producer Quincy Jones gave Jackson the nickname "Smelly." Jones tried to explain that the word didn't mean "stinky", it meant "cool."

⭐ At one point Jackson was going to Disneyland three or four times a day. To mingle with the crowd unnoticed, he sported wigs, hats, fake beards, glasses, and fake noses. Finally, he gave up his disguises and traveled around the park in a wheelchair so he could get pushed right to the head of every line.

⭐ Jackson also wore bizarre disguises when he canvassed door-to-door for the Jehovah's Witnesses. Sometimes he donned a total-body disguise he called his "fat suit." When fat-suited Jackson appeared on the doorstep of one home, a large dog lunged at him. Jackson dropped his religious literature and ran away, ripping off pieces of his fat suit as he dashed down the street.

⭐ Jackson built a secret gallery at Neverland Ranch, his Southern California home. Objects on display in "Michael's Treasure Room" included: one hundred antique dolls, a glass case with $1 million in jewels, porcelain figures of himself alongside Disney characters, and a $200,000 portrait of Jackson, Albert Einstein, George Washington, Abraham Lincoln, the *Mona Lisa*, and the movie alien-character ET, all wearing sunglasses and a white sequined glove.

⭐ For a time, Jackson kept six mannequins in his room. He dressed them in evening gowns with feather boas, named each one, and had conversations with them. Explained the rock star, "I like to imagine talking to them."

⭐ Jackson spent a lot of time with one young friend, trying to fly. Jackson and the boy would close their eyes, hold hands, stand in the middle of his room and concentrate on floating to the ceiling. "I'd get bored after half an hour or so," recalled the youngster years later, "but Jackson just kept standing there with his eyes closed, wishing he could fly. Once he asked Tinkerbell to sprinkle him with pixie dust. No, I'm sure he wasn't kidding."

⭐ Sometimes Jackson spent the whole day speaking in a "doo-doo language." He called everyone "doo-doo-head." Said Jackson on one of his doo-doo days: "I'm hungry. I wonder what I'll have. Maybe some doo-doo."

**Bubbles the chimp appeared at a celebrity fashion show in 1987 carrying a picture of his pet rock star, Michael Jackson.** [photo courtesy of Archive Photos]

⭐ On September 4, 1993, Jackson paid $26 million to settle a lawsuit involving six counts of claimed sexual battery. When reporters in Buenos Aires gathered outside his hotel window to ask about his alleged misdeeds with young boys, Jackson waved a copy of the magazine *Child* out the window. The headline on the magazine read: "46 Fun Baby Games."

⭐ Following in the footsteps of his father-in-law Elvis Presley, Jackson acquired a chimp named Bubbles in 1984. Among the perks Bubbles enjoyed: twenty matching designer outfits and his own hotel room when he traveled.

🐶 Jackson talked baby talk to Bubbles, changed his diapers, and even shaved the chimp's rear because Bubbles couldn't "wipe himself."

⭐ Eventually Jackson got jealous of his chimp. "I'm the star," whined Michael, "not that chimp!"

⭐ After Bubbles slugged Jackson, Jackson consulted with chimp expert Jane Goodall, then decided to send his former companion to a private zoo. Explained Jackson, "Bubbles just isn't that cute anymore."

⭐ Jackson enjoyed releasing fake news to the tabloids. At one point, Jackson posed for a picture in a hyperbaric chamber. Jackson then gave a tabloid reporter the exclusive rights to sell the story as long as the reporter used the word "bizarre" three times in the piece. Jackson then complained when the tabloid ran the story.

⭐ Jackson began wrapping three of his fingers in surgical tape because he heard Howard Hughes did it.

⭐ Former President Ronald Reagan sent a telegram to Jackson which read, "Your deep faith in God and adherence to traditional values are an inspiration to all of us." Later that year Jackson traveled to the White House to meet the prez, but when he stepped into the Diplomatic Reception Room he got frightened, ran away, and hid in the presidential bathroom. Nancy Reagan just shook her head in amazement.

⭐ Jackson traveled to the Ivory Coast village of Krinjabo and was crowned "King of Sanwis." Throughout the entire trip Jackson held his nose. When the press said that this was putting Africa down, his spokesman said, "Under no circumstances would we be here if we thought your country smelled."

⭐ Before he made love to his wife Debbie Rowe, Michael dressed up as Peter Pan and danced around the room. Another time he put on a horse's head and galloped around on a broomstick. Explained Debbie, "It made him feel romantic."

💰 One day Jackson entertained himself by sitting on the floor of his living room, tearing up $100 bills, throwing them in the air, and saying, "Isn't it pretty. Money makes the best confetti."

# The Jackson Family

## FACTS OF LIFE

**RINGLEADERS:** (All the children were born in Gary, Indiana.): Maureen Reilette (Rebbie)—born May 29, 1950; Sigmund Esco (Jackie)—born May 4, 1951; Toriano Adaryll (Tito)—born October 15, 1953; Jermaine la Juaen—born December 11, 1954; LaToya Yvonne—born May 29, 1956; Marlon David—born March 12, 1957; Steven Randall (Randy)—born October 29, 1962; Janet Damita Jo—born May 16, 1966; Katherine (mother)—born Kattie B. Scruse, May 4, 1930, Barbour County, Alabama; Joe (father)—born Joseph Walter Jackson, July 29, 1929, Fountain Hill, Arkansas.

## SELECTED HITS (and Misses)

**SONGS:** "Big Boy" (The Jackson 5—1968), "I Want You Back" (The Jackson 5—1970), "You're in Good Hands" (Jermaine—1973), "Shake Your Body (Down to the Ground)" (The Jackson 5—1979), "Young Love" (Janet—1982), "Come Give Your Love to Me" (Janet—1982), "Centipede" (Rebbie—1984), "Control" (Janet—1986), "Rhythm Nation" (Janet—1989), "Love Will Never Do Without You" (Janet—1989), "If" (Janet—1993), "Velvet Rope" (Janet—1997).

**TV:** *The Jacksons: An American Dream* (miniseries—1992).

# QUICKIE BIO

America's First Family of Pop has made dysfunction a spectator sport. Born in Gary, Indiana, to father Joe and mother Katherine, youngsters Jackie, Tito, Jermaine, Marlon, and Michael started performing locally as the Jackson 5. The group began winning local talent contests and signed with Motown Records in 1969. After a string of mega-smash hits, Michael went solo. The rest of the family, save Janet, has been riding Michael's coattails ever since. In 1994, the Jackson brothers reunited for the Victory tour. Claimed the tour's promoter, Don King, "Anybody who sees this show will be a better person for years to come." Obviously, the Jacksons themselves never saw the show.

## THE JACKSON FAMILY DOES THE DUMBEST THINGS

⭐ Poppa Joe Jackson used to go into young Michael's room, light up matches, and hold them to his son's feet. When Michael screamed, Daddy Joe just laughed.

⭐ Joe didn't let his kids play out in the street near their home in Gary, Indiana. He said he was trying to protect them from violence. At the same time, Joe was allegedly whopping all his kids with razor straps, belts, wire coat-hangers, rulers, switches, and fists. The Jacksons probably would have been a lot safer out on the street.

⭐ Joe was an avid gun collector. He liked to pull guns out of his bureau, aim them at his children, and pull the trigger.

⭐ In late 1979, mother Katherine called hubby Joe at his Sunset Boulevard office in Los Angeles. When Joe's girlfriend, Gina Sprague, answered the phone, Katherine slammed it down, put Randy and Janet in the car, drove to the office, ran inside, and yelled, "Bitch! I told you we were gonna get you!" Mommy Jackson pulled Sprague out of her chair and dropped her on the floor. All three Jacksons then dragged her out of the office and into the hallway. Randy held Sprague against the wall while Katherine reportedly beat her and ripped off her necklace. When a security guard arrived on the scene, Janet warned him, "Leave, mister. This is a family affair."

⭐ Jermaine Jackson married Hazel Gordy, daughter of Motown Records exec Berry Gordy. Jermaine later had an illegitimate child by another woman. Jermaine often showed up at Jackson family reunions with his wife, his girlfriend, and his illegitimate child.

"Snakes are intellectually limited, but once you've been around one and get to know his ways, you can tell when he likes you," commented LaToya Jackson. She was talking about reptiles, not her ex-husband.
{photo courtesy of Archive Photos]

⭐ When Katherine heard her son Marlon's solo album *Baby Tonight* (1987), she commented, "Marlon can't sing. Why doesn't he just hang it up? He has no talent."

⭐ Narcissist Tito named his three sons Tito. The trio began performing as 3T and in 1996 charted a minor hit called "Anything."

⭐ LaToya Jackson claimed that her family tried to kidnap her twice to keep her from an alleged former brothel owner named Jack Gordon.

⭐ LaToya eventually made Gordon her manager and married him. Moments after the ceremony, LaToya turned to her husband and said, "I just want you to know one thing. We are not married."

LaToya draped her nude body with snakes for a layout in *Playboy* magazine.

 LaToya later opened up a telephone psychic network. Callers to the line were greeted with: "Hello, I'm LaToya. And I have brought together some of the world's most gifted psychics to help answer your most personal questions."

 Janet didn't pose with snakes. Instead she talked to Jafar, her pet giraffe; Lola, her pet llama; her four pet dogs; and her pet deer. "They were wonderful listeners," said Janet. "And I really felt they understood what I was feeling."

 To get over depression, Janet had a coffee enema. "Your body cells hold emotions," Janet told a reporter. "And with the enema you can bring out the sad cells or—whatever it is."

 To please her boyfriend Rene Elizondo, Janet offered to have either her nipple or her privates pierced. Rene chose the nipple. Janet also had the middle of her nose pierced. She explained it was for "a spiritual reason which I don't talk about."

# Mick Jagger

## FACTS OF LIFE

**ORIGIN:** Born Michael Phillip Jagger, July 26, 1943, Dartford, England.

**FORMATIVE YEARS:** Attended London School of Economics and considered being a journalist "but it seemed too much like hard work."

**FAMILY PLANNING:** Had an illegitimate child by Marsha Hunt; Married Bianca Perez Morena de Macias, May 13, 1971; divorced 1978; Married Jerry Hall (model), November 21, 1990.

**ROMANTIC INTERESTS:** "I had my first sexual experience with boys at school," said Mick. "I think that's true of almost every boy." Later romantic interests included Andrew Loog Oldham (his manager), Chrissie Shrimpton (ingenue), P.P. Arnold (one of the singing Ikettes), Brian Jones (bandmate), Bebe Buell (groupie), Pamela Des Barres (groupie), Marianne Faithfull (singer), Eric Clapton (musician), David Bowie (see: *David Bowie*), Angela Bowie (David Bowie's wife), Linda Ronstadt (singer), Anita Pallenberg (see: *Keith Richards*), Carly Simon (singer), Rudolph Nureyev (dancer), Cornelia Guest (debutante—see: *Boy George*), Carla Bruni (model).

## SELECTED HITS (and Misses)

**SONGS:** (With the Rolling Stones) "Time Is On My Side" (1964), "Sympathy for the Devil" (1969), "Angie" (1973), "Miss You" (1978), "Emotional Rescue" (1980), "Hang Fire" (1982), "Just Another Night" (Mick Jagger solo—1985), "Dancing in the Street" (Mick Jagger and David Bowie—1985), "Mixed Emotions" (1989).

**FILMS:** *Ned Kelly* (1970), *Performance* (1970), *Cocksucker Blues* (1972), *Running Out of Luck* (1986), *Freejack* (1992), *Bent* (1997).

## QUICKIE BIO

Mick Jagger was introduced to rhythm-and-blues by a black cook on an American army base in England. Entranced by the sound, Jagger got into the British blues scene and dropped out of college to play with the Rolling Stones. Along with pal David Bowie, Jagger became pop culture's leading omnisexual. "I'd rather die than be forty-five and still singing 'Satisfaction,'" said a young Jagger. By the late 1990s, Jagger was well into his fifties and was still singing "Satisfaction." Jagger continues to push the envelope of sexuality even as a middle-aged man. In 1997, he appeared as a transvestite nightclub hostess in a movie appropriately titled *Bent*. "Mick?" observed Rolling Stone guitarist Keith Richards, "He's a lovely bunch of guys."

## MICK JAGGER DOES
## THE DUMBEST THINGS

★ To annoy Rolling Stones bandmate Brian Jones, Jagger seduced Pat Andrews, the mother of Jones's second illegitimate kid. Then Jagger went ahead and seduced Jones.

★ Two groupies slept with Jones. When they were finished they said he was "great, but he's no Mick Jagger." Then the enterprising duo had sex with Keith Richards. Again they said, he was "great, but he's no Mick Jagger." Finally, the girls managed to sleep with Jagger himself. Their comment: "He's great. But he's no Mick Jagger."

★ While eating at a London restaurant on Kings Road, Jagger was confronted by a gentleman seated at the next table. "Are you a man or a woman?" the gentleman asked. Jagger stood up, unzipped his pants and presented the evidence.

★ When his girlfriend Chrissie Shrimpton tried to commit suicide in December 1966, Jagger visited her in the hospital. He inquired about her health, then told her he was seeing singer Marianne Faithfull. Then he stopped paying her hospital bills. Then Mick dropped Faithfull and she tried to commit suicide.

In 1970, Jagger portrayed a retired bisexual rock star in the film *Performance*. One of his costars was Anita Pallenberg, who was seeing Keith Richards at the time. During one romantic scene, Pallenberg stuck her tongue in Jagger's nostril and really got the Stone rolling. The scene

was so hot, it was cut from the film. But an uncut version of the film later won an award at a porno festival in Amsterdam.

⭐ In 1972, Jagger and Russian ballet star Rudolph Nureyev met TV commentator/star Geraldo Rivera at a party. Jagger and Nureyev nuzzled up to Rivera. Nureyev told Jagger, "He's a virgin, you know." "Oh, well," Jagger chuckled. "We can break him in." Rivera escaped intact.

⭐ For a while, Jagger introduced Bebe Buell as "the mother of one of my illegitimate children." Jagger got jealous when Bebe informed him that Steven Tyler of Aerosmith was actually the father of her daughter, who grew up to be the actress Liv Tyler.

⭐ Jagger had an emerald inserted into the middle of his upper right incisor. When people mistook it for a bit of spinach, he switched to a ruby. Then he got sick of people talking about a spot of blood on his lip, so he implanted a diamond.

⭐ Jagger's first wife Bianca Perez Morena de Macias tried to keep him in line by "losing" expensive pieces of jewelry. Whenever Jagger made a play for another woman, de Macias would interrupt by saying, "God, I've lost my $40,000 bracelet!" Jagger called it "one of her little stunts."

⭐ Another one of de Macias's stunts was to go out with men on her own. One of her lovers was Jack Ford, the son of former president Gerald R. Ford. Jack and de Macias had their picture taken together in the Lincoln bedroom of the White House.

⭐ Model Jerry Hall had a more direct method for keeping her hubby Jagger in line. Whenever she saw a woman make a pass at Jagger, she jabbed her with her elbows, stomped on her toes, or kicked her in the shins. "In Texas," she explained, "we tell other girls where to get off."

⭐ When her elbows didn't work, Hall relied on her mouth. "Even if you have only two seconds, drop everything else and give him a blow job," advised Hall. "That way he won't really want sex with anyone else."

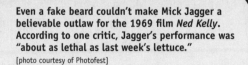

Even a fake beard couldn't make Mick Jagger a believable outlaw for the 1969 film *Ned Kelly*. According to one critic, Jagger's performance was "about as lethal as last week's lettuce."

[photo courtesy of Photofest]

# Rick James

## FACTS OF LIFE

**ORIGIN:** Born James Ambrose Johnson, Jr., February 1, 1948, Buffalo, New York.

**FORMATIVE YEARS:** Joined the navy to see the world. Saw enough and went AWOL.

**FAMILY PLANNING:** Married Tanya Anne Hijazi in 1997.

**ROMANTIC INTERESTS:** "Chicks always run up, feeling my ass and nuts and touching my dick and thinking I'm supposed to f*** right there on the floor."

## SELECTED HITS (and Misses)

**SONGS:** "You and I" (1978), "Super Freak" (1981), "Give It to Me Baby" (1981), "Cold Blooded" (1983), "17" (1984), "Spend the Night with Me" (1985), "Loosey's Rap" (1988), "Mama's Eyes" (1997), "Urban Rhapsody" (1997).

## QUICKIE BIO

Rick James was the nephew of the Temptations' Melvin Franklin, a connection that helped him break into the music biz in the late 1970s. James's resounding 1982 anthem "Super Freak" was such a good tune that it became

106

a hit again in 1990 when songster M.C. Hammer sampled it for the hit "U Can't Touch This." "Super Freak" James not only played music, he produced music for movie star Eddie Murphy (remember "Party All the Time"?) and other L.A. scenemakers. When the hits stopped happening in the late 1980s, James stumbled from his platform boots and fell all the way to prison. After his release from jail, he released the 1997 album *Urban Rhapsody*. One of his earlier album titles would have been more appropriate: *Bustin' Out of L Seven*.

## RICK JAMES DOES
## THE DUMBEST THINGS

⭐ When James was growing up, his mother ran a gambling operation. "Most parents want their kids to be doctors and lawyers," recalled James. "My mother wanted us to be numbers racketeers."

⭐ At age fifteen James joined the U.S. Naval Reserves. He went AWOL and fled to Canada. There he moved into an apartment with Canadian rocker Neil Young. The two played together in a group called the Mynah Birds. James claimed that he was the one who convinced Young to go electric. Whether or not James was the godfather of grunge, the Mynahs broke up in 1965 when James was arrested for his naval indiscretions.

⭐ When James hit it big in Los Angeles, he moved into a mansion once owned by William Randolph Hearst. Said James, "I was living large inside a Citizen Kane fantasy."

⭐ James used his "large living" to develop a violent Jekyll-and-Hyde personality. "The Rick James image is one thing," he sighed. "James Johnson, me, is another."

⭐ By the late 1980s, the evil James had completely taken over James Johnson, Jr. One night, James and his girlfriend, Tanya Anne Hijazi, partied with another woman. James and Hijazi were later arrested for assault with a deadly weapon, false imprisonment, making terrorist threats, furnishing narcotics, and, as if that wasn't enough (and, gee, don't you think it ought to be?), forced oral copulation.

⭐ During the encounter, James told the woman that what he was doing was good for her. (Huh?) James explained that he was torturing her so that she could learn how people live in California.

⭐ After hideously abusing the woman, James gave her $320. "Here you go," said the rocker. "Go buy yourself something nice." The charges against James were dropped.

A year later, James and Hijazi invited a different woman over to their L.A. hotel room. Charges resulting from this romantic evening included assault with a deadly weapon, torture, false imprisonment (again), forced oral copulation (again), terrorist threats (again), and—your favorite and mine—aggravated mayhem.

✪ James pled no-contest to assault, drug, and false-imprisonment charges. He maintained that he was still a romantic kind of guy. "People look at [me and Tanya] like we're Bonnie and Clyde," said the remorseful James, "but we really love each other."

✪ After serving three years in California's Folsom Prison, James Johnson gazed back at his Rick James side and despaired, "I think about this character that I've created and it bums the f*** out of me sometimes." Even so, Johnson resurrected the Rick James character for a 1997 comeback tour. Now that's a *real* bummer.

"The black Marquis de Sade," said Rick James, describing his own well-deserved reputation.
[photo courtesy of Photofest]

# Jefferson Airplane

## FACTS OF LIFE

**RINGLEADERS:** Grace Slick (singer)—born Grace Barnett Wing, October 30, 1939, Chicago, Illinois; Marty Balin (vocals)—born Martyn Jerel Buchwald, January 30, 1942, Cincinnati, Ohio; Paul Kantner (guitar)—born March 12, 1941, San Francisco, California.

### Selected Hits (and Misses)

**SONGS:** "Somebody to Love" (1967), "White Rabbit" (1967), "Volunteers" (1969), "Ride the Tiger" (1974), "Miracles" (1975), "We Built This City" (1985), "Nothing's Gonna Stop Us Now" (1987), "It's Not Over ('Till It's Over)" (1987).

**FILM:** *One P.M.* (1969).

### Quickie Bio

In 1965, Marty Balin and Paul Kantner named their band the Jefferson Airplane in honor of a fictional blues character, Blind Thomas Jefferson Airplane. However, the band didn't take off until sharp-tongued socialite Grace Slick jumped on board. A regular attraction at the Fillmore West, the Airplane helped define the San Francisco psychedelic sound and launched their own record label—Grunt Records. The Airplane crashed in 1972, then took flight again as the Jefferson Starship. Various Starship incarnations continued to cruise through the 1990s, though a 1989 Jefferson Airplane reunion was voted "Most Unwelcome Comeback" by *Rolling Stone* magazine.

## JEFFERSON AIRPLANE DOES THE DUMBEST THINGS

⭐ Slick kept two medicine cabinets in her house, "one for recreational purposes, the other for medicinal routines." She explained further, "I was always afraid of getting the mouthwash mixed up with the mescaline or taking tablets of aspirin instead of acid."

⭐ During a performance at the Whiskey-a-Go-Go, Balin took too much acid, not aspirin. He became mesmerized by a pair of very large breasts in the audience. Then he fell off the stage.

⭐ Slick was performing at an outdoor concert in L.A. when it started to rain. The psychedelic rocker took her shirt off. "I don't want to get it wet," she reasoned.

⭐ Grace Slick was too embarrassed to take her clothes off when she was cruising with music star David Crosby on his yacht off Florida. "I was embarrassed because these women all had perfect figures, no tan lines, and long blond hair. I had kinky brown hair. I was skinny at that point, with no boobs—one of them's bigger than the other—and knobby knees." Crosby called her "the Chrome Nun."

⭐ Slick later jumped onstage during a performance of Crosby, Stills, Nash and Young. Drunk, she performed silent karate moves until promoter Bill Graham pulled her off the stage.

⭐ When Slick appeared on the TV show *The Smothers Brothers Comedy Hour*, she performed in blackface.

⭐ At the Fillmore East in 1969, Grace walked out onto the Manhattan stage dressed as Adolf Hitler.

⭐ One of the band members went to bed with a girl named Detroit Frieda. He got the clap. She came back to town a month later. He went to bed with her again. Guess what? He got the clap *again*.

⭐ Kantner was busted onstage in Miami for telling the kids to burn the place. The cops escorted him to the police station. Kantner noted that the cops were drinking bourbon. He spiked their bourbon with acid.

⭐ At Altamont, Balin jumped offstage to keep the Hell's Angels from beating up a fan. The Hell's Angels beat up Balin, then jumped onstage to pummel Paul Kantner. Slick observed, "Ya gotta keep bodies off each other unless you wanna make love," then kept on singing. When a friend later commented on Slick's courage, the singer confessed that she had been blind, not brave. "I had forgotten to put my contacts in that morning."

★ Invited by Tricia and Pat Nixon to attend a Finch College reunion at the White House, Slick invited political activist Abbie Hoffman to be her escort. Slick filled up her jacket pockets with LSD to dose the president. But the folks at the door wouldn't let Hoffman enter the event.

★ After delivering a daughter fathered by Kantner, Slick told the nurse, "We're naming her 'god' with a small g; we want her to be humble." However, the birth certificate read "China Wing Kantner."

★ The Airplane started a record label called Grunt Records. Slick and Kantner signed a band led by Reality de Lipcrotch. Lipcrotch wanted to release albums that would disintegrate as they were being played.

★ TV talk-show host Geraldo Rivera once asked Slick what it was she had always wanted to be. Slick answered, "Blond with big boobs."

# Billy Joel

## FACTS OF LIFE

**ORIGIN:** Born William Martin Joel, May 9, 1949, Hicksville, New York.

**FORMATIVE YEARS:** Dropped out of Hicksville High.

**FAMILY PLANNING:** Married Elizabeth Weber (secretary), 1973, divorced July 1982; Married Christie Brinkley (model), March 23, 1985, divorced August 25, 1994.

**ROMANTIC INTERESTS:** "I know I'm perceived as a mainstay of soft rock—which to me is like soft cock. I hate that....I don't have a soft cock—I got a hard cock."

### Selected Hits (and Misses)

**SONGS:** "Brain Invasion" (1970), "Piano Man" (1973), "The Entertainer" (1974), "New York State of Mind" (1976), "Just the Way You Are" (1977), "Scenes From an Italian Restaurant" (1977), "Only the Good Die Young" (1977), "Big Shot" (1978), "Uptown Girl" (1983).

**TV:** "I don't do TV. Only by mistake. Or if someone shysters me."

### Quickie Bio

Following in the footsteps of his classically trained father, Billy Joel studied keyboards and played with bands at Hicksville High. Joel's first big break came when he recorded with joke-rock acts the Shangri Las and the

Detergents. The Long Island musician eventually worked his way through Los Angeles piano bars into the soft heart of sap-rock, selling millions of records and wedding supermodel Christie Brinkley. By 1997, Brinkley had split, and Joel had decided to start writing classical music. "I'm tired of writing pop songs," declared Joel. While the world prepared for Billy Beethoven, the pop-dissing Joel prepared for his 1998 world tour with another "classical" musician—Elton John.

## BILLY JOEL DOES
## THE DUMBEST THINGS

✪ As a youth, Joel once teetered on the brink of suicide. "I went into the closet and said, 'I'm gonna kill myself,'" confessed the singer. "There was chlorine bleach and I said, 'Nah, that's gonna taste bad.' So I took the Pledge. All I ended up doing was farting furniture polish."

✪ Joel went through a psychedelic phase with a band called the Hassles. Groovy Billy wrote the song "Hour of the Wolf." Sighed Joel, "I was a lousy hippie."

✪ Hassled by the Hassles, Joel formed a band called Attila. Attila was an organ-and-drums heavy-metal act. Joel posed for the *Attila* album cover in medieval armor standing next to bloody sides of beef. Recalled Joel years later, "It was a very noble experiment."

✪ After Attila broke up, Joel checked himself into a psychiatric hospital. Then he headed for California and got ripped off by his manager (whose name was Artie Ripp). Eventually Joel suggested his wife become his manager. "Why don't you manage me?" asked Joel, who may have been temporarily insane. "You know how dumb musicians can be and you've been hanging around me long enough." His wife agreed. Recalled a proud Joel, "I figured this would be the first case of 'Artist Screws Manager.'"

✪ Billy Joel later claimed he got screwed by his wife/manager. He fired her, divorced her, then hired her brother to be his new manager. Joel later fired his brother-in-law and slapped him with a $90 million lawsuit.

✪ After his divorce, Joel claimed he was looking for a woman who would love him even if he "killed forty million people and slashed their tongues out and raped most of them."

"I don't have a soft cock. I've got a hard cock," argued Billy Joel in *Rolling Stone* magazine.
[photo courtesy of Photofest]

★ Joel found Brinkley in a Caribbean piano bar in 1983. "There's something beyond her look," said the intellectual Joel. "She's nicely rounded which is very important in bed."

★ Joel was shocked in 1973 when his song "Piano Man" started climbing the charts. "This is a hit song?" asked the ivory-tickler. "You gotta be kidding me. It's just the same chorus over and over again."

★ Joel's band thought the 1977 hit song "Just the Way You Are" was absolutely the worst. Exclaimed Joel's drummer, "I won't play that oily cocktail lounge cha-cha/samba crap!"

★ When critic Ken Tucker called Joel "the great spoiled brat of rock," the piano man threw a fit. Onstage during a concert, Joel ripped the review apart and yelled out to his adoring fans, "F*** you, Ken Tucker."

★ Joel said he admired Paul McCartney "because his voice can pull off these real dopey records." Not as dopey as yours, Billy.

# Elton John

## FACTS OF LIFE

ORIGIN: Born Reginald Kenneth Dwight, March 25, 1947, Pinner, England.

FORMATIVE YEARS: Dropped out of Pinner County Grammar School.

FAMILY PLANNING: Married Renate Blauel, February 14, 1984; divorced November 18, 1988.

ROMANTIC INTERESTS: According to his first fiancée Linda Ann Woodrow, "When we rolled into bed, he was clumsy, and, frankly, didn't have a clue." Other lovers reportedly included John Reid (his onetime manager) and David Furnish (an advertising executive).

## SELECTED HITS (and Misses)

SONGS: "Country Comfort" (1970), "Rocket Man (I Think It's Gonna Be a Long, Long Time)" (1972), "Crocodile Rock" (1972), "Candle in the Wind" (1973), "Bennie and the Jets" (1973), "The Bitch Is Back" (1974), "Lucy in the Sky with Diamonds" (1974), "Philadelphia Freedom" (1975), "Mama Can't Buy You Love" (1979), "I Guess That's Why They Call It Love" (1983), "I Don't Wanna Go On with You Like That" (1988), "Can You Feel the Love Tonight" (1994), "Candle in the Wind 1997" (Lady Diana version—1997).

FILMS: *Born to Boogie* (1972), *Tommy* (1975), *The Lion King* (soundtrack—1994).

# QUICKIE BIO

A spiring concert pianist Reggie Dwight won a scholarship to London's Royal Academy of Music in 1958. Dwight turned down the sponsorship and instead began pounding out the blues. After playing the club circuit and impersonating the Bee Gees on cut-rate albums, Dwight changed his name to Elton John, teamed up with seventeen-year-old lyricist Bernard Taupin, and began churning out hits. John's flamboyant outfits and outrageous stage shows made KISS look bland. John split with Taupin in 1977, then became the king of animated rock with the extraordinary success of his soundtrack for the 1994 cartoon feature *The Lion King.* In 1997, John made history when his Lady Diana tribute "Candle in the Wind 1997" became the biggest-selling single of *all* time, surpassing Bing Crosby's "White Christmas." England's Queen Elizabeth was so impressed by the money Elton raised that the next year she knighted him Sir Reginald Kenneth Dwight. There was no report of what the Queen thought when Elton showed up at his fiftieth birthday party wearing an $80,000 ensemble including a white wig topped with a silver ship and a fifteen-foot ostrich feather train carried by two nearly nude hunks. "All hail Elton, the queen who would be king!"

## ELTON JOHN DOES THE DUMBEST THINGS

Anatomy was the reason John chose his middle name, Hercules. "I asked myself 'Am I hung like a horse?'" recalled Elton, "And the answer was yes, so I gave myself that name as it seemed very appropriate." Hercules was the name of a horse on the British TV sitcom *Steptoe and Son.*

★ While living with his fiancée Linda Ann Woodrow and close pal Bernie Taupin, John became depressed. Taupin and Woodrow found him in the kitchen with his head in the gas range trying to kill himself. However, it was only a halfhearted attempt. "He'd only turned the gas on to 'low,' and left the kitchen window open," Taupin recalled. "And he'd thought to take a cushion to rest his head on."

★ By the 1970s, John was fixated on camp fashion items—especially glasses. He collected hundreds of pairs of spectacles, including a heart-shaped rimless pair tinted in red, white, and blue; a pair with little hoods that could be pulled down; a pair with windshield wipers; and a solid gold pair. Of the latter, John said, "I'm so afraid of losing them that they're strictly for my eyes only."

"I am not your usual sex idol, am I?" gushed Elton John
[photo courtesy of Photofest]

⭐ At different times, John has appeared before audiences dressed as Uncle Sam, Prince Charming, Donald Duck, Ronald McDonald, Mozart, Santa Claus, and Rod Stewart's wife Rachel Hunter.

⭐ John's least successful costume creation was a pair of wooden pants. Sighed John, "Not very good for moving about, I'm afraid."

⭐ On a 1972 American tour, John tap-danced while a midget sprinkled him with glitter. Another tour featured deep-throated porn star Linda Lovelace and look-alikes posing as the Queen of England, Mae West, Batman, Robin, and the Beatles.

⭐ Elton's sex life exploded in the 1970s. "I would walk into a club and see someone I hadn't even met and I would already have them on the conveyor belt," confessed John. "They'd come out with a Versace shirt and a Cartier watch at the other end."

⭐ Designer Gianni Versace was a big buddy of John's. "Come on, you bitch. You bitch, where are you?" said Versace to John over the phone. "Come on, let's go shopping."

💰 It's no wonder Versace encouraged Elton John to shop. The singer regularly shelled out $85,000 and more for Versace-designed outfits. The

balding singer once spent $850,000 on a single day's shopping spree. "For Elton," said an associate, "when the going gets tough, the tough go shopping."

 Elton loved to shop, but he hated carrying things. When asked to push a shopping cart for a Citibank commercial, Elton reportedly exclaimed, "Are you mad? I'll look like a big, fat homeless person pushing that thing!"

⭐ John's temper tantrums, known as "Reggie's Little Moments," were as legendary as his stage shows. "I could be unbelievably horrible and stupid," recalled Elton. "On tours, I'd get on a plane, then get off it, maybe six or eight times. I'd walk out of a hotel suite because I didn't like the color of the bedspread. I remember looking out of my room at the Inn on the Park one day and saying, 'It's too windy. Can someone please do something about it?'"

⭐ In 1975, John brought his relatives along to enjoy "Elton John Week" in Los Angeles. John reportedly took sixty Valiums, jumped into the hotel pool, and yelled "I'm going to die!" His grandmother sighed, "I suppose we've all got to go home now."

⭐ John has dyed his hair every color from orange to green to silver. Eventually, John's exhausted locks just fell out. The balding superstar went to Paris to endure a hair transplant. After the procedure, he came out from the clinic, his head wrapped in gauze. When he tried to get into a waiting car, he whammed his head against the car door. Fearing that he had knocked out his hair plugs, he rushed back into the clinic to have them checked.

⭐ When on the road, Elton used a bunch of different aliases including Sir Tarquin Budgerigar, Bobo Latrine, Jr., Sir Horace Pussy, and Binky Poodle-clip.

⭐ John was absent at the Science Fiction Movie Awards in 1978, but luckily, partner Bernie Taupin was there to announce history's dumbest performance of a rock song—William Shatner's spoken-word rendition of "Rocket Man."

⭐ John first recorded the 1973 hit "Candle in the Wind" as a tribute to Marilyn Monroe. His 1997 remake of the song as a tribute to the late Princess Diana blasted sales records. However, some rockers didn't appreciate Elton Hercules John's herculean effort on behalf of Lady Diana. The Rolling Stones' Keith Richards commented that John was only good for "writing songs for dead blonds." "He's so pathetic, poor thing," spat John in retaliation. "It's like a monkey with arthritis trying to go onstage and looking young."

# The Kinks

## FACTS OF LIFE

**RINGLEADERS:** Ray Davies (singer)—born June 21, 1944 London, England; Dave Davies (guitar)—born February 3, 1947, London, England; Mick Avory (drums)—born February 15, 1944, Hampton Court, Surrey, England.

## SELECTED HITS (and Misses)

**SONGS:** "You Really Got Me" (1964), "All Day and All of the Night" (1964), "Tired of Waiting for You" (1965), "Lola" (1970), "Apeman" (1970), "Acute Schizophrenia Paranoia Blues" (1971), "Come Dancing" (1983).

**FILMS:** *The Virgin Soldiers* (soundtrack by Ray Davies—1969), *Absolute Beginners* (Ray Davies—1986).

## QUICKIE BIO

After elder brother Ray Davies dropped out of art school to play rock and roll with his group for British debutantes, younger brother Dave Davies joined them to form the Kinks. The band hit it big in the early 1960s, then careened along a career path that followed the twisted psychodrama of the Davies brothers. In 1993, the brothers summed up their relationship in the song "Hatred (A Duet)" which featured the line *"Hatred is the only thing that keeps us together."*

# THE KINKS DO
# THE DUMBEST THINGS

⭐ Ray once tried to be like Keith Moon and destroy his hotel room. "I threw a Guinness bottle against the wall," explained Ray. "It bounced back and hit me on the head and knocked me out."

⭐ On their first American tour in 1965, the Davies boys behaved so badly that their manager quit and went to work for Sonny and Cher. The band missed so many concerts and got into so many fights that they were banned from performing in the United States for four years by the American Federation of Musicians.

⭐ The stress of being a celebrity wore heavily on Ray in 1966. At one point he stuffed money in his sock, ran to his publicist's office, and punched him out. The police chased Davies down the street. A pedestrian, who happened to be a psychiatrist, saved Davies by putting him into a cab and sending him home.

⭐ Onstage in England in 1965, Dave sported two black eyes given him the night before by his drummer and housemate Mick Avory. At the start of the evening's second song, Avory took offense to Dave and clobbered him again—this time with a cymbal. Dave was knocked unconscious and needed ten stitches in his head. Avory laughed off the incident to the press. "The idea," he said, "was to wave stuff around and generally go mad."

⭐ Onstage in Washington, D.C., fourteen years later, Avory threw another cymbal at Dave, and chased him offstage.

⭐ A prominent fashion designer came to a party at Ray's home. The designer made disparaging remarks about Ray's clothes. Ray didn't mind that. But when the designer compared Ray to Mick Jagger, Ray punched the guy. Ray later wrote a song about the incident—"Dedicated Follower of Fashion."

⭐ In 1971, brothers Ray and Dave were dining in Manhattan. Dave tried to steal one of Ray's french fries. Ray stabbed his brother in the chest with a fork.

⭐ During one performance, Ray introduced a song sung by Dave with the words, "Let's let the little twerp express himself as best he can." "I don't know why I do that," sighed Ray later. "It's appalling, horrible."

⭐ During a Boston performance of the Kinks' rock epic *Preservation*, Dave got so mad at brother Ray that he left the stage and played the *whole* show from behind a curtain.

⭐ When Ray took his driving test, he knocked down a woman carrying groceries. He ran out of the car to help her but forgot to set the parking brake. The driving instructor had to stop the moving vehicle. Ray gave up. "I was only learning to drive because I thought I should be a regular person," said Ray. "But that was stupid."

⭐ Ray had as much difficulty with women as with cars. He left his second wife to take up with hard-partying songster Chrissie Hynde of the Pretenders. Brother Dave didn't think much of Ray's latest girlfriend. When Ray brought her onstage, Dave stomped off. He came back a moment later and spit in Hynde's face.

⭐ Ray asked a photographer to take a picture of the couple for their mantel. The only problem was, they had no mantel. Ray had destroyed it with a TV set during a fight with Hynde.

# KISS

## FACTS OF LIFE

**RINGLEADERS:** Gene Simmons (bass, vocals)—born Chaim Witz, August 25, 1949, Haifa, Israel; Paul Stanley (guitar, vocals)—born Paul Stanley Eisen, January 20, 1950, Queens, New York; Ace Frehley (guitar, vocals)—born Paul Frehley, April 22, 1951, Bronx, New York; Peter Criss (drums, vocals)—born George Peter Criscoula, December 27, 1945, Brooklyn, New York.

## SELECTED HITS (and Misses)

**SONGS:** "Black Diamond" (1974), "Room Service" (1975), "Rock and Roll All Nite" (1975), "Detroit Rock City" (1976), "Beth" (1976), "Hard Luck Woman" (1976), "I Love It Loud" (1982), "Forever" (1990), "Lick It Up" (1993).

**TV:** *KISS Meets the Phantom of the Park* (telefeature—1978).

## QUICKIE BIO

Schoolteacher Gene Simmons and Paul Stanley came up with the KISS concept in 1973. They began with crude face paint and cheap S & M leather-wear but quickly graduated to full-blown fire-breathin', blood-hurlin', dry-ice-and-smoke-bombs mega–rock productions. KISS's comic book approach generated top-selling albums and a flood of KISS merchandise including pinball machines, belt buckles, masks, dolls, board games, credit cards, and even comic books. Simmons, the Mickey Mouse of rock, lost some of his marketing appeal when he dated Cher and then Diana Ross. However, the mouse roared back with a blockbuster 1996 reunion tour. KISS earned more money onstage than any other rock band that year. Now, *that's* scary.

# KISS DOES THE
# DUMBEST THINGS

⭐ After graduating from Richmond College, Simmons became a school teacher. Why did he quit to form KISS? "I wanted to kill those little pricks," he said.

⭐ Paul Frehley's nickname (other than "Ace") was "Scraps," because in KISS's early days he'd eat whatever was left over on everyone else's plates.

⭐ During KISS's first big show, with Iggy Pop and Blue Oyster Cult in 1974, Simmons tried to breathe fire. Instead, he set his own hair on fire.

⭐ Simmons bragged that he mated with 3,000 women during the 1970s. His dream girl? One that's "got big tits that'll knock you in the face. Someone you can wrap your loins around and swap spit with." Or, a woman with nipples like "coat hangers."

⭐ In 1975, a fan won a dream date with Simmons in a magazine promotion. An embarrassed Simmons was forced to take off his platform boots to fit in her Volkswagen.

⭐ Frehley created the double-S lightning strokes in KISS's logo—very similar to the SS logo used by Nazi troopers. He then claimed he wasn't familiar with the Nazi version.

⭐ Peter Criss had such a hard time remembering his lines for the 1978 TV movie *KISS Meets the Phantom of the Park,* that his entire part had to be redubbed.

⭐ In the early 1980s, Criss got drunk and fired his revolver at a Christmas tree. Why the tree? Apparently because his wife hadn't let him be the one to put the star on top.

⭐ In 1980, Stanley searched for an expensive New York co-op. He was turned down by the management of several buildings before he got smart and started wearing a short-haired wig to interviews.

⭐ During one of KISS's rare periods of financial problems, Frehley proposed the band get ordained by the Universal Life Church and become preachers.

⭐ Simmons told the press in 1980 that he had plans for a "KISS World," as in Disney World, a traveling amusement park, and a special KISS line of cars manufactured by Chrysler. "I don't want Mickey Mouse to have a

"There's nothing like knowing you're helping the youth of America undress," sighed Gene Simmons of KISS.

[photo courtesy of Photofest]

corner on that market," said Simmons, "There's nothing that Super-man, King Kong, or Mickey Mouse have got that we haven't or can't have."

On their 1992 album *Revenge*, Stanley and Simmons penned the line *"The bigger the cushion, the better the pushin'."* Oops, the line was almost exactly the same as a line from Spinal Tap's 1984 song "Big Bottom." *("The bigger the cushion/the sweeter the pushin'")* Stanley and Simmons claimed that they'd never heard of Spinal Tap. Yeah, guys. You never heard of Alice Cooper either.

# k.d. lang

## FACTS OF LIFE

**ORIGIN:** Born Kathryn Dawn Lang, November 2, 1961, Consort, Alberta, Canada.

**FORMATIVE YEARS:** Briefly attended Red Deer College on a volleyball scholarship, then dropped out and hung around with a slacker named Drifter.

**FAMILY PLANNING:** "My goals are not to be a wife or necessarily a mother."

**ROMANTIC INTERESTS:** Came out sexually at a young age and confessed that her teenage lovers included "anyone I could get my hands on, basically." Later admitted, "When a person is attracted to me, they're not thinking about my genitals."

## SELECTED HITS (and Misses)

**SONGS:** "Big-Boned Gal" (1987), "Crying" (duet with Roy Orbison—1987), "Constant Craving" (1992), "Miss Chatelaine" (1993), "You're OK" (1996), "Don't Smoke in Bed" (1997).

**FILM:** *Salmonberries* (1991).

**TV:** *The Last Don* (miniseries—1997).

## QUICKIE BIO

lang grew up a girl jock in Alberta, Canada, before blasting onto the music scene in the 1980s as an androgynous Canadian cowgirl. She first tried country, but then decided Nashville was "an ugly little city." She then helped usher in the era of "lesbian chic," and became a radical vegetarian torch singer. Her 1997 album *Drag* celebrated the sensuality of smoking.

## k.d. lang DOES
## THE DUMBEST THINGS

- ★ k.d. lang insisted that people write her name in lowercase letters.

- ★ In her early days, lang was a performing artist. During one show, she crawled around onstage in garbage bags and participated in a twelve-hour (actual time) reenactment of Barney Clark's heart-transplant surgery. For the show, lang used a heart made from pickled beets.

- ★ lang confessed that she learned a lot about show-biz by watching crows. According to lang, "They sort of teach me how to dance."

- ★ In 1982, lang performed in a musical in Edmonton, Canada. The director told her to act like Patsy Cline. lang looked at the director and asked, "Who's Patsy Cline?"

- ★ By 1987, lang had decided that she was Patsy Cline. "I think I am the reincarnation of Patsy Cline," said lang. "You may think Patsy Cline died in a plane crash in 1963, but she's living right here in my merry body, I tell ya."

- ★ Five years later, lang wasn't so sure. "She's kind of moved on," said lang, who'd given up recording country music. "I'm sure she's picked some young singer to pick on now."

- 🐶 lang picked up politics. She appeared in an ad campaign sponsored by PETA (People for the Ethical Treatment of Animals). In the ad, lang declared, "Meat Stinks."

- ★ Ranchers in her hometown of Consort, Canada, didn't agree. A sign at the edge of the small town read, "Consort: Home of k.d. lang." After her anti-meat comments, someone spray-painted the sign with the words "Eat Beef Dyke." A radio-station manager took a more reasonable approach to the meat controversy. "If she thinks meat stinks," said the manager, "she hasn't had the opportunity to smell cauliflower that's been in the refrigerator too long."

- ★ The controversy didn't really bother lang. "Even my dog's a vegetarian," she shrugged. "Eats couscous, soy protein, garlic, and broccoli."

★ Vegetarian lang admitted that she nibbled on a lot of sage while writing music. Explained the singer, "It's like getting stoned without smoking a joint."

★ After the meat stink died down, lang attended PETA's annual "Fur is a Drag" party in New York City. Surrounded by female impersonators, lang herself dressed in, er, um, drag. One magazine editor wondered, "What is the world coming to, when dykes are dressing up like fags who dress up like women?"

★ At the party, a female impersonator came out of the women's bathroom and told lang that a lot of fans in the bathroom wanted to meet her. "What do they look like?" lang asked. "Oh, they're young and cute and sexy," the impersonator said. lang told her personal assistant, "Go check out the bathroom."

★ lang wore a wedding dress to the Canadian Juno Awards in 1985. lang told baffled reporters, "I thought it was appropriate. But lots of people don't get it."

★ When lang won the Grammy for Best Female Vocal Performance of 1992, she was thrilled. "What can I do to top this?" she asked reporters backstage at the ceremony. "Best Male Vocalist?"

# Led Zeppelin

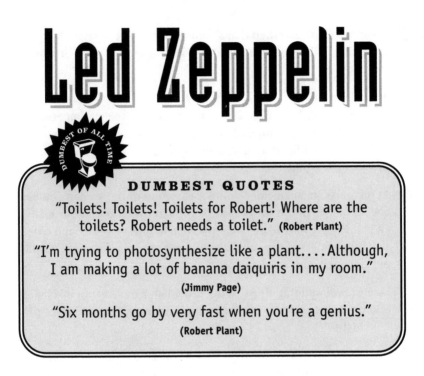

**DUMBEST OF ALL TIME**

## DUMBEST QUOTES

"Toilets! Toilets! Toilets for Robert! Where are the toilets? Robert needs a toilet." **(Robert Plant)**

"I'm trying to photosynthesize like a plant.... Although, I am making a lot of banana daiquiris in my room."
**(Jimmy Page)**

"Six months go by very fast when you're a genius."
**(Robert Plant)**

## FACTS OF LIFE (and Death)

**RINGLEADERS:** John "Bonzo" Bonham (drummer)—born May 31, 1948, Bromwich, England, died September 25, 1980 of a "pulmonary edema" caused by choking to death after drinking heavily; Robert Plant (vocals)—born August 20, 1948, West Bromwich, England; Jimmy Page (guitar)—born James Patrick Page, January 9, 1944, Middlesex, England; John Paul Jones (bass)—born John Baldwin, June 3, 1946, Sidcup, England.

## SELECTED HITS (and Misses)

**SONGS:** "Communication Breakdown" (1969), "Whole Lotta Love" (1969), "The Immigrant Song" (1970), "Stairway to Heaven" (1971), "Black Dog" (1972), "Kashmir" (1975), "Sick Again" (1975), "Fool in the Rain" (1980), "Ozone Baby" (1982).

**FILMS:** *The Song Remains the Same* (1976), *Death Wish II* (soundtrack by Jimmy Page—1982).

## QUICKIE BIO

Named for a favorite expression of The Who's Keith Moon ("This gig is "going down like a lead Zeppelin"), the band took off in 1968, led by veteran session guitarist Jimmy Page. Zeppelin burned through the charts as it left a trail of debauched devastation throughout England, Europe, and North America. Though the group disbanded with the death of drummer John Bonham in 1980, Led Zeppelin proved to be one of the most popular rock bands of all time. By the late 1990s, American radio stations had broadcast "Stairway to Heaven" more than three million times, for a total playing time of over forty-four solid years. No one was more sick of "Stairway" than Led Zeppelin singer Robert Plant, who referred to the most popular rock tune in history as "that bloody wedding song."

## LED ZEPPELIN DOES
## THE DUMBEST THINGS

★ In 1967, CBS-TV tried to turn Robert Plant into the next Tom Jones. Plant recorded a lushly orchestrated Italian ballad titled "Our Song." It sold about 800 copies.

★ Led Zeppelin was as famous for its exotic sexual exploits as for its music. One evening, two young girls were lounging in the bathtub of Led Zeppelin's hotel suite. Page walked in. He giggled, "We figured you need something to keep you company." Then he threw four live octopuses into the tub. The young ladies wound up enjoying the octopuses more than the rockers. "Oh my god," squealed one of them, "I've gotta get one of these. It's like having an eight-armed vibrator!"

★ While staying at the Hotel Château Marmont in Los Angeles, Bonham borrowed a white coat and a room-service cart. He lifted a girl named Candy onto the cart, removed her clothing, and said, "It's time for some surgery, my dear." Bonham went to the bathroom and emerged with a shaving brush, shaving cream, and razor. Page, Plant, Jones, and Bonham took turns shaving Candy's privates. At the end of the operation, Plant gasped in horror. "Bonham, how could you?" he said, staring at the girl on the cart. "This is mine. This is my f***ing brush."

Then there was the infamous "mudshark incident," which was actually more like a red herring. In 1969, Led Zeppelin checked into Seattle's Edgewater Inn. The place was a favorite with musicians because guests could fish from their rooms. The band hauled in some fish. Then they hauled in a seventeen-year-old redhead named Jackie. She mentioned she really liked being tied up. The obliging Englishmen ordered a rope from room service. Next, Jackie removed her clothes and the boys tied her to the bed. Then the road manager entertained the band by taking a red snapper and introducing it to the girl's private parts.

"You don't serve urine cocktails all the time," explained Robert Plant of Led Zeppelin.
[photo courtesy of Photofest]

⭐ Led Zeppelin later cheered on another adventurous female fan while she made love with her pet Great Dane. The boys in the band even provided strategically placed bacon for the Great Dane's pleasure.

⭐ Eva Von Zeppelin, a direct descendant of Count Ferdinand Von Zeppelin, called the band a bunch of "screaming monkeys." When Eva threatened to keep Led Zeppelin from playing in Copenhagen, the band changed their stage name for the gig. They called themselves the Nobs, a slang term for peckers.

⭐ In 1970, the band held a press conference in a Copenhagen art gallery. A critic started conversing with Bonham about a painting. Bonham cut him short and asked, "Do you want to know what I think of this paintin'?" The critic answered, "Yes." Bonham lifted the artwork off the wall and smashed it on the critic's head. Bonham asked, "Are there any other paintings you'd like me to critique tonight?"

⭐ During a 1971 North American tour, Led Zeppelin's road manager was in bed with some friendly girls. Bonham was watching TV, but he couldn't concentrate with all the grunting and groaning. Bonham took one of the girls' shoes and pooped in it. After the show the next night, the same girl yelled out at Bonham, "Remember me? You s*** in my shoe yesterday! I just wanted to thank you for a wonderful night!"

-  Bonham got so fed-up with Page's Japanese girlfriend that he pooped in her purse.

- Bonham got equally fed up with a Tokyo disc jockey who wouldn't play Led Zeppelin recordings. The DJ sat in a cage that rose and fell like an elevator. Bonham unzipped his pants and took aim. Bull's-eye!

On a 1974 flight from London to New York, Bonham got drunk and lazy. So lazy that he peed in his first-class seat rather than bother to go to the restroom. When he began to get uncomfortable, he walked back to tourist class and offered his first-class seat to a roadie. "That's bloody nice of you, Bonham," said the unsuspecting passenger as he moved forward. "That's just wonderful."

- Zeppelin's manager Peter Grant attended a party in 1974. Grant went up to Bob Dylan, but didn't recognize him. "Hi," said Grant, "I manage Led Zeppelin." Dylan shot back, "Hey, I don't come to you with my problems."

# John Lennon

**DUMBEST QUOTE**

"You know what they say about the Japanese is right! They all do look alike." (John Lennon)

## FACTS OF LIFE (and Death)

**ORIGIN:** Born John Winston Lennon, October 9, 1940, Liverpool, England, died December 8, 1980, murdered by a fanatical fan in New York City.

**FORMATIVE YEARS:** "My whole school life was a case of 'I couldn't care less.'"

**FAMILY PLANNING:** Married Cynthia Powell (art student) August 23, 1962; divorced November 8, 1968; Married Yoko Ono (artist) March 20, 1969.

**ROMANTIC INTERESTS:** Brian Epstein (manager), Joan Baez (musician), May Pang (his maid).

## SELECTED HITS (and Misses)

**SONGS:** (With the Beatles) "Please Please Me" (1963), "Twist and Shout" (1963), "A Hard Day's Night" (1964), "I Want to Hold Your Hand" (1964), "Help!" (1965), "Nowhere Man" (1966), "Strawberry Fields Forever" (1967), "I Am the Walrus" (1967), "Hey Jude" (1968), (Solo) "Cold Turkey" (1969), "Instant Karma" (1970), "Imagine" (1971), "Whatever Gets You Through the Night" (1974), "Dream" (1975), "(Just Like) Starting Over" (1980), "Woman" (1980).

**FILMS:** *How I Won the War* (1967), plus his movie collaborations with the other Beatles: *A Hard Day's Night* (1964), *Help!* (1965), *The Magical Mystery Tour* (1967), *Yellow Submarine* (animated—1968), *Let It Be* (1970), *The Compleat Beatles* (1982).

**TV:** *The Mike Douglas Show* (Lennon and Ono as cohosts of a talk program—1972).

## QUICKIE BIO

John Lennon met Liverpool buddy Paul McCartney in 1957 when the younger McCartney jumped onstage with Lennon and started playing trumpet. Lennon and McCartney began playing together with the Quarrymen, then changed their name to the Beatles. Manager Brian Epstein transformed the Rude Boys into mop-tops and took America by storm in 1964. Lennon's romance with artist Yoko Ono, and the disintegration of the Beatles in 1970, left many fans shaking their heads. Whether it was rock and roll, the Maharishi, world peace, or househusbandry, Lennon enthusiastically embraced life in ways that were brilliant, not-so-brilliant, and, well, just plain dumb.

## JOHN LENNON DOES THE DUMBEST THINGS

✪ On Good Friday, 1962, Lennon hung a life-size image of Jesus on the cross from the balcony of his Hamburg hotel room. When nuns from a nearby Catholic church stood in the street gazing at the sacrilegious icon, the fun-loving mop-top pelted them with water-filled condoms, then peed out the window yelling, "Raindrops from heaven!"

✪ The owner of the Star Club in Hamburg got so fed up with Lennon and his bandmates that he screamed, "Schmeiss diese englischen Arschlosche 'raus!" ("Throw these English a**holes out!")

✪ The world press screamed in March 1966, when Lennon announced to British interviewer that the Beatles were "more popular than Jesus."

✪ Lennon later told the other Beatles, "I am Jesus Christ come back again." But no one seemed to care. When Lennon introduced himself as the Messiah to a complete stranger, the man looked at Lennon and said, "Oh, really? Well, I loved your last record...."

✪ In the politically charged climate of the 1960s, Lennon returned his prestigious Member of the British Empire award to the Crown with the following note. "Your Majesty, I am returning this MBE in protest against Britain's involvement in the Nigeria-Biafra thing, against our support of America in Vietnam, and against 'Cold Turkey' slipping down the charts. With love, John Lennon of Bag."

"I guess the world thinks we're an ugly couple," mused John Lennon about himself and his wife, Yoko Ono. [photo courtesy of Photofest]

⭐ Lennon's inspiration for the 1967 song "Good Morning" came from a TV ad for Kellogg's Corn Flakes.

⭐ In 1967, Lennon decided that a TV repairman named John Alexis Mardas was his guru. Lennon called him Magic Alex and gave him a bunch of money to build a flying saucer, an artificial sun, and "loud-paper"—wallpaper which was really a speaker system. None of the inventions worked.

⭐ A few days after Lennon married Yoko Ono in Gibraltar in March 1969 (just days after Paul and Linda McCartney tied the knot), the newly-weds held a "bed-in" at the Hilton Hotel in Amsterdam. Lennon and Ono sat fully clothed on their bed from ten A.M. to ten P.M. talking about peace. They only left their bed long enough to allow room service to change the sheets.

⭐ Silly as it was, the "bed-in" made a lot more sense than "bagism." Lennon and Ono had themselves sewn inside white bedclothes and crouched silently on a low table at a hotel in Vienna. When stunned reporters refused to believe that the rock stars were actually in the bag, Ono began wailing a Japanese folk song.

📺 Lennon and Ono's films were almost as dumb as their politics. *Smile* was a 52-minute close-up of Lennon's mouth with the sound of birds chirping in the background. *Up Your Legs Forever* showed hundreds of thighs in motion. *Film No. 4* revealed several hundred wobbling bottoms. *Fly*

showed a fly crawling around a woman's crotch. *Self-Portrait* revealed the intimate details of Lennon's own crotch. The movie was supposed to show Lennon getting an erection. Evidently, the subject never came up.

 In early 1974, Lennon took a break from recording in Los Angeles and dined at a restaurant with maid/girlfriend May Pang. Lennon drank too much, visited the ladies' bathroom, found a sanitary napkin and taped it to his forehead. The rowdy crew then moved to the Troubadour Club. Lennon, outfitted in his new headgear, shouted obscenities at the performers and everyone else in the club. When the waitress refused to serve him, Lennon slurred, "Don't you know who I am?" The irritated waitress responded, "You're some a\*\*hole, with a Kotex on his head."

Lennon gave up music in 1975 to become a househusband. One morning, Ono decided to torment her hubby by deliberately placing cat poop on the floor of their New York City apartment. Lennon stepped on the feline droppings, grabbed Ono, and threatened to burn off her hair. He then went back to his bedroom and listened to the self-hypnosis tapes *I Love My Body* and *There's No Need to Be Angry.*

 Lennon's kids continued their father's legacy of controversial political statements. In 1998, Sean Lennon, son of John and Yoko, announced that government agents had conspired to kill his father. Proclaimed Sean, "Anyone who thinks that Mark Chapman was just some crazy guy who killed my dad for his personal interests is insane, I think, or very naïve." Others, including half-brother Julian Lennon, thought Sean was insane, or very naïve.

# Little Richard

## FACTS OF LIFE

**ORIGIN:** Born Richard Wayne Penniman, December 5, 1932, Macon, Georgia.

**FORMATIVE YEARS:** Dropped out of school.

**FAMILY PLANNING:** Never married.

**ROMANTIC INTERESTS:** "Everybody take off your clothes," Little Richard said to kick off an orgy. "Take 'em all off right now."

## SELECTED HITS (and Misses)

**SONGS:** "Get Rich Quick" (1951), "Tutti-Frutti" (1955), "Long Tall Sally" (1956), "Lucille" (1957), "Jenny, Jenny" (1957), "Good Golly Miss Molly" (1958), "Ooh! My Soul" (1958), "Holy Mackerel, Don't You Want a Man Like Me" (1965).

**FILMS:** *Mr. Rock and Roll* (1957), *The Girl Can't Help It* (1957), *Down and Out in Beverly Hills* (1986), *Purple People Eater* (1988).

## QUICKIE BIO

After singing gospel and peddling cure-alls with a traveling medicine show, Little Richard started pounding his piano, and screaming lyrics like "Awop-bop-a-loo-momp Alop-bam-boo." He started recording in 1951 and never stopped. During his five decades in show business (plus stints as a born-again preacher), Richard saw it all, smelled it all, and shouted about it all *"Ooh, may soul!"*

## LITTLE RICHARD DOES
## THE DUMBEST THINGS

⭐ As a young boy, Richard decided to give a birthday present to Miz Ola, one of his neighbors in Macon, Georgia. He wanted to do something creative. So he defecated, wrapped it up in a box and left it for his elderly friend. When Miz Ola opened the box, she screamed, "I'll kill him," and jumped off her porch without her walking cane. "God bless Miz Ola," Richard recalled in his autobiography. "She's dead now."

⭐ After picking up sex tips from local gay hustlers like Madame Oop, Sis Henry, and Bro Boy, Richard began driving around with a woman named Fanny. Richard didn't like the driving as much as he liked watching Fanny have sex in the back of the car with excited pedestrians. Richard and Fanny ran into trouble when they decided to fill 'er up at a local gas station. Richard was arrested for lewd conduct and told to get out of Macon.

⛓️ When he wasn't busy driving or performing, Richard liked to watch people "take out and urinate" in the restroom of the Trailways bus station in Long Beach, California. Richard didn't enjoy it when one of the restroom visitors turned out to be an undercover cop.

In the morning after hosting an orgy, Little Richard often entertained his guests by reading passages from the Bible. Praise the Lord!
[photo courtesy of Photofest]

⭐ Richard enjoyed organizing after-show orgies even more than hanging out in restrooms. According to Richard, "I would pay a guy who had a big penis to come and have sex with these ladies so I could watch them."

⭐ In the morning after an orgy, Richard often entertained his guests by reading passages from the Bible.

⭐ Richard liked to share the sexual wealth. In the dressing room before a gig, Richard introduced his girlfriend Angel to Texas rocker Buddy Holly. The lead Cricket started having sex with Angel while boyfriend Richard watched. "He finished and went to the stage still fastening himself up," remembered Richard. "He came and went."

⭐ One night, Richard and three or four of his male friends decided to have super-sex with a beautiful girl. They all took off their clothes. Then they covered the girl's body with cocaine. Next, they snorted all the cocaine. Then they got so whacked-out they forgot to have sex.

⭐ In 1957, Richard decided that rock music was devilish. He joined the ministry and sold all his future song royalties for $10,000. In the 1980s, Richard decided that rock wasn't so bad after all. He sued (but failed) to regain the royalties.

⭐ Richard tried to revive his career in the 1990s. In 1997, he performed a version of "The Curly Shuffle" for a TV tribute to the Three Stooges, complete with his trademark howls.

# Courtney Love

**DUMBEST QUOTES**

"Don't eat cheese. There are a million things to eat that are not cheese." (Courtney Love)

"I think when you get married it should be forever. Even though I did get married once and it was annulled." (Courtney Love)

"I'm a total drag-queen fag." (Courtney Love)

## FACTS OF LIFE

**ORIGIN:** Born Courtney Michelle Harrison, July 9, 1964, San Francisco, California.

**FORMATIVE YEARS:** Reform-school graduate.

**FAMILY PLANNING:** Married James Moreland (aka Falling James of the L.A. band Leaving Trains) in 1989; divorced; Married Kurt Cobain, February 24, 1992; widowed April 5, 1994.

**ROMANTIC INTERESTS:** Billy Corgan (musician), Trent Reznor (musician—see: *Nine Inch Nails*), Ian McCullough (musician).

## SELECTED HITS (and Misses)

**SONGS:** (With the band Hole) "Retard Girl" (1991), "Teenage Whore" (1991), "Pretty on the Inside" (1991), "Doll Parts" (1994), "Miss World" (1994), "Asking for It" (1994).

**FILMS:** *Sid and Nancy* (1986), *Straight to Hell* (1987), *Basquiat: Build a Fort, Set It on Fire* (1995), *The People vs. Larry Flynt* (1996), *Feeling Minnesota* (1996).

## QUICKIE BIO

The love child of a Deadhead and a trust-fund hippie therapist, Courtney Love worked as a stripper, party girl, and all-around troublemaker as she struggled to break into the entertainment biz. In 1989, she placed an ad for musicians in a Los Angeles paper and from the respondents formed the band Hole. When she first got together with future husband Kurt Cobain, Love's Hole was making more money than Cobain's music group, Nirvana. That changed quickly. So did Love—after the suicide death of her millionaire husband in 1994. Fans who saw the thoroughly reprocessed rock star on the covers of *Harper's Bazaar* and *US* had to ask themselves, "Where's Courtney?"

## COURTNEY LOVE DOES THE DUMBEST THINGS

✪ In her younger years, Love was poor but fashionable. "I always felt like half a person when I was poor and would run out of perfume," she told *Mademoiselle* magazine. "I'd find a way to get it even when I was on food stamps."

✪ While onstage with her band Hole, Love enjoyed performing faux fellatio on fans, pelting the audience with radishes, and throwing fits. She liked to pose with one foot on the monitor to maximize crotch-shot possibilities. Once she gave her underwear to a fan in exchange for a Nine Inch Nails hat. She then set the hat on fire.

✪ Love had a hard time dealing with tour sponsors. In 1995, Molson's beer paid Hole $400,000 to play a gig near the Arctic Circle. "F****in' Molson's, man," the ungrateful Love said. "I douche with it, I wash my face with it, I smash chicks in the head with it."

✪ Love later appeared at a Seattle benefit dedicated to stopping violence against women. Backstage at the anti-violence concert, Love slapped a woman and began wrestling with her on the floor.

✪ In 1995, Love jumped into a mosh pit, then punched out two fans for groping her. The fans sued Love. Love showed up for trial in Orlando, Florida, reportedly so sedated she had to be helped into her chair. During the courtroom sessions, Love leaned over to the plaintiffs' lawyers and said, "Hey, are you the prosecutors? Well, can I be O.J. and you can play Christopher Darden?" Just like O.J., Love was found not guilty.

"I found my inner bitch and ran with her," snarled **Courtney Love.** [courtesy of Archive Photos/Express Newspapers]

 In May 1991, Love spotted Cobain at a Butthole Surfers concert. She walked up to the guitarist and punched him in the stomach. Cobain punched Courtney back. According to Courtney, their romance was "a mating ritual for dysfunctional people."

⭐ At a later meeting, Cobain and Love got even closer. "We bonded over pharmaceuticals," explained Love. "I had Vicodin extra-strength...and he had Hycomine cough syrup."

⭐ A pregnant Love told *Vanity Fair* magazine in 1992, "If there ever is a time that a person should be on drugs, it's when they're pregnant, because it sucks."

- Later, while Love was giving birth, she worried about the fact that she had been shooting heroin while pregnant with her child. Chanted Love, "You will only have one head."

- Love tried at one point to preserve Cobain's DNA. She performed oral sex on Cobain, spit into a cup, and stuck the gooey mess in the freezer. Later, Courtney learned that the freezer wasn't cold enough for cryogenic preservation. The sperm spoiled.

- Love was always the jealous kind. Mary Lou Lord, one of Cobain's old girlfriends, got the full Love treatment. Love complained to the press, "Mary Lou Lord once gave Kurt a blow job and has built a career on it."

- Later, Love complained about complaining about Mary Lou Lord. She made up a term for giving free press to worthless people. She called it "Mary Lou Lording."

- Things got wacky when Mary Lou Lord showed up at a party for Love backstage at the Palladium in Los Angeles. While Danny DeVito and rock star Perry Farrell looked on, Love jumped up and pushed Lord. Lord ran out of the room. Love ran after her screaming, "I'm gonna kill you!" Love's boobs flopped out of her outfit as she ran. A bouncer tried to stop Lord, but only managed to pull off her wig, her jacket, and her shirt. Lord ran out onto Sunset Boulevard, with Love in hot pursuit. Lord finally lost Love by hiding behind a telephone pole.

- Love didn't like Madonna any more than she liked Mary Lou Lord. At the MTV Music Awards Show in 1995, Love burst in on an interview with Madonna. Love grabbed a mike, took a seat, and started dissing Madonna for not watching Hole perform. While Madonna looked on nervously, Love fell off her chair and stuck her legs straight up in the air.

- By 1997, Love was more interested in being a reporter than a rock star. She interviewed Fleetwood Mac's Stevie Nicks for *Spin* magazine and then interviewed her beautician, Kevyn Aucoin, for *Details* magazine. "Let's talk about Cher," said the former wild woman of Grunge. Replied Aucoin, "I think as a society we really owe her a great deal."

- In the same interview, Aucoin admitted that after working with Love, he "cried for like two days." We can understand why.

# Madonna

## FACTS OF LIFE

**ORIGIN:** Born Madonna Louise Ciccone, August 16, 1958, Bay City, Michigan.

**FORMATIVE YEARS:** High-school cheerleader.

**FAMILY PLANNING:** Married Sean Penn, August 16, 1985; divorced 1989; Had a daughter, Lourdes, in late 1996 by her personal trainer Carlos Leon.

**ROMANTIC INTERESTS:** Antonio Banderas (actor), Warren Beatty (actor), Sandra Bernhard (comedian), Dennis Rodman (basketball player), Vanilla Ice (see: *Vanilla Ice*), Andy Bird (twelve years younger).

## SELECTED HITS (and Misses)

**SONGS:** "Lucky Star" (1983), "Like a Virgin" (1984), "Material Girl" (1984), "Papa Don't Preach" (1986), "Like a Prayer" (1989), "Erotica" (1992), "I'll Remember" (1994), "Don't Cry for Me, Argentina" (1997).

**FILMS:** *A Certain Sacrifice* (1980), *Desperately Seeking Susan* (1985), *Shanghai Surprise* (1986), *Who's That Girl?* (1987), *Bloodhounds of Broadway* (1989), *Dick Tracy* (1990), *Truth or Dare* (1991), *A League of Their Own* (1992), *Shadows and Fog* (1992), *Body of Evidence* (1992), *Four Rooms* (1995), *Girl 6* (1996), *Evita* (1996).

## QUICKIE BIO

As a high-school cheerleader, Madonna wore flesh-colored panties, just to shock people. In later years, the Material Girl made a career out of shocking people with her sexually charged (and highly lucrative) music, movies, and stage performances. She was always one of her own biggest fans. "I'm everything," she proudly proclaimed. After a stormy marriage to actor Sean Penn, Madonna decided she didn't even need a mate—except for sperm donation. Certainly, she didn't need a hubby for sex. She wrote a book on the subject—a 1992 tome that displayed Madonna enjoying herself in a variety of different modes. The title of Madonna's literary masterpiece? *Sex*.

## MADONNA DOES
## THE DUMBEST THINGS

✪ In the early days of her career, Madonna got the attention of record-company "suits" by dropping popcorn into her cleavage during business meetings and sassily fishing it out.

✪ Madonna's past caught up with her in 1985 when both *Playboy* and *Penthouse* reprinted nude pictures of her in her more hirsute—and hungry—days. The photos revealed that Madonna was not a natural blond.

✪ At Sean Penn and Madonna's 1985 Malibu, California, wedding, Penn anticipated the invasion of an airborne press corps by marking the words F*** YOU in the nearby sand.

✪ Penn was as violent with the home folks as with the press. After Christmas in 1989, a furious Penn allegedly bound up Madonna like a holiday turkey for a few hours in a fit of rage. Madonna promptly filed for divorce—for the second time.

✪ "All the men I've stepped over to get to the top…" said Madonna of her many sexual conquests, "every one of them would have me back because they all still love me and I love them." Sure, Madonna.

✪ In 1989, Madonna inked a $5 million deal to do a Pepsi commercial. She then offended Catholic Pepsi drinkers by performing steamy altar sex in the video for the song "Like A Prayer." Pepsi broke off the deal after only one airing of the expensive commercial. Italian TV flat-out banned it. In 1991, some American Catholic leaders called on Pope John Paul II to excommunicate Madonna for blasphemy.

✪ Comedian Sandra Bernhard was once romantically linked to Madonna, although the "affair" probably involved more publicity than passion. Still, the couple, referred to in the press as "the Snatch Batch," had a very public friendship in the early 1990s—and a very public falling-out. Ex-Madonna-friend Bernhard acidly commented that "every time Madonna farts, [the press] picks up on it. They want to see how it smells. I hate to break the news, but it smells like everybody else's farts."

✪ Sandra—Meet Cher! Cher told a TV audience that Madonna could "be a little more magnanimous and a little less of a c***."

⭐ Madonna was no slouch at slagging others. The Material Girl, who built her career as a Marilyn Monroe knockoff, accused rock singer Gwen Stefani of stealing her moves, her look, and even (gasp!) her hair. After Madonna's jabs, Stefani and her band No Doubt were pulled from Madonna's best friend Rosie O'Donnell's TV talk-show lineup. O'Donnell said it was due to "scheduling difficulties."

⭐ While auditioning models for the *Sex* book photo sessions, Madonna asked two questions: "Do you mind getting naked?" and "Would you mind kissing me?"

⭐ At the press party for the book, Madonna herself arrived dressed as Little Bo Peep and carried a lamb.

⭐ Madonna made a 1994 appearance on David Letterman's TV talk show and uttered the f-word thirteen times. She then demanded the host sniff her undies. Letterman politely declined.

Madonna's pet chihuahua Chiquita was reportedly depressed over the attention lavished on Madonna's new baby, Lourdes. So Madonna sent the pooch to a canine shrink. Guess that little $7,500 diamond choker from Tiffany's just wasn't enough for the yapper!

"I won't be happy until I'm as famous as God," bragged Madonna.
[photo courtesy of Photofest]

# The Mamas and the Papas

## FACTS OF LIFE (and Death)

**RINGLEADERS:** John Phillips (vocals)—born John Edmund Andrew Phillips, August 30, 1935, Parris Island, South Carolina; Michelle Phillips (vocals)—born Holly Michelle Gilliam, April 6, 1944, Long Beach, California; Denny Doherty (vocals)—born November 29, 1941, Halifax, Canada; "Mama Cass" Elliot (vocals)—born Ellen Cohen, September 19, 1941, Baltimore, Maryland, died London, England July 29, 1974, of a heart attack while choking on food.

## SELECTED HITS (and Misses)

**SONGS:** "California Dreamin'" (1965), "Monday Monday" (1966), "I Saw Her Again" (1966), "Words of Love" (1966), "Dedicated to the One I Love" (1967), "Creeque Alley" (1967), "Twelve Thirty (Young Girls Are Coming to the Canyon)" (1967), "Dream a Little Dream of Me" (Cass Elliot—1968).

**FILMS:** *Brewster McCloud* (coproduced by John Phillips—1970), *The Last Movie* (Michelle Phillips—1979), *Dillinger* (Michelle Phillips—1973), *Valentino* (Michelle Phillips—1976), *American Anthem* (Michelle Phillips—1986), *Let It Ride* (Michelle Phillips—1989), *Army of One* (Michelle Phillips—1994).

**TV:** *Secrets of a Married Man* (Michelle Phillips—telefeature, 1986), *Assault and Matrimony* (Michelle Phillips—telefeature, 1987), *Rubdown* (Michelle Phillips—telefeature, 1993).

## QUICKIE BIO

After dropping out of four universities, John Phillips dropped into the music business. He started touring the folkie circuit with Denny Doherty before coupling with Michelle Gilliam and Cass Elliot to form the Mamas and the Papas. The hard-partying Los Angeles band recorded a series of autobiographical hits. At one point, Phillips was romantically pursuing Gilliam, Cass was romantically pursuing Doherty, and Doherty was trying to escape on his motorcycle. By the end of the 1960s, the band had fallen into retirement. Phillips and Gilliam spawned actress MacKenzie Phillips, then divorced and wrote tell-all bios about one another. As of 1997, no one had revived the act as the Grandmas and the Grandpas.

## THE MAMAS AND THE PAPAS DO
## THE DUMBEST THINGS

★ In the early 1960s, the folk-singing John Phillips traveled to Cuba with a friend to help Fidel Castro. He never saw Castro, but he did spend a week getting drunk, singing on a Havana TV show, and watching stag movies.

★ Phillips left his first wife Susan for Mama Michelle. Susan was understanding about the whole thing. She even let Phillips and Gilliam stay over in her house and use her bed. Phillips and Gilliam got so physical they snapped a leg off the bed. Ex-wife Susan complained, "It's bad enough you broke the bed, but you could have at least made it."

★ John Phillips was one of the organizers of the 1967 Monterey International Pop Festival, one of rock's first big benefit concerts. During the festivities, Phillips's ex-wife Susan called to tell him that she was serving him with papers for nonpayment of child support. "I'm the charity case you have to help," said Susan, "You're setting up this wonderful benefit to save the world. Oh, that's so cute I could barf."

★ The Mamas and the Papas were an incestuous family. One morning in 1965, John Phillips walked into Doherty's room. Doherty was under the sheets. Phillip's wife Gilliam was sitting on the bed, getting into her clothes. Phillips was furious. The group had just signed a record deal. "Who the hell signs a five-year deal to work together when the other guy in the group's got a thing going with your wife?" John asked himself. "I'm not that crazy." He was. Phillips *and* Doherty *and* Gilliam kept the contract.

★ Elliot was tried in London in 1967 for failure to pay a hotel bill. As the group left the courtroom, TV cameras showed Doherty and John

Phillips taking hash brownies from Elliot's purse and gobbling them down.

★ In Paris, John Phillips and friend Scott McKenzie, who recorded Phillips's song "San Francisco (Be Sure to Wear Some Flowers in Your Hair)," bought a bottle of champagne, hired eight prostitutes, and partied together on a bed beneath a ceiling mirror. Mused Phillips, "We're so dumb, Scott, we really are. What are we doing wrong?" "Don't make me laugh," said Scott, "It's late. We haven't got much time...."

✈ Papa John took his Rolls-Royce out for a spin one night in Los Angeles. He left the expensive car in valet parking—for six weeks. He also left a royalty check for $250,000 sitting in the glove compartment.

★ John Phillips was as careless with drugs as he was with cars and money. One day, Phillips's dog Trelawny, otherwise known as Mr. T, gobbled up a bag of mescaline capsules. Mr. T ran in circles for three days, then stared at himself in the mirror for twelve hours. Said Phillips, "He [Mr. T] was more human than anything else after swallowing all that mescaline."

★ John Phillips wrote the music for *Man on the Moon*, a musical that opened on Broadway in 1974. Brendan Gill of *The New Yorker* said the show "came as close to being totally mindless as any stage work that I can recall." Phillips observed, "God knows how much money had all come down to one 'dumb' evening of theater on the Great White Way."

👓 John Phillips was arrested in 1980 for trafficking in "tens of thousands of dosage units of controlled prescription drugs." Sitting in a New York City jail after the bust, Papa John had a confrontation with some guards. One goosed him with a billy club. Another asked him for an autograph. A third guard leaned over to the rock star and asked, "Hey, Johnny. Did Mama Cass really choke on a ham sandwich or what?"

★ Phillips was convicted, fined, and ordered to lead anti-drug seminars. While he was preaching to kids to stay off drugs, the Papa became a serious alcoholic. He received a liver transplant in 1995.

# Marilyn Manson

## FACTS OF LIFE

**ORIGIN:** Born Brian Warner, January 5, 1969, Canton, Ohio.

**FORMATIVE YEARS:** Studied journalism in college.

**FAMILY PLANNING:** When asked about his relationship to kids, Manson responded, "I'm not discouraging or promoting child abuse or child molestation."

**ROMANTIC INTERESTS:** "I don't have a conventional relationship."

## SELECTED HITS (and Misses)

**SONGS:** "Smells Like Children" (1994), "Cake and Sodomy" (1994), "Antichrist Superstar" (1997), "Dried Up, Tied, and Dead to the World" (1997).

**FILM:** *Lost Highway* (1997).

## QUICKIE BIO

Inspired by Ozzy Osbourne, Alice Cooper, KISS, and David Bowie, journalism student Brian Warner got together with friends to create the really scary rock band Marilyn Manson and the Spooky Kids. Manson got his big break when he interviewed Trent Reznor. Reznor sensed a kindred spirit and produced Manson's records. Manson might have been just another industrial shock rocker who enjoyed *The Cat in the Hat* if officials in New Jersey, South Carolina, and other states hadn't tried to ban his shows in 1997. Not since Ice-T and his song "Cop Killer" had any performer generated such public outrage—and such fabulous record-selling publicity.

# MARILYN MANSON DOES
# THE DUMBEST THINGS

⭐ While touring with Nine Inch Nails, Reznor's band, Manson performed oral sex on his guitar player onstage for about thirty seconds. Six years earlier a girl had performed oral sex on Manson onstage.

⭐ Manson denied the rumor that he was a child actor who appeared on the show *Mr. Belvedere.* "I've masturbated during the show when it was on TV," Manson explained, "but I've never been on it."

⭐ Manson also denied rumors that he forced people to mutilate boxloads of puppies and performed satanic rituals in which he stabbed teenage girls.

⭐ Manson did rip up Bibles, scream obscenities, and use the American flag as toilet paper as a regular part of his stage act.

⭐ Manson and bandmate Twiggy Ramirez performed a porno snuff scene in the film *Lost Highway.* "It was all very 'Marilyn Manson,'" said Manson.

⭐ Manson claimed that he took on his anti-Christ persona because he was abused as a child. "I used to get picked on for carrying my KISS lunchbox to school…" explained Manson. "It's the kind of abuse that stays with you forever."

**"I pity anybody who has to spend a day with me,"** moped Marilyn Manson.
[photo courtesy of Joseph Sia/Archive Photos]

⭐ Manson had a collection of fifteen prosthetic limbs which he took with him on tour.

⭐ At a Miami club, Ramirez and Marilyn played with a glow bracelet. Ramirez first wrapped the bracelet around his own pecker. Then Manson tried to insert the bracelet into Ramirez's member. Ramirez wound up biting off the end (of the bracelet) and spraying the glow stuff around the club.

🕯 Fans have asked Manson to cut them and put cigarettes out on their faces. One lucky fan got Manson to autograph his testicles. "He used a felt pen," enthused the fan. "It was like a turn-on."

⭐ Marilyn Manson and his buddies invited a deaf girl to join them for a party. The deaf girl stripped naked except for her boots. Manson made a helmut out of a large ham, adorned it with bacon, sausage links, and chicken gizzards and put it on the deaf girl's head. Then he put pimento loaf on her nipples and pieces of bologna on her back. Manson referred to the incident as "meat and greet."

⭐ During the same party, Manson asked Twiggy Ramirez and another friend to tape their penises together to see if the deaf girl could swallow them in one gulp. They couldn't figure out how to tape their penises together side by side, so they taped them end to end. Manson said the girl played them like a "dick harmonica." At the end of the harmonica solo, the deaf girl asked to take a shower. Manson asked her if he could pee on her before she turned on the water. "Just not on my boots," said the meat covered deaf girl. "And don't get it in my eyes. It stings."

# Linda McCartney

## FACTS OF LIFE and Death

ORIGIN: Born Linda Louise Eastman, September 24, 1942, Scarsdale, New York, died April 17, 1998, in Arizona of cancer.

FORMATIVE YEARS: Dropped out of the University of Arizona in Tucson.

FAMILY PLANNING: Married Bob See 1962; divorced 1963; Married Paul McCartney, March 12, 1969 (she was pregnant by him at the time).

ROMANTIC INTERESTS: Al Kooper (musician).

## SELECTED HITS (and Misses)

SONGS: (With husband Paul): "The Lovely Linda" (1970), "Singalong Junk" (1970), "Bip Bop" (1971), "Mary Had a Little Lamb" (1972), "Silly Love Songs" (1976), "Cook of the House" (1976).

FILM: *Rupert Bear and the Frog Song* (cartoon—1985).

## QUICKIE BIO

Beatles-hungry Linda McCartney broke into the rock business by intercepting an invitation to a Rolling Stones press party and snapping a series of attention-grabbing, crotch-level photos of the hosts. In 1967, Paul

McCartney was out "pullin' birds" at a London club, when Linda pulled him and never let go. Living proof that money, love, and fame can't buy talent, Sir Paul spent a quarter century pretending that his wife was actually a real musician. Linda is the highest-paid air vocalist in entertainment history. Remember Beatles fans: McCartney spent more time performing with Linda than he did with the Fab Four.

## LINDA McCARTNEY DOES
## THE DUMBEST THINGS

✪ When Linda came to visit Paul in London in 1968, Paul complained to a friend that "an American groupie" was "flying in. I've thrown her out once," explained Paul, "had to throw her suitcase over the wall, but it's no good, she keeps coming back."

✪ In the late 1960s, Linda and Paul's house at St. Johns Wood in England was a rock-and-roll zoo, filled with cats, dogs, chickens, guinea hens, ducks, geese, and pet droppings. When visitors, like Paul's stepmother, tried to spray the bugs crawling around the kitchen, Linda intervened in order to protect her animals.

Linda and Paul were obsessed with sheep. Their 1971 album was titled *Ram*. To promote *Ram*, Linda and Paul produced a record titled *Brung to Ewe by Hal Smith*, complete with the sound of bleating sheep.

A lot of Linda and Paul's songs didn't make any sense at all. Like the tune "Bip Bop." "The song just goes nowhere," recalled Paul. "I still cringe every time I hear it."

✪ The tune "Kreen-Akrore" featured Linda and Sir Paul imitating animal noises to celebrate life in the Brazilian rain forest.

✪ Linda, a vegetarian, was fixated on food. She first vocalized her obsession in the song "Cook of the House," a tune that began with the sound of potatoes frying.

✪ One Thanksgiving, creative Linda served her family a macaroni turkey.

✪ Linda and Paul's most distasteful vegetarian stunt occurred in 1996. The couple bought space in *The New Yorker* magazine for "Paul's Furs." The ad urged customers to "save thousands" by calling for a "Free Fur Video." The video turned out to be a gruesome animal snuff tape, and the number turned out to be a PETA (People for the Ethical Treatment of Animals) phone line.

✪ Though Linda didn't like meat, she liked herbs an awful lot. In 1980, Linda and Paul landed at Japan's Narita Airport to begin a tour. The first piece of McCartney luggage opened by the Japanese customs inspectors contained a bag full of joints. Paul spent the next ten days in a local jail, singing "Yesterday" again and again as requested by his guards. Paul later described the incident as "incredibly dumb."

✪ In 1984, Paul and Linda were busted in Barbados for possession of pot. They plead guilty and flew to London with their kids. After landing at Heathrow Airport, the couple was arrested for transporting pot. Linda later rationalized her actions by explaining, "I don't smoke it in front of the kids."

✪ During one tour, a disgruntled roadie allegedly miked and recorded Linda's off-key crooning during "Hey Jude." When shock-jock Howard Stern played the offensive screeching on his popular radio program, Linda obtained a cease-and-desist order.

✪ Linda McCartney's death in 1998 was a sad event and a public relations fiasco. McCartney's publicist first told the media that Linda had passed away in Santa Barbara, CA. Then he changed the story, saying that she had actually died in Tuscon, Arizona. Then he went out of his way to deny rumors of an assisted suicide, causing the media to speculate that perhaps it was an assisted suicide.

✪ Sir Paul McCartney's epitaph was a lot more understandable. He simply urged mourners to "go veggie."

# Metallica

**DUMBEST QUOTES**

"I'd like to get a beer-holder on my guitar
like they have on boats." **(James Hetfield)**

"Sometimes we spit towards each other to wake up.
A good loogie can really get someone's attention."
**(James Hetfield)**

## FACTS OF LIFE

**RINGLEADERS:** James Hetfield (vocals, guitar)—born August 3, 1963, Los
Angeles, California; Kirk Hammett (guitar)—born November 18, 1962, San
Francisco, California; Lars Ulrich (drums)—born December 26, 1963, Gen-
toss, Denmark; Dave Mustaine (guitar)—born September 13, 1961, La Mesa,
California.

## SELECTED HITS (and Misses)

**SONGS:** "Seek and Destroy" (1983), "Creeping Death" (1984), "For Whom
the Bell Tolls" (1984), "Master of Puppets" (1986), "One" (1988), "Enter Sand-
man" (1991), "The Unforgiven" (1992), "Nothing Else Matters" (1992).

## QUICKIE BIO

Danish drummer Lars Ulrich, the son of a professional tennis player,
teamed with singer James Hetfield and lead guitarist Dave Mustaine in
the early 1980s to form a band. They quickly found out what their teenage
L.A.-area audiences wanted—violent, sci-fi filled, heavy-metal music. Borrow-
ing the name Metallica from a San Francisco heavy-metal fanzine, and lyrical
ideas from H.P. Lovecraft, the band invested almost a decade in schnapps-
demented touring before cleaning up their act and scoring a hit with the
1988 song "One." Critics described them as "ugly guys, singing ugly things to
ugly music." But like an ugly building, Metallica became respectable in its old
age. In 1997, a Finnish cello quartet wrote classical interpretations of classic
Metallica and released it on an album titled *Apocalyptica*.

# METALLICA DOES
# THE DUMBEST THINGS

⭐ Mustaine didn't last long with Metallica. When a drunken Hetfield kicked Mustaine's dog, a drunken Mustaine punched Hetfield and left the band. Mustaine went on to lead his own heavy-metal band, Megadeth. Mustaine summed up his Metallica years as "magical yet impossible."

⭐ On a low-budget 1983 tour, Metallica saved money by sharing hotel-room beds. "Actually, no one snores much," recalled Hammett. "We drool a lot."

⭐ Metallica protested when the band's management suggested they change the title of their first major album to *Kill 'Em All.* The original title: *Metal Up Your A\*\*.*

⭐ Toward the end of the *Kill 'Em All* tour, Metallica spotted a fan wearing a homemade shirt that read, "Alcoholica, Drank 'Em All." Metallica ripped off the idea and printed up Alcoholica shirts of their own.

⭐ On their first visit to London, Metallica was arrested for vandalizing a movie theater. "We climbed on top of the marquee kicking the lights down on people," recalled Hetfield. "It was just one of those things we had to do when we were drunk."

⭐ Critics complained that the Metallica song "Fade to Black" encouraged kids to commit suicide. Metallica vehemently denied that they encouraged youngsters to do anything. "If somebody is dumb enough to just follow somebody else, that's their own fault," explained Hetfield. "When you're a role model, you have a responsibility and you lose your creative juices. Why worry about what other people think?"

⭐ On a 1987 break from Metallica, Hetfield played surprise gigs at San Francisco clubs with a band he called Spastic Children. The band wanted to end one show with a nude encore, but were strongly discouraged by the club owners. So they played in their underwear instead. Another Hetfield band featured a song about Larry Singleton, a California man who went to jail for raping a woman and hacking her arms off.

⭐ During a 1992 tour with Guns N' Roses, Metallica set off a fiery special effect which accidentally set fire to Hetfield. "I was playing guitar—and then all of a sudden I was not playing guitar anymore," recalled Hetfield who was taken to a hospital and treated for second- and third-degree burns.

At the end of the 1992 tour, Kirk Hammett pulled down his pants, mooned a TV camera and shouted, "That's what I think of the Guns N' Roses tour."

When Metallica released an album with an all-black cover, many people were reminded of the "none more black" album of another heavy-metal act. "Spinal Tap," sighed Ulrich. "That joke came up five minutes after I told it to the first person outside the inner sanctum."

Metallica's Hammett later met Spinal Tap's Nigel Tufnel at the 1992 MTV Music Awards. Hammett introduced himself by saying, "Hey man, I'm Kirk from Metallica and our record is all black." Tufnel looked up very matter-of-factly and said, "I can respect that."

After recording "One," a song sympathetic to a war veteran, and then "Don't Tread on Me," a war anthem, Metallica was labeled as "jingoistic" by some critics. "That was definitely a word we had to look up," Hammett said.

What will Ulrich do if Metallica comes to an end? "I'm going to put an ad in the paper saying, 'Stupid drummer looking for stupid people to play music with.'"

Inspired by the Million Man March in Washington, D.C., Metallica held its own mass gathering in a Philadelphia parking lot. The one-and-a-half hour free show was billed as the Multimillion Decibel March.

# Milli Vanilli

## FACTS OF LIFE and Death

**RINGLEADERS:** Robert Pilatus—born May 14, 1966, New York City, died April 2, 1998, in Frankfurt, Germany of a reported overconsumption of alcohol and pills; Fabrice Morvan—born May 14, 1966, Guadeloupe, West Indies.

## SELECTED HITS (and Misses)

**SONGS:** "Girl You Know It's True" (1989), "Baby Don't Forget My Number" (1989), "Girl I'm Gonna Miss You" (1989), "Blame It On the Rain" (1989), "All or Nothing" (1990).

## QUICKIE BIO

One of the biggest scandals ever in music history involved two pretty boys who lip-synched pop hits. Rob Pilatus and Fab Morvan were marginally talented, very attractive, European-raised young men who had that driving ambition *to be famous at any cost.* Frank Farian, a German producer, harnessed that ambition to create Milli Vanilli. When the band reached the United States, they scored three number-one hits, sold ten million records, and picked up a Grammy as Best New Artist of the Year in 1989. However, the team fought with Farian, and the producer revealed to the press that Milli Vanilli never actually sang their hit songs. *Horrors!* Despite the fact that record producers have a long history of manufacturing rock bands (see: *The Monkees, The Partridge Family, The Spice Girls*), the Milli Vanilli boys (and their career) took it on the fashionable chin. Milli Vanilli's record company didn't seem to care. "Embarrassing?" scoffed a company spokesperson. "We sold seven million albums."

# MILLI VANILLI DOES
## THE DUMBEST THINGS

⭐ In their pre-Milli Vanilli days, Rob Pilatus and Fab Morvan tried modeling. However, they weren't tall enough. So they tried singing. Sort of.

⭐ Farian matched the pint-sized singers with a tune he'd produced with studio singers in 1987. Farian wasn't worried about the fact that Milli Vanilli didn't sing on the record. After all, he'd done the same thing about ten years earlier with a song called "Pop Muzik" and a band called the "M" Factor.

⭐ The German-bred duo did not even speak English well when they first recorded. Milli Vanilli was coached phonetically in order to be able to perform at least some of their songs live.

✍ During one live performance, the Milli Vanilli tape-loop jammed, and repeated the same line over and over and over again. After dancing the same steps a few times, the boys bolted backstage and fixed the machine.

⭐ After the lip-synching revelation, lawyers launched a class-action suit against Milli Vanilli. When the suit was finally settled, purchasers of Milli Vanilli recordings and concert tickets were offered a small cash

"We can sing as well as any pop star in the Top Ten," bragged Rob Pilatus (left) of Milli Vanilli. Too bad the boys didn't sing on their 1989 Grammy Award-winning hit record. [photo courtesy of Reuters/Ed Nachtrieb/Archive Photos]

rebate. No one brought up the fact that the records probably sounded better without Milli Vanilli.

- ✪ Just as shocking as the truth about Milli Vanilli's vocal prowess was the revelation that the tiny braids and curly dreads adorning the boys' heads were also fake.

- ✪ Pilatus was devastated by Milli Vanilli's plunge into disgrace. In 1991, he threatened to commit suicide by jumping from the balcony of a Sunset Boulevard hotel in Los Angeles. He didn't jump. Instead, he plunged back into the recording studio with Fab and released an album called *Rob and Fab.* The disc sold fewer than 2,000 copies.

- ✪ With their Grammy gone and record sales in the toilet, Milli Vanilli agreed to make a commercial for Carefree sugarless gum in which they lip-synched the jingle.

- ✪ Selling chewing gum didn't bring Rob happiness. After pulling a boozy all-nighter in Los Angeles in February 1996, he mistook someone's Cutlass for his Mercedes and got into a fight. Pilatus was arrested and didn't have enough money to post bail. He eventually was ordered into drug rehab, reportedly for the tenth time. As a further blow to his ego, the LAPD press relations office kept referring to Pilatus as "the Milli Vanilli guy." Two years later Pilatus died in a German hotel room after consuming pills and alcohol.

# The Monkees

## FACTS OF LIFE

**RINGLEADERS:** Mickey Dolenz (drums)—born March 8, 1945, Tarzana, California); Davy Jones (vocals)—born David Jones, December 30, 1945, Manchester, England; Michael Nesmith (guitar)—born December 30, 1942, Houston, Texas; Peter Tork (bass)—born February 13, 1944, Washington, D.C.

## SELECTED HITS (and Misses)

**SONGS:** "Last Train to Clarksville" (1966), "I'm a Believer" (1966), "A Little Bit Me, A Little Bit You" (1967), "Pleasant Valley Sunday" (1967), "Daydream Believer" (1967), "Valleri" (1967), "Zor and Zam" (1968), "Tapioca Tundra" (1968), "She's Movin' In with Rico" (1968).

**FILMS:** *Head* (1968), *Night of the Strangler* (Mickey Dolenz—1973).

**TV:** *Circus Boy* (Mickey Dolenz [using the name Mickey Braddock] series, 1956–58), *The Monkees* (series, 1966–68), *33⅓ Revolutions Per Monkee* (1969).

## QUICKIE BIO

The Monkees were one of rock's most successful "fake" bands. In 1966, Hollywood TV producers hired Mickey Dolenz, Davy Jones, Michael Nesmith, and Peter Tork to star as the band in a sitcom styled after the Beatles' successful film *A Hard Day's Night*. The Monkees didn't play any instruments on their first two hit albums. And when they did play their own instruments, they didn't play very well. However, the Monkees actually tried very hard to be real. Unfortunately they didn't succeed. By 1970, their shining star had burned out like a goofy prop "idea" light-bulb. Since then, various partial re-unions of the band have met with various levels of disinterest. Except by those who are fascinated by UFOs and JFK. "There are a stack of people who think the Monkees were a conspiracy," sighed Nesmith in the mid-1990s. "These tend to be people who live in the desert in a house made out of hub-caps."

## THE MONKEES DO
## THE DUMBEST THINGS

✪ Stephen Stills, later of Crosby, Stills and Nash fame, tried out to be a Monkee. The producers didn't go for him because his hair was falling out and he had bad teeth.

✪ Stills suggested his friend Peter Tork. Tork walked into the wall as he entered the audition, and got the job.

✪ When the Monkees ate their first meal together, Jones was shocked by Dolenz's table manners. "I've never seen anybody eat like that in my life, man," said the former star of British theater. "You eat like a pig." Jones then grabbed two handfuls of salad and smashed them into his own face.

✪ Before the Monkees' sitcom premiered, the band made a promotional appearance in front of TV-station executives. Dolenz shaved with a microphone. Jones pretended to be a duck. "That's the Monkees?" said one station exec. "Forget it!"

✪ Nesmith never really bought into the whole Monkees thing. "I told them that the music they were producing was garbage, patently designed to sell, with no redeeming social value at all," he complained. "And they all looked at me as if I had a bug up my nose."

✪ Child actors Dolenz and Jones didn't really care about the music. They cared about close-ups. Dolenz slipped the cameraman $25 to make sure he got the most close-ups. Then Jones slipped the guy $35, and stole the show.

✪ When Jones wasn't busy in front of the camera, he was busy in his twelve- by fourteen-foot windowless dressing room. Jones smuggled groupies into the box and used it as his love nest. "I'd be kissing one girl," Jones explained, "going to another, saying, 'Wait a minute I'll be with you in a second.'"

⭐ Tork didn't get to sing any songs on the Monkees' first album. So he insisted that he be allowed to sing a "meaningful" song on the second album. The result? "Your Auntie Grizelda," a novelty number featuring a chorus of vocalized armpit-fart noises, sung by Tork.

⭐ Tork made the most of his fame when he went to the Monterey International Pop Festival in 1967. Tork saw Brian Jones of the Rolling Stones backstage. The two shook hands. Then Tork said, "You know there's about a hundred photographers just dying to get that shot; would you mind again?" Jones obliged, but said softly under his breath, "How embarrassing."

⭐ The Monkees' plotless feature-film *Head* in 1968 was even more embarrassing. Written by actor Jack Nicholson, the cast included former Mouseketeer Annette Funicello, boxer Sonny Liston, football player Ray Nitschke, and Carol Doda, known as "Miss Super Breasts." The film featured the Monkees as dandruff in Victor Mature's hair, and intercut Monkees concert footage with shots of Vietnam War atrocities and old movie clips.

⭐ In 1967, the Monkees hit the road with Jimi Hendrix as their opening act. Monkees fans disliked Hendrix and booed him. In New York, Hendrix got fed up, flipped the fans the bird, and walked off the tour. "Oh God, I hate them!" Hendrix later said of the headliners. "Dishwater!"

⭐ For many years after the tour, certain groupies debated the question of "whose was bigger," Jimi's or the aptly-named Peter's.

⭐ In 1972, Tork was caught with hash in El Paso and sentenced to four months in prison. "It was not the worst thing that ever happened to me," confessed the convicted Monkee.

# Keith Moon

**DUMBEST OF ALL TIME**

## DUMBEST QUOTES

"I am the best Keith Moon–type drummer in the world." (Keith Moon)

"They're always saying I'm a Capitalist pig. I suppose I am, but, ah...it ah...it's good for my drumming, I think." (Keith Moon)

## FACTS OF LIFE (and Death)

**ORIGIN:** Born Keith John Moon, August 23, 1947, Wembley, England, died September 7, 1978, London, England, of an overdose of Heminevrin, a drug used to treat alcoholism.

**FORMATIVE YEARS:** Dropped out of school at age fifteen.

**FAMILY PLANNING:** Married Kim Kerrigan (model) March 1966; divorced 1973.

**ROMANTIC INTERESTS:** According to his biographer, "Much of the time he just can't be bothered."

## SELECTED HITS (and Misses)

**SONGS:** (see: *The Who*)

**FILMS:** *200 Motels* (1972), *That'll Be the Day* (1974), *Tommy* (1975), *Sextette* (with Mae West—1978), *The Kids Are Alright* (1979).

## QUICKIE BIO

Keith Moon held down twenty-three different jobs before he donned an orange suit, got drunk, and auditioned for The Who in 1964. For the next fourteen years, the surf music-loving drummer stayed with The Who and stayed drunk. A brilliant musician and even more brilliant party animal, Moon the Loon did more to promote excessive waste than any other member of his generation. According to his personal assistant, "Moon simply behaves like a lunatic virtually all the time." "The one thing that scares me is drugs," confessed Moon. "The public aspect of my life is an illusion anyway...an hallucination. I don't need an hallucination within an hallucination." Moon's hallucinations came to an end with his death by drug overdose in 1978. He was the only member of The Who who actually died before he got old.

## KEITH MOON DOES
## THE DUMBEST THINGS

★ Moon revealed his distinctive personality early on in life. His art teacher described him as "retarded artistically, idiotic in other respects."

★ Moon despised hippies. When they handed him flowers he would smile, take them, and eat them.

★ In 1967, Moon declared that his twentieth birthday was actually his twenty-first and began to celebrate at a Holiday Inn in Flint, Michigan. When the manager came in at midnight and asked Moon to quiet down, the drummer went ballistic. He threw the birthday cake at the manager. Then he raced down the hallway, grabbed a fire extinguisher, sprayed the cars in the parking lot, destroyed his hotel room, jumped into the hotel swimming pool, stripped naked, tripped on a doorsill, and knocked out his two front teeth. The Holiday Inn banned The Who forever.

★ On the TV variety show *The Smothers Brothers Comedy Hour* in 1967, Moon decided to augment the standard The Who pyrotechnic display, and loaded his drum kit with an enormous charge of gunpowder. At the end of "My Generation," Moon detonated his drums. He was blasted off the riser. Cymbal shrapnel cut his arm. The explosion fried a camera, the studio monitors, and guitarist Pete Townshend's hair (not to mention affecting the hearing in his left ear). When Tommy Smothers walked out with his signature guitar around his neck, Townshend grabbed the guitar and smashed it on the ground.

✈ While driving his sports car at more than 100 miles per hour, Moon decided to shift into low gear. The rear wheels locked. The car turned somersaults, end over end, and came to rest a few feet from a sixty-foot drop. A police officer rode up to the wreck on a bicycle, looked over the damage, and said, "Hello, Keith. I knew it was you."

"Sig Heil!" shouted Keith Moon, drummer for the Who, while walking through a Jewish neighborhood in London dressed as a Nazi. (Moon is now dead.) [photo courtesy of Archive Photos/Fotos International]

✪ Moon wrecked his Rolls-Royce one Christmas Day. When the police came to investigate, Moon was full of holiday cheer. "Have a drink, dear boys!" he said. Then he couldn't remember where the liquor cabinet was. A few minutes later he appeared with a Japanese television set in his arms. "Here, chaps," he said. "A token of my friendship." Moonie fell flat on his face, smashed the set, stood up, and passed out. He was never prosecuted for the accident.

✪ In 1971, Moon went out for a joy ride with his mates. He wound up running over his chauffeur's head by mistake.

✪ Moon later took a one-legged man with him on a "fun" ride. Moon, laughing hysterically, headed straight for a truck on the wrong side of the road. His passenger took off his false leg and started pounding Moon. Their car careened into a ditch. The handicapped passenger pounded Moon a bit more, then strapped his leg back on and walked off.

✪ In the early 1970s, Moon sat on the hood of his Rolls-Royce and was driven around London stark naked. His driver pulled up in front of a West London club. Moon put on a pair of underpants and entered. Once inside, he ripped off his underwear and jumped up onto Mick and Bianca Jagger's table. The Jaggers took one look at the Moon and quickly departed.

⭐ Moon and a friend put on Nazi uniforms and went into a Jewish neighborhood in London shouting, "Sieg heil!" They entered a bakery and screamed for German bread. The Jewish lady behind the counter chased the Nazi jokesters into the street, hitting them with her heaviest loaf.

⭐ After his wife Kim left Moon in 1973, she sighed, "He'll get up in the morning and decide to be Adolf Hitler for the day. And he is Adolf Hitler."

⭐ After being released from drug rehab, Moon got on an airplane and immediately relapsed. He threw his food all over the plane, then tried to fight his way into the cockpit. Later, he passed out, woke up, and screamed. He jumped out of his seat and played the *Lone Ranger* theme over the public-address system. Upon landing, Moon stood at attention in the aisle, with his pants around his ankles. The other passengers applauded his performance.

🎹 Moon brought six hookers into an Indian restaurant, sat them on the bar, and announced, "And now for your delectation and delight, the one and only, the great, the astonishing, the astounding Moonio will perform his world famous multi-clitoral stimulation—before your very eyes and entirely without a safety net!" Moon proceeded to lap his way down the bar to the delight of the girls and the horror of the restaurant owner.

⭐ Moon developed his own language. For example, the following terms for male genitalia: bacon assegai, beef torpedo, cobblers, cricket set, mutton javelin, plonker, pork sword, and wanger.

⭐ Moon went to a Monkees concert in 1968. Just before the show started, he jumped up in the crowd and started chanting, "We want The Who."

⭐ On the set of the film *Countdown* (1968), a crew member handed Moon a pay envelope. Moon tore open the packet, took out 170 one-pound notes, tore them up, then threw them into the air and danced around singing, "We're millionaires, aren't we?"

# Jim Morrison

## FACTS OF LIFE (and Death)

**ORIGIN:** Born James Douglas Morrison, December 8, 1943, Melbourne, Florida, died July 3, 1971, Paris, France of a "heart attack induced by respiratory problems."

**FORMATIVE YEARS:** Dropped out of the Film School at the University of California.

**FAMILY PLANNING:** Married Patricia Kennealy (witch), June 24, 1970, in a non-traditional ceremony.

**ROMANTIC INTERESTS:** Mary Frances Werbelow (beauty-pageant contestant); Pamela Courson (called herself "Jim's creation"); Rosanna White (Jim liked her organic shampoo); Gloria Stavers (editor, *16* magazine); "presidential groupies" in Mexico (Jim picked one out at the anthropology museum).

## SELECTED HITS (and Misses)

**SONGS:** "Break On Through" (1967), "Light My Fire" (1967), "Love Me Two Times" (1967), "Hello, I Love You" (1968), "Touch Me" (1969), "Roadhouse Blues" (1970), "The Celebration of the Lizard" (1970), "Love Her Madly" (1971), "Riders on the Storm" (1971).

**FILM:** *The Doors* (Oliver Stone's fictional feature about Morrison and the Doors—1991).

## QUICKIE BIO

Inspired by Rimbaud, Blake, Huxley, acid, and booze, Jim Morrison broke through the doors of perception and joined with Los Angeles musicians to form the Doors in 1965. His Lizard King good looks, leather pants, and drunken stage performances earned him legions of fans and jail time. As his drinking got out of control, Morrison walked into as many doors as he walked through. His gravesite in Paris became a popular attraction. Hard-core believers still wonder, "Is Jim really buried there?" Yup.

## JIM MORRISON DOES
## THE DUMBEST THINGS

✪ While still in college in Los Angeles, Morrison went out drinking, then went to the library. After checking out the chicks, he whipped out his pecker and began to take a leak between the bookshelves.

✪ A friend invited Morrison over to dinner to celebrate Morrison's twenty-sixth birthday. Morrison got drunk, pulled his member out of his pants, and passed out. Then he began to pee. Morrison's friend filled up three crystal goblets.

✪ When a girlfriend refused to sleep with him, Jim grabbed her wrist and held a carving knife to her stomach. Just then, a friend of Morrison's came into the apartment. Morrison let go of the girl and laughed, "Hey now, what's this? A knife? Now, where did that come from?"

✪ Morrison and his girlfriend Pamela once had a violent argument over the average life-expectancy of a golden retriever.

✪ During a 1968 performance in San Francisco, a drunken Morrison began to whirl the microphone around his head like a lariat. Promoter Bill Graham rushed out onto the floor waving his arms. Morrison let go of the mike, smashed Graham in the forehead, and knocked him down.

✪ Morrison got inebriated with singer Janis Joplin. Morrison grabbed Joplin by the hair, pulled her head towards his crotch, and held her there. She broke free and ran to the bathroom. He fled in a car. Joplin chased him and began hitting him on the head with a bottle of Southern Comfort. Morrison laughed.

✪ Morrison asked a pal to drop him off at another friend's pad after heavy drinking. Morrison pounded on the door, then passed out on the doorstep. It turned out to be the home of a sixty-eight-year-old woman who promptly had Morrison arrested for public drunkenness.

- Morrison spotted a friend's sister standing in a boutique. He yelled out, "Whoooopeeee, look at those tits!" An elderly woman thought Morrison was yelling at her. She chased him around the store, hitting him with her handbag.

- In March 1969, Morrison was arrested for exposing himself onstage in Miami. Morrison eventually went to trial for profanity, indecent exposure, lewd behavior, and public drunkenness. During the courtroom case, the prosecutor asked Morrison if he had indeed exposed himself. Morrison replied, "I don't remember. I was too drunk." Morrison was later convicted of exposing himself but found *not guilty* of public drunkenness.

- After the Miami bust, a drinking buddy asked Morrison why he had exposed himself onstage. Morrison replied, "I wanted to see what it looked like in a spotlight."

- At lunch in Paris just before his death in 1971, Morrison drank two Bloody Marys and a bottle of Chivas Regal. He then struck up a conversation with two French businessmen. Said the slobbering American, "You look stupid. Are you a**holes?" No, Jim. You are—er, were.

# Mötley Crüe

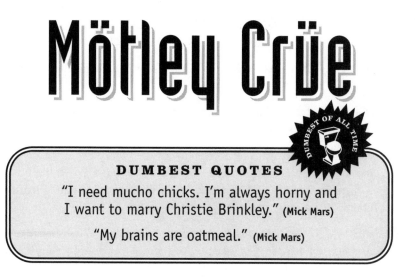

## DUMBEST QUOTES

"I need mucho chicks. I'm always horny and I want to marry Christie Brinkley." (Mick Mars)

"My brains are oatmeal." (Mick Mars)

## FACTS OF LIFE

**RINGLEADERS:** Vince Neil (vocals)—born Vincent Neil Wharton, February 8, 1961, Hollywood, California; Mick Mars (guitar)—born Bob Deal, April 3, 1955, Terre Haute, Indiana; Tommy Lee (drums)—born Thomas Lee Bass, October 3, 1962, Athens, Greece; Nikki Sixx (bass)—born Frank Carlton Serafino Ferranno, December 11, 1958, San Jose, California.

## SELECTED HITS (and Misses)

**SONGS:** "God Bless the Children of the Beast" (1983), "Smokin' in the Boys' Room" (1985), "Girls, Girls, Girls" (1987), "Slice of Your Pie" (1989), "She Goes Down" (1989), "Dr. Feelgood" (1989), "Without You" (1990), "Home Sweet Home" (1991).

## QUICKIE BIO

Los Angeles rockers Tommy Lee, Nikki Sixx, and Vince Neil got together in 1981 to form Mötley Crüe. The boys developed a trash-glam image while thrilling their fans with mainstream heavy-metal music and a bevy of larger-than-life women. A conviction for vehicular manslaughter (Vince), a near-death drug experience (Nikki), and multiple divorces brought the band huge publicity by the late 1980s. After Neil left the band in 1992, record sales plummeted. Even so, Lee managed to snag busty *Baywatch* TV star (and five-time *Playboy* cover girl) Pamela Anderson. Anderson and Lee's naughty home videos, Neil's return, and a new album, *Generation Swine*, brought the band back into the public eye in 1997. However, the public seemed to be more interested in looking at Anderson than in listening to Mötley Crüe.

# MÖTLEY CRÜE DOES
# THE DUMBEST THINGS

★ One of the Crüe's earliest stage gimmicks was lighting their pants on fire.

★ When the band tried to take their show into Canada in 1982, Canadian customs confiscated Neil's studded and spiked stage paraphernalia and classified it as "deadly weaponry."

★ On tour with Ozzy Osbourne in 1984, the Crüe mixed up a big bowl of food, pissed in it, and dumped it on Osbourne's head. Enthused Tommy, "It's fun!"

★ In 1984, Mötley Crüe was thrown out of Germany. Why? Because the band tossed mattresses out of their hotel window to watch them bounce off parked cars.

★ According to Sixx, the band was sued by a number of male and female fans. "Quite a few times, girls have been raped at our concerts," recalled the musician. "Some have claimed to have gone deaf while we were onstage. Someone lost their eyes in a fight, so we get assault charges because we were onstage when they got the s*** kicked out of them. It goes on and on. We have a lawsuit pending from this guy who thinks he's me."

★ In Japan, Lee and Sixx took some pills on a train, drank fifteen bottles of sake, and split a fifth of Jack Daniel's—in *less* than an hour. Then the two poured food on some Japanese passengers and chucked the empty bottle of Jack Daniel's through the window. Sixx was arrested, and later admitted, "I'm a raving lunatic when I'm wasted."

★ Sixx claimed he once shot whiskey into his arm when he ran out of heroin.

★ Sixx shot up too much heroin in 1987, in addition to consuming Valium, cocaine, whiskey, and beer. "I kinda remember waking up," recalled Sixx, "[and a paramedic] telling me I'd died, then been revived."

After his heart stopped beating for two minutes, paramedics did indeed give Sixx two shots of adrenaline to bring him back from death. After leaving the hospital, Sixx hitchhiked back to his home—and shot up some more heroin. Later he wrote the song "Kickstart My Heart."

★ When the Crüe sobered up after Sixx's near death, hard-partying comedian Sam Kinison gave the boys a hard time. "What're you gonna do now?" Kinison asked. "Go out and wreck a salad bar?"

**Tommy Lee's tally whacker! Now on Video!**
[photo courtesy of Photofest]

⭐ The band turned from drugs to romance. Neil saw a woman mud-wrestling one night and fell in love. Neil offered the woman $3,000 a week if she would stop mud-wrestling (with anyone but him). She agreed to the deal. The two were married—and later divorced.

⭐ Mick Mars was married and divorced three times. He had a hard time dating as well. In 1993, he went out target shooting with a girlfriend and accidentally shot her in the stomach.

⭐ Drummer Tommy Lee married model Elaine Bergen and divorced her thirty days later. In 1986, he married TV starlet Heather Locklear. Just before the marriage fell apart, Locklear left the following message for Tommy on their answering machine. "Sorry to interrupt you when you're doing an interview, dear, but I just want to give you the message that the dog's poop needs to be cleaned up. I love you. 'Bye."

⭐ Tommy divorced Locklear in 1993. Two years later he married five-time *Playboy* cover girl Pamela Anderson. The cute couple appeared in *Screw* Magazine, *Hustler,* and *Penthouse* and sent video tapes of their wedding night to *Playboy.*

In 1997, more Anderson-and-Lee tapes emerged—this time supposedly stolen from Tommy's secret safe. The tapes allegedly revealed (among other things) Anderson lubricating Lee's stick shift as he drove down the road, Anderson mating with Lee on board a rented love boat, and an aroused Lee honking the boat's horn with his own personal drumstick.

⭐ Late in 1997, Lee put his drumstick on the big screen. After passing a video camera through the crowd at a San Antonio concert and asking female fans to flash their breasts, Lee pointed the camera at his exposed drumstick and started shooting. For a few moments, Lee's pecker appeared behind him on an enormous video screen.

⭐ At one point Anderson got fed up with all the nasty fake photos of her displayed on the Internet. A disgusted Anderson asked Lee to look at one particularly naughty image—a shot of Anderson having sex with Raquel Welch. "Yuuuuck," said Anderson. "Why would anyone want to see that?" Said husband Lee, "Do you mind moving over a little so I can get a better look?"

⭐ Tommy finally lost it in 1998 when he watched an x-rated video of wife Pamela making love with rocker Bret Michaels. Tommy got so mad he kicked his wife and broke one of her fingernails. Pam called the police, who took Tommy away. Pam later filed for divorce and screamed to the tabloids, "I never want to see him or his tattooed body again!" Tommy was sentenced to six months in jail.

# Nine Inch Nails

## FACTS OF LIFE

**RINGLEADERS:** Trent Reznor (vocals, keyboards, sax, tuba)—born Michael Trent Reznor, May 17, 1965, Mercer, Pennsylvania.

## SELECTED HITS (and Misses)

**SONGS:** "Suck" (1989), "Sin" (1989), "Head Like a Hole" (1989), "March of the Pigs" (1994), "Happiness in Slavery" (1995), "Perfect Drug" (1997).

**FILMS:** *Natural Born Killers* (soundtrack—1994); *Lost Highway* (soundtrack—1997).

## QUICKIE BIO

Teenage musician Trent Reznor transformed an interest in the group KISS into a ghoulie-rock empire. His 1989 creation Nine Inch Nails churned out hammer-of-the-gods rhythms that found a huge audience as part of Perry Farrell's 1991 Lollapalooza rock carnival. With an ever-changing lineup of musicians, Reznor turned industrial rock into an industry. When Marilyn Manson interviewed Reznor for a school paper, Reznor was so impressed he made Manson a star. According to Reznor, it was tough to make Manson's act spooky enough. "After three minutes," he confessed, "it's not scary anymore."

## NINE INCH NAILS DOES THE DUMBEST THINGS

⭐ Fans believed that the name Nine Inch Nails referred to the nails that crucified Jesus or the fingernails on the Statue of Liberty. According to Reznor, the name had *no* meaning.

Peek-a-boo! Trent Reznor of the band Nine Inch Nails was so afraid of Courtney Love that he hid from her. [photo courtesy of Photofest]

✪ On tour with Guns N' Roses, Nine Inch Nails was booed by a crowd of 65,000. One audience member threw a sausage link up onstage. Sighed Reznor, "That was a penis shrinker."

✪ Reznor hated Axl Rose. According to Reznor, Rose was surrounded by people who said things like, "'Yes, Mr. Rose, that does smell good, can I flush it for you?'"

✪ At one point, a drunken Reznor tried to fight his way offstage. Once he gained composure, he noticed that his road manager's face was a bloody mess. Explained the bruised staffer, "You punched me four times in the mouth!"

✪ Reznor made a fatal mistake when he brought his dog to a 1994 concert in Columbus, Ohio. The dog leapt from a third-floor balcony and fell fifty feet to its death.

🖥 While making the video for the song "Down With It," Trent Reznor played dead. The video crew wanted to get a dramatic shot of the rock star pretending to be a corpse, so they tied a camera to a helium balloon and let the balloon rise up into the air. Unfortunately, the balloon drifted away, and finally landed in a farmer's field. The farmer found the video and turned it over to the FBI. Federal agents thought the video was a snuff film and launched an investigation.

 The video for "Sin" featured gay men smeared with blood and close-ups of genital piercings.

 During a recording session, Reznor decorated the studio with pictures of male organs cut out of gay porno magazines.

 Reznor's video for "Happiness in Slavery" featured a person being slowly dismembered while watching a Nine Inch Nails video. The video was rejected by MTV reps who informed Reznor, "We don't show the human form in any kind of bondage." "What about Madonna?" Reznor asked. "Madonna is Madonna," they replied.

 When Reznor relocated to Los Angeles in 1992, he rented the house where Sharon Tate and others were brutally murdered by the "family" of Charles Manson. Reznor claimed he was unaware of the connection but nicknamed the house "Le Pig," in reference to the word *pig* written on the walls in blood during the grisly 1969 murders.

 Reznor recorded his fellow Goth Marilyn Manson in the macabre manse. Manson said it was "something they'd wanted to do for a long time." The house was demolished not long after Reznor moved out.

 Courtney Love toured with Nine Inch Nails in 1994 and developed a major crush on Reznor. One night, she went to see him in his hotel room. Reznor peeped through the door, saw Love, and pretended he wasn't in. Love convinced a maid to let her into the locked room. Reznor jumped from his balcony to the one of his manager's suite to hide from Love. Love was furious. "Nine inches? I don't think so," she fumed. "Four inches is more like it."

# The Notorious B.I.G.

## FACTS OF LIFE (and Death)

**ORIGIN:** Born Christopher Wallace, May 21, 1972, Brooklyn, New York, died March 10, 1997, Los Angeles, California, in a drive-by shooting.

**FORMATIVE YEARS:** Dropped out of high school.

**FAMILY PLANNING:** Married Faith Evans (singer) 1994; divorced 1997.

**ROMANTIC INTERESTS:** "I done had every kind of bitch. Young bitch, old bitch, users, mothers, grandmothers, dumb bitches...."

## SELECTED HITS (and Misses)

**SONGS:** "Give Me the Loot" (1994), "Machine Gun Funk" (1994), "Big Popps" (1995), "Somebody Got to Die" (1997), "My Downfall" (1997), "Hypnotize" (1997).

## QUICKIE BIO

A self-described neighborhood thug who found a better life (although a short one), Christopher Wallace made his name as a drug-dealing hustler in New York City before breaking into showbiz. A born storyteller who rapped just for fun, Wallace laid down some of his material on tape and sent it to the magazine *The Source*. The songs found their way to rap producer Sean "Puffy" Combs who helped transform Wallace into The Notorious B.I.G. Biggie hit it big with his 1994 album *Ready to Die*. Unfortunately, life imitated art. The East Coast Biggie spent the next three years picking fights with a bunch of people, including West Coast rap star Tupac Shakur. Rivals Biggie and Tupac both met the same fate as victims of drive-by shootings. Biggie was cremated. His ex-wife Faith Evans owns half his ashes. His ex-girlfriend and rap star Lil' Kim owns the other half of his remains, which she reportedly kisses every morning.

## THE NOTORIOUS B.I.G. DOES THE DUMBEST THINGS

✪ On a visit to New Jersey in 1995, Biggie had a difference of opinion with the friend of a concert promoter. Biggie allegedly robbed the man and broke his jaw.

✪ When a couple of fans came up to Biggie to get an autograph in 1996, Biggie swung at them with a baseball bat, chased them down the street, threatened to kill them, smashed the windows of their car, reached into the vehicle, and punched at them. Though he pled guilty to criminal mischief and harassment, Biggie was philosophical about the incident. Mused the rap star, "I say grow from your mistakes."

✪ Biggie married Faith Evans eight days after he met her. When a reporter asked if the whirlwind romance was working out, Biggie responded, "She ain't speaking to me right now."

🐶 Biggie didn't have any pets. But he did like to say, "Tupac, at one point, was my dog."

✪ When Tupac claimed on record that he had mated with Biggie's wife Faith, Biggie joked, "If Faith has twins, she'll probably have two pacs. Get it? Tu...Pac's."

✪ In 1997, Biggie canceled plans to perform in London. "I don't want to go to Europe right now," he explained while munching on a sausage pizza. "The food is horrible."

✪ Biggie's last album, *Life After Death . . . Till Death Do Us Part,* was released after his own death in a drive-by shooting. Biggie's favorite cut on the album? "You're Nobody Till Somebody Kills You."

✪ Folks in the black community seemed confused about Biggie's legacy. A teacher at a Brooklyn day-care center told her students all about the rap star. "He's from around here and he succeeded in life," said the teacher. "I want them to know they can accomplish their goals." Comedian Chris Rock had a different opinion about Biggie and his fellow murdered rapper, Tupac Shakur. "I loved Tupac and Biggie, but school is going to open on their birthdays," said Rock. "There won't be pictures of the two hanging in Grandma's kitchen."

# Ted Nugent

## FACTS OF LIFE

ORIGIN: Born December 13, 1948, Detroit, Michigan.

FORMATIVE YEARS: Attended an all-boys Catholic school and confessed, "I didn't know you could beat off until 1972."

FAMILY PLANNING: Married with children. "My kids actually like that terminally-unemployable, soulless rap bulls\*\*\*."

ROMANTIC INTERESTS: "Life is one big female safari and Dr. Ruth [Westheimer] is my guide."

# SELECTED HITS (and Misses)

**SONGS:** "Journey to the Center of the Mind" (1968), "Tooth, Fang and Claw"(1974), "Dog Eat Dog" (1976), "Cat Scratch Fever" (1977), "Wango Tango" (1980), "Fred Bear—American Hunter's Theme Song" (1990).

**FILM:** *State Park* (performed song for the soundtrack, "Love Is Like a Chainsaw"—1988).

**TV:** *Spirit of the Wild* (1996).

## QUICKIE BIO

The Motor City Madman played in a bunch of high-school bands before making his first recordings with the Amboy Dukes. In the 1970s, Ted Nugent hit with songs like "Cat Scratch Fever" and "Stranglehold." He made a good run up the charts with his 1980s band Damn Yankees, but eventually traded heavy-metal music for heavy metal weaponry. A lifelong hunting enthusiast (and not just for girls), Nugent founded a bow-hunting camp for kids, started his own pro-gun radio talk show, and considered running for Congress as a conservative.

## TED NUGENT DOES
## THE DUMBEST THINGS

✪ A teenage Nugent enjoyed lying on the roof of his car, sticking his arms through the windows, and driving. Sometimes, he slipped his car into neutral and danced on the hood while moving down the highway. Observed Nugent, "No one would drive with me."

✪ Nugent was rock's answer to *George of the Jungle*. Ted liked to swing on a rope onstage wearing a rabbit-skin loincloth. "With no bottom panel," explained Nugent, "so the women could enjoy me."

✪ In 1978, Nugent carved his autograph into a fan's arm with a bowie knife.

✪ Nugent showed equally poor taste when he jammed on a song called "Bomb Iran." The song advocated applying molten-lead enemas to the Ayatollah. Nugent later described the ballad as "very political, gung-ho America."

✪ When a female reporter asked Nugent why he didn't wear tuxedos on his album covers, Nugent replied, "Why did you decide not to douche yourself with molten lava?"

TED NUGENT 181

"Basically I'm just an erector set looking for some bolts," mused Ted Nugent.
[photo courtesy of Photofest]

⭐ At the end of one of Nugent's rehearsals, a visiting guitarist pulled out a machine gun and opened fire. Bullets ripped through Nugent's equipment cases and trashed a limousine parked outside. After surviving the gunfire, Nugent said, "I've gotta get some of those blanks for my .45s."

👀 Nugent never got the blanks, but he did find some flaming arrows. He shot the arrows into the audience during a 1993 show in Cincinnati, Ohio, and was fined $1,000 for violating the local fire code.

⭐ Nugent made a video to promote the positive aspects of hunting. He set his educational video to the tune of his big hit—"Stranglehold."

Nugent went on safari to Africa. "It's kind of like [Manhattan's] Four-teenth Street," Nugent said upon his return. "But without all that concrete which tends to mess you up."

 Ted wrote a book called *Blood Trails* in which he gave a detailed account of 120 kills. For example, "The Zwickey 2 Blade had penetrated the entire skull, slicing the brain and severing a big vein. Yum, yum!!"

 Nugent took to the Detroit airwaves in December 1996, to host a talk-radio show. The headbanging version of Rush Limbaugh covered a variety of controversial topics including, "Unions—Money for Nothing," "Bad Guys—Good Ones Are Dead Ones," and "Gun Control—Giving Criminals the Upper Hand." Right-wing presidential candidate Bo Gritz called Nugent his "hero." Proclaimed the heroic Nugent, "If I'd have made the army, we wouldn't have had all that trouble in Vietnam, 'cause I would have won it in a year."

 In 1986, Nugent the hero brought a nineteen-year-old fan onstage and ripped off her clothes. When the police gave him no trouble, Nugent explained, "I did such a good job, they didn't have the heart to arrest me."

 Nugent once addressed an anti-drug rally and said, "[Jimi Hendrix] thought I was stupid, and I thought he was God. Now he's dead, and I'm still Ted." Too bad.

# Oasis

## FACTS OF LIFE

**RINGLEADERS:** Noel Gallagher (guitar, vocals)—born May 29, 1967, Manchester, England; Liam Gallagher (vocals)—born September 21, 1972, Manchester, England; Bonehead (guitar)—born Paul Arthurs, June 23, 1965, Manchester, England.

## SELECTED HITS (and Misses)

**SONGS:** "Shakermaker" (1994), "Cigarettes and Alcohol" (1994), "Whatever" (1994), "Wonderwall" (1995), "What's the Story, Morning Glory" (1995), "Champagne Supernova" (1995).

## QUICKIE BIO

When Noel Gallagher joined his little brother Liam's group in 1991, he turned a Manchester, England, bar band into a surly, swearing rock supernova. Named for a Manchester club where the Beatles once played, Oasis quickly became the darlings of the British tabloids, and the Gallaghers generated more sibling-rivalry ink than anyone since Ray and Dave Davies of the

Kinks. Spiteful, nasty, and eminently quotable, Oasis charted major hits, cut short a major U.S. tour, and threatened to rule rock. Until 1997, that is, when Oasis record sales went a bit flat, leaving the Gallagher boys swearing at each other and everyone else.

## OASIS DOES THE DUMBEST THINGS

 In high school, Noel Gallagher liked to sniff glue and steal things. "How we ever managed to do any burgling I don't know," he recalled. "We were all off our tits on drugs."

 On one crime spree, Noel and his mates locked a milkman in a public toilet and stole his milk truck. Driving the vehicle down the road, Noel's gang asked themselves, "What are we gonna do with a milk float [truck] and like 20,000 bottles of milk?"

 At a bar in England, Noel Gallagher was talking with rock superstar George Michael. Two girls came into the bar, stared at the celebrities, and threw up. Then they bent down, fingered through the barf, picked out some undigested tablets of the drug Ecstasy, and popped them back in their mouths. Scoffed the bartender, "Oasis fans."

 In 1993, Oasis boarded a ferry from England to Amsterdam for the band's first overseas gig. On the ride over, the boys got into the whiskey. Liam got into a fight with the ferry security guards and wound up in the brig. Liam swore at the guards so much they finally drew a chalk line on the floor and ordered him to lie down with his nose on it. The squirming rock star stayed there for three hours. The band was not allowed to disembark in Amsterdam.

 At a 1994 Los Angeles performance, Liam was so wrecked on speed he could hardly perform. His solution? Go backstage and snort more speed. When Liam returned, Gallagher yelled at him for doing drugs. Then Liam attacked Noel with his tambourine.

 Unhappy at finding Liam partying during a recording session, Noel chased him around the studio with a cricket bat.

 Before a 1995 gig in Buffalo, New York, Liam and Noel duked it out so bad, they canceled the show.

 Then they canceled the entire American tour. Explained Noel, "All the rows that ever started, we've been drunk—'Look at your shoes, you dickhead.' 'Who are you calling a dick?', 'Calling you a dick.' 'Who's a dick?'—And before you know it, you're hailing a Concorde."

- Long-absent father Gallagher invited his sons for a healing reunion at a Dublin hotel. Noel, Liam, and Dad shook hands, shared a few drinks, and wound up punching each other out.

- Rivalry between the Gallaghers even found its way to the altar. After little Liam married older actress Patsy Kensit in April 1997, Noel turned around and did the same two months later with publicist Meg Matthews. While Liam had a civil ceremony in London, Noel was married by an Elvis impersonator in the same

**Liam Gallagher of the band Oasis showed appreciation for his fans at the 1996 MTV Video Music Awards by gobbing on them.** [photo courtesy of Reuters/Jeff Christensen/Archive Photos]

Las Vegas chapel where Mickey Rooney married each of his eight wives. Neither Gallagher brother invited the other to his wedding.

- Noel firmly believes in the existence of alien life. Liam does not. "If I saw an alien, I'd tell him to f*** right off," said Liam, "because whatever planet he came from, they wouldn't have the Beatles or any decent f***ing music."

- The Gallagher brothers greatly admired the music of the Beatles, but *not* the Beatles themselves. Referring to Paul McCartney's classical projects, Liam scoffed, "Sitting around with a bunch of old lesbians writing doesn't sound classical to me. I've written three classical albums."

- The Gallaghers didn't think much of the British royal family either. Snarled Noel Gallagher, "I think they should all be shot."

- On route to Australia for a 1998 concert tour, Liam Gallagher got drunk on the plane, screamed obscenities, and threatened to stab the pilot. After landing in Australia, Gallagher head-butted an unsuspecting tourist, breaking his nose.

# Sinéad O'Connor

## FACTS OF LIFE

**ORIGIN:** Born December 12, 1966, Dublin, Ireland.

**FORMATIVE YEARS:** As a child, O'Connor considered running away from home. But since her father was a sprinter, O'Connor felt that he would have caught her, and decided to stay put.

**FAMILY PLANNING:** She had a child by boyfriend/drummer John Reynolds in 1987, and a second child in 1996.

**ROMANTIC INTERESTS:** Refused to utter the name of one of her boyfriends but did tell the press "make sure you say he's a little s***."

## SELECTED HITS (and Misses)

**SONGS:** "Mandinka" (1988), "Nothing Compares 2 U" (1990), "The Emperor's New Clothes" (1990), "You Do Something to Me" (1990), "You Made Me the Thief of Your Heart" (1994).

**FILMS:** *Butcher Boy* (1997).

## QUICKIE BIO

One of rock's reigning queens of self-righteousness, Sinéad O'Connor had a tumultuous upbringing. Her parents split up when she was eight years old, and she was regularly beaten by her mother. Her father was finally able to gain custody, but under his care O'Connor became a thief and was sent off to reform school. O'Connor later enrolled at the Dublin College of Music and supported herself by working as a Kiss-o-gram French maid. She broke into the big time after working with U2 guitarist The Edge. However, she made a real name for herself by insulting people.

## SINÉAD O'CONNOR DOES
## THE DUMBEST THINGS

⭐ While at reform school, O'Connor wanted to cop a buzz. So she chugged a large dose of her boyfriend's asthma medication. The nuns at the school thought that O'Connor was trying to commit suicide and extended her stay by six months.

⭐ O'Connor claimed that she never hated her abusive mother because "I chose her as my mother before I was born. You see what I mean?"

⭐ In 1990, O'Connor refused to perform a gig in New Jersey *if* the national anthem was also played. Her initial protest was against the idea of American patriotism. Then she added a protest against censorship in music. As a result, many radio stations banned her music. Frank Sinatra told an audience that he wanted to kick her ass. "I can't hit Frank Sinatra back; he's an old man," said Sinéad. "I'd probably kill him."

⭐ A few months later, O'Connor visited a Beverly Hills health-food store. After the expedition, an employee was fired. The offense? Playing "The Star-Spangled Banner" while O'Connor was shopping.

🔲 The Irish lass refused to appear on the TV show *Saturday Night Live* in May of 1990 because the host for show was the offensive comedian Andrew "Dice" Clay. When O'Connor did finally appear on the program in 1992, she managed to be offensive on her own. After an a cappella version of Bob Marley's song "War," O'Connor held up a picture of Pope John Paul II, then tore it up and proclaimed, "Fight the real enemy." A stunned Lorne Michaels, the show's producer, said afterward, "We were sort of shocked, the way you would be at a house guest pissing on a flower arrangement in the dining room."

✪ In 1995, O'Connor punched out two Israeli photographers and damaged their equipment. The scuffle happened during a visit to Jerusalem's Holy Sepulcher Church.

✪ Two years later, O'Connor ignited another church-related firestorm when she portrayed the Virgin Mary in *Butcher Boy*. In the film, O'Connor, as the Virgin, appeared in a vision to a teenager and encouraged him to go on a murder spree.

✪ When an interviewer asked O'Connor if she wanted a number one record, the Irish rock star replied, "No, absolutely not. That's not the kind of artist that I am, luckily. Otherwise I'd never be taken seriously."

**"Fight the real enemy,"** shouted Sinéad O'Connor on *Saturday Night Live,* referring to Pope John Paul II. In 1996, Sinéad threw a cup of coffer on her real enemy, a photographer. [photo courtesy of Big Pictures/Archive Photos]

# Ozzy Osbourne

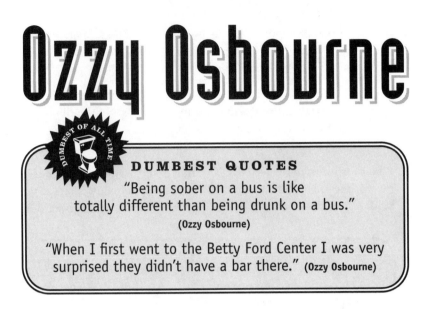

## DUMBEST QUOTES

"Being sober on a bus is like totally different than being drunk on a bus."
**(Ozzy Osbourne)**

"When I first went to the Betty Ford Center I was very surprised they didn't have a bar there." **(Ozzy Osbourne)**

## FACTS OF LIFE

**ORIGIN:** Born John Michael Osbourne, December 3, 1948, Birmingham, England.

**FORMATIVE YEARS:** Was kicked out of school, arrested for burglary and assaulting an officer at age seventeen, and served time in prison.

**FAMILY PLANNING:** Married Thelma, 1971; divorced 1981; Married Sharon Arden (manager) July 4, 1982.

**ROMANTIC INTERESTS:** "I screwed all the groupies when it was safe...."

## SELECTED HITS (and Misses)

**SONGS:** "Iron Man" (with Black Sabbath—1972), "Die Young" (1980), "Suicide Solution" (1981), "Children of the Grave" (1982), "Diary of a Madman" (1981), "Shot in the Dark" (1986), "Close My Eyes Forever" (with Lita Ford—1989), "Mama, I'm Coming Home" (1992).

**FILM:** *Trick or Treat* (1987).

## QUICKIE BIO

In the 1920s, entertainers traveled with carnivals and bit the heads off chickens. People called them geeks. In the 1970s, 1980s, and 1990s, a rock star toured with various bands, and bit the heads off doves and bats. People called him Ozzy. Ozzy Osbourne and some mates formed Black Sabbath in

1969. For years, Osbourne took LSD, drank booze, and delivered hard-rocking occult goodies to hordes of devoted fans. Osbourne left Black Sabbath in 1980, reuniting with his surviving bandmates periodically over the years. As a solo performer, Osbourne thrived with his late-1990s Ozzfest road shows. When the aging Osbourne failed to show for a 1997 gig with Marilyn Manson in Columbus, Ohio, the fans rioted. That's Osbourne. Driving them crazy even when he's not there. Some would say that Osbourne hasn't been there for years.

## OZZY OSBOURNE DOES THE DUMBEST THINGS

✪ Osbourne developed a satanic reputation during the years he spent performing with Black Sabbath. However, Osbourne never took his occult shtick seriously. "The devil-worship thing was a marketing invention of the record company," he explained. "We played along to put dough in our pockets."

During a 1982 Florida tour, Osbourne and his bandmates decided to have some fun with airplanes. They pulled into a small airport. The tour bus driver, also a pilot, who was flying on cocaine, climbed aboard a plane and took off with guitarist Randy Rhoads. When he saw his wife standing next to the tour bus, the driver/pilot tried to run her over. Ooops! The pilot missed his wife, but hit the bus and crashed, killing himself, Rhoads, and another passenger. Osbourne emerged unscathed and completed the tour.

✪ In 1978, Osbourne declared that he was an alcoholic. He quit his band and retired from performing. Instead of drinking on the road, the rocker decided to open up a bar. Osbourne quickly drank up the inventory, squandered his money, and got back together with a band.

✪ When Osbourne lived with his first wife Thelma, they kept chickens. One day it was Osbourne's turn to feed the chickens. But he was too busy drinking. Thelma kept bugging him. So finally Osbourne went outside with a shotgun and blasted them.

✪ In 1981, Osbourne busted into a meeting of record-company executives, pulled a pigeon out of his pocket, and bit off its head. The executives thought the publicity stunt was disgusting. Osbourne didn't. "The bird was [already] dead," explained the sharp-toothed rocker.

 Osbourne's most famous animal act involved a bat, *not* a pigeon. In the winter of 1982, Osbourne entertained his fans by throwing meat out into the audience. A fan in Des Moines, Iowa threw a dead bat back at

"I hate being pigeon holed," said Ozzy Osbourne who bit the head off a dove in 1981. Later he acquired a taste for bats.
[photo courtesy of Photofest]

Osbourne. According to Osbourne, "I didn't know it was a bat at the time....I thought it was one of those rubber toy things, but as soon as I crunched [its] head I then realized, 'Oh my god, what have I done?!'"

★ Osbourne suffered through a series of rabies shots—and a zillion questions about his bat diet. Complained Osbourne, fifteen years later, "You get pretty damn tired of it when people still to this day go, 'So Ozz, did you really bite the head off a bat?'"

★ Osbourne never bit the head off any of his pets. But he did take his dog Baldrick into the doctor to have its face surgically altered. According to an Osbourne spokesperson, "He's been looking more handsome every day." Not Osbourne. The dog.

★ Osbourne's Black Sabbath bandmate Tony Iommi gave himself some body-altering surgery at one point. "I can't use right-handed instruments now," explained Iommi, "because I snipped the ends of my fingers off."

★ In later years, Osbourne tried to change his public persona. Family man Osbourne posed for *People* magazine in a bubble bath with his children and explained, "The kids don't need to be reminded of who I am."

Osbourne didn't treat his wives as well as his kids. He dragged his first wife around by the hair and chopped out all the doors in their home. The not-so-happy couple split up in the early 1980s.

 Osbourne married his second wife on the beach in Hawaii. At the end of the ceremony, Osbourne, sporting fake fangs, nibbled his bride's neck and sang "Fangs for the Memory."

 In 1989, Osbourne threatened not just to bite his bride, but to kill her. He was promptly hauled off to jail. The case fell apart when his wife (who was also his manager) refused to press charges.

 While dining with a group of record-industry big shots at a restaurant in Germany in 1981, Osbourne jumped up on the table, kissed a man on the lips, and peed into a carafe of wine.

Before a San Antonio concert in 1982, Osbourne remembered the Alamo. Osbourne put on his wife's green evening gown, grabbed a bottle of brandy, and posed for pictures in front of the former mission. He then peed nearby and was arrested for public intoxication and urinating on the Alamo grounds.

 In 1991, Osbourne arrived at a record shop for an in-store promotion. There was only one problem: the store was promoting Guns N' Roses, *not* Ozzy Osbourne.

 Before Ozzfest 1997, Osbourne watched reruns of the old TV series *The Beverly Hillbillies*. The program inspired Osbourne to sanctify water in a secret ceremony and offered it up to his adoring fans. The price for drinking California spring water "personally blessed by Osbourne"? $2.75.

# The Partridge Family

## FACTS OF LIFE

**RINGLEADERS:** Keith Partridge (guitar, vocals)—born David Cassidy, April 12, 1950, New York City; Danny Partridge (bass)—born Danny Bonaduce, August 13, 1959, Broomhall, Pennsylvania.

## SELECTED HITS (and Misses)

**SONGS:** "I Think I Love You" (1970), "I Woke Up in Love This Morning" (1971), "It's One of Those Nights (Yes Love)" (1972), "Am I Losing You?" (1972), "Friend and Lover" (1973).

**FILMS:** *H.O.T.S.* (Danny—1979), *Instant Karma* (David—1990), *Spirit of '76* (David—1991).

**TV:** *The Survivors* (David—series, 1969–70), *The Partridge Family* (series, 1970–74), *Goober and the Ghost Chasers* (Danny—cartoon series, 1973), *Partridge Family: 2200 A.D.* (cartoon series, 1974–75), *Murder on Flight 502* (Danny—telefeature, 1975), *David Cassidy—Man Undercover* (David, 1978–79), *The Night the City Screamed* (David—telefeature; 1980).

## QUICKIE BIO

Picking up where the chart-topping Monkees left off, the Partridge Family was a made-for-TV rock band that starred in its own self-titled sitcom. The squeaky-clean show about a rockin' mom and her kids was loosely based on a late 1960s band called the Cowsills. Yes, Mother Cowsill did indeed play rock with her kids. To make things really confusing, David Cassidy's real-life stepmother Shirley Jones starred as Cassidy's *Partridge Family* mom. None of the Partridges except for Cassidy and Jones sang or played instruments on the records released by the band. However, David Cassidy emerged as one of the great teen idols of the 1970s. Everyone was even more stunned when David and his TV brother Danny Bonaduce slipped—for a time—down the slope of drugs, sex, and debauchery. Said TV talk-show host Geraldo Rivera to the former child rock star, "Bonaduce, they just can't kill you, can they?"

## THE PARTRIDGE FAMILY DOES THE DUMBEST THINGS

⭐ Aggressive female fans of Cassidy bared their breasts for him as he entered the TV studio. Cassidy may have been young, but he was a quick learner. "When some female comes up to your car, with no bra on, a shirt open to her navel, showing off her tits, and says, 'Hi,'" explained the teen idol, "you know what's going on."

⭐ Bonaduce also figured out what was going on. He supposedly lost his virginity at age thirteen to a girl who had come to *The Partridge Family* TV set hoping to meet Cassidy.

"I was 21 years old, my dick was always hard, and they [the groupies] were so willing," said David Cassidy describing the perks of being one of the stars of *The Partridge Family.* [photo courtesy of Photofest]

⭐ Cassidy knew he had a lot to offer the girls. He called himself Harry the Horse. Others agreed with Cassidy's opinion of himself. "Oh wow," said the Butter Queen, a notorious groupie, to Cassidy. "You've got it all over Mick Jagger."

⭐ When Cassidy hit the sack with Gina Lollobrigida, the veteran Italian movie bombshell bought $200 worth of fruit and arranged it around the youth as he lay in bed. Then she gobbled up her fruit salad.

⭐ Just before a concert in New Jersey, Cassidy had to take a pee. He didn't see a bathroom in his trailer, so he peed in a cup. Then he heard some giggles. He found two teenage girls who had been hiding in his trailer for twenty-one hours. Cassidy screamed, "Get the f*** out of here!" and tossed the cup at them.

⭐ Cassidy became so popular that his solo tours turned deadly. During a London show, a thousand people were injured and a teenage female fan was crushed to death. Government officials in Australia declared Cassidy a hazard to public health.

⭐ After his days with *The Partridge Family*, Bonaduce became a hazard to his own health. In 1990, he was arrested in Florida on a drug charge. In 1991, he was arrested for assaulting a transvestite prostitute in Phoenix, Arizona. The police speculated that Bonaduce paid the transvestite for his/her services, but tried to get his money back when he discovered that she was really a he. Bonaduce left the scene of the crime driving 125 miles per hour in a 25 mph zone.

⭐ Bonaduce later got into the media biz. He hosted a nationally-seen TV talk show which died a quick death. Then, in 1996, he took part in a promotion for a Detroit station. The former *Partridge* kid chugged beer, sang a song with a band called the Critics, and participated in something called "Slot Machine in Your Pants." The gimmick involved dumping cans of fruit down someone's pants and pulling the person's arm like a Vegas slot machine. Sighed Bonaduce, "I'm lucky to have a job."

⭐ Bonaduce had the call letters of a radio station and the name of a station manager tattooed to his rear end. He thought it would help him keep his job.

# Pink Floyd

## FACTS OF LIFE

**RINGLEADERS:** Roger Keith "Syd" Barrett (vocals, guitar)—born January 6, 1946, Cambridge, England; David Gilmour (vocals, bass)—born March 6, 1946, Cambridge, England; Roger Waters (vocals, guitar)—born September 6, 1944, Great Bookham, England; Nick Mason (drums)—born January 27, 1945, Birmingham, England.

## SELECTED HITS (and Misses)

**SONGS:** "Arnold Layne" (1967), "Careful With That Axe, Eugene" (1969), "Pigs on the Wing (Part 1)" (1977), "Pigs on the Wing (Part 2)" (1977), "Comfortably Numb" (1979), "Get Your Filthy Hands Off My Desert" (1983).

**FILMS:** *Tonite Let's All Make Love in London* (1968), *The Body* (soundtrack, including "Womb Bit," "More Than Seven Dwarfs in Penis-Land," and "Dance of the Red Corpuscles"—1970), *The Valley* (soundtrack—1972), *Pink Floyd Live at Pompeii* (1972), *The Wall* (1982).

**TV:** *What If It's Just Green Cheese?* (soundtrack—BBC British network show about the *Apollo 11* moon landing, 1969).

## QUICKIE BIO

British architecture students Roger Waters and Nick Mason teamed up with art student Syd Barrett in 1966 and began performing at a London club called the Spontaneous Underground. Barrett dubbed the group The Pink Floyd Sound after American blues singers Pink Anderson and Floyd

"Dipper Boy" Council. Some who attended the Spontaneous Underground performances didn't even realize that there was a band onstage. However, it was the dawn of the psychedelic era, so it was happening, man. It wasn't happening when Barrett went crazy and left the band in 1968. But David Gilmour took his place. Pink Floyd managed to capture their momentary lapses of reason on record, and evolved into one of the most successful rock acts of all time. Their 1972 album *Dark Side of the Moon* spent more than twenty-five years on the *Billboard* best-seller charts. The band continued to fight, tour, sue each other, and record into the 1990s. Barrett, on the other hand, watched the "telly" and enjoyed the quiet life of an apartment dweller in Cambridge, England.

## PINK FLOYD DOES
## THE DUMBEST THINGS

✪ Floyd's first hit record was "Arnold Layne," a ditty about a kleptomaniac transvestite.

✪ For a time, Barrett roomed with a fellow described as "one of the original acid-in-the-reservoir, change-the-face-of-the-world acid missionaries." Barrett's visitors were so afraid of getting dosed with LSD that they refused all drinks in the house and were even fearful of the tap water.

✪ Barrett kept his girlfriend under lock-and-key for three days. When the girl escaped, Barrett locked himself in the room.

▣ A triumphant first American Pink Floyd tour in 1967 was canceled after just eight weeks, mainly because of Barrett. When Floyd appeared on TV's *American Bandstand,* Barrett forgot to mouth the words to the songs he was supposed to lip-synch. Instead of answering questions on *The Pat Boone Show,* Barrett just gave the TV cameras a catatonic stare.

✪ One of Barrett's last songs was called "Have You Got It Yet?" Barrett played the song over and over for Waters. Each time he played it, he played it differently. Waters couldn't follow, so Barrett kept asking him, "Have you got it yet?"

✪ One evening, the band went onstage and left Barrett behind in the dressing room. Barrett crushed up a handful of Quaaludes, mixed them with a full tube of Brylcream, plastered his hair, and joined the boys onstage. Observers watched Barrett's hairdo melt "like a guttered candle."

✪ When a reporter tried to interview Barrett about his religious beliefs, the founder of Floyd said, "Right, right. Now, look up there—can you see the people on the ceiling?"

⭐ The cover of the album *Atom Heart Mother* featured a picture of a cow. But not just any picture of a cow. According to the designer, it was "the ultimate picture of a cow; it's just totally cow."

⭐ In 1971, Floyd performed at a "garden party" at a lake in a London suburb. The garden party climaxed with a display of fireworks as an inflatable octopus shrouded in dry ice rose from the lake. The show impressed the audience, but killed all the fish in the lake.

⭐ Pink Floyd created a forty-foot inflatable pig for a 1977 photo shoot. During the session, the pig balloon broke free of its moorings and drifted toward London's Heathrow Airport. Pilots coming into Heathrow were amused to hear British aviation officials warn, "Pig on the loose!" The Pink Floyd pig eventually crashed safely in a farmer's field.

⭐ At a 1980 performance of the concept album *The Wall,* fireworks ignited the stage curtains. Pieces of burning fabric fell down on the audience. The crowd cheered. They thought it was part of the show.

During the 1980s, Waters and Gilmour waged a war for the Floyd psychedelic franchise. Gilmour said, "Roger is a dog in the manger." Waters reportedly paid an artist to print a roll of toilet paper with Gilmour's face on every sheet. An observer characterized the feud as "Waters's megalomania versus Gilmour's pent-up frustrations, superheated into a rage for simple vengeance."

⭐ In 1988, the band transformed the Grand Canal in Venice, Italy, into a Floyd set and played a free concert. Described later as "the rape of Venice," the event led to the resignation of Venice's mayor and the entire city council.

Fifty-six truckloads of equipment were needed for Floyd's 1990 American tour. In Pittsburgh, the rockers shared their hotel with a convention of blind bowlers. During the performance of the song "Sorrow," the power went off for ten minutes. Shrugged Gilmour, "The song was getting a bit boring anyway." Floyd started referring to the tour as, you guessed it, *Spinal Tap.*

# Iggy Pop

## FACTS OF LIFE

**ORIGIN:** Born James Newell Osterberg, April 21, 1947, Muskegon, Michigan.

**FORMATIVE YEARS:** University of Michigan dropout.

**FAMILY PLANNING:** Married Wendy Weisberg, 1968; divorced a month later; Married Suchi.

**ROMANTIC INTERESTS:** "One of my big ambitions is to make love to a flight attendant."

## SELECTED HITS (and Misses)

**SONGS:** "I Wanna Be Your Dog" (with the Stooges—1969), "Lust for Life" (1976), "I'm Bored" (1979), "Blah Blah Blah" (1986), "Knucklehead" (1996).

**FILMS:** *Sid and Nancy* (1986), *The Color of Money* (1986), *Cry-Baby* (1990), *Hardware* (1990), *Tank Girl* (1994), *Dead Man* (1995), *Private Parts* (1997), *The Brave* (1997).

**TV:** *The Adventures of Pete and Pete* (series, 1993–94).

## QUICKIE BIO

In 1967, a mild-mannered Detroit teenager transformed himself into Iggy Pop (named for a local junkie known as "Iggy the Iguana") and formed the band the Psychedelic Stooges. Pop's self-wounding stage act got the attention of David Bowie and other rock royalty, but the rocker never managed to turn his reputation into major record sales. He flew high when his music appeared in the 1996 cult hit film *Trainspotting,* then crashed when he injured himself during a 1997 concert tour. Sighed the fifty-something Pop, "It's kind of terrible to be a middle-aged musician and not know how to do anything else."

## IGGY POP DOES
## THE DUMBEST THINGS

⭐ When Pop showed up for his army physical, the sergeant asked him to strip down to his underwear. Pop stripped, then took his place in line with an enormous woody (11 inches by 1¾ inches according to Pop's estimation). The sergeant shouted, "Where's your *underwear?*" then led Pop away for a battery of psychological tests. Pop failed.

⭐ Pop later pulled out his biggie and showed it to Ginger (Tina Louise) from the TV show *Gilligan's Island.* Said Pop, "It's the kind of thing I really don't need to garnish." What, the biggie?

⭐ After playing four nights with the Stooges in New York, Pop ran out of things to do onstage. So he pulled out his pecker. "I didn't know what to do with it," explained Pop. "So I zipped it back and walked off."

⭐ While in New York in 1971, Pop met David Bowie. After partying through the night, Pop declared that "the only good rocker [was] a dead rocker." Then he hit himself over the head with a beer bottle and passed out.

⭐ After landing a record deal and a six-figure advance with the help of David Bowie, Pop appeared at a London press conference. Bowie arrived drunk and kissed the Detroit rocker on the lips. Pop punched his mentor in the nose.

⭐ Instead of wrecking his instruments onstage, Pop wrecked himself. He burned himself with swirling microphone cords, jumped chest-first into broken glass, and forced himself to puke. On one occasion, Pop told audience members to beat him up. They did.

⭐ At a show in Rome, Michigan, Pop ripped through his pants and covered his crotch with shaving cream. The creamy codpiece did not satisfy the local police, who arrested him and pulled him from the stage.

⭐ During a 1970 gig with Alice Cooper, Pop jumped into the crowd and smeared himself with peanut butter.

⭐ Pop later performed an entire show while zippered inside a military duffel bag.

★ Pop's personal hygiene was as questionable as his stage act. He sometimes kept a glass next to his bed at night. An empty one. That way, if he had to pee, he didn't have to walk all the way to the bathroom.

★ Pop got depressed after the Stooges broke up for the second time. He ate a bunch of Quaaludes, Valiums, and Seconals and went out to dinner. He flipped. The cops picked him up and gave him the choice of jail or a mental hospital. Pop chose the mental hospital. The next day, he broke out of the facility, consumed the rest of his stash, then committed himself to a hospital—again.

★ On the 1990s children's TV show *The Adventures of Pete and Pete,* Pop played the part of "Mr. Mecklenberg," whom Pop described as "a boomer dad with a corncob up his a\*\*." When his kiddie costars asked the aging rocker to autograph his album *FunHouse,* Pop admitted, "I felt stupid because I put the f-word on it."

★ Pop worked on the soundtrack for the 1997 flop film *The Brave.* "Often when we were creating the music," Pop explained at the Cannes Film Festival, "the engineer and I looked at each other and we would say, 'What would Yanni do?'" Pop does Yanni? No wonder the film tanked.

★ While at Cannes, Pop and his band played a gig for a gaggle of movie stars. According to some reports, Pop spat during one of his songs, and the loogie landed close to Demi Moore. To make her feel better, Pop invited Demi onstage to help him sing "I Wanna Be Your Dog."

★ Pop's most humiliating performance occurred in the summer of 1997. Pop jumped off the stage into the arms of his adoring fans. Oooops! Turns out, there weren't enough fans in the audience to catch the airborne rock star. Pop fell straight to the ground, dislocated his shoulder, and had to cancel the rest of his tour.

# Elvis Presley

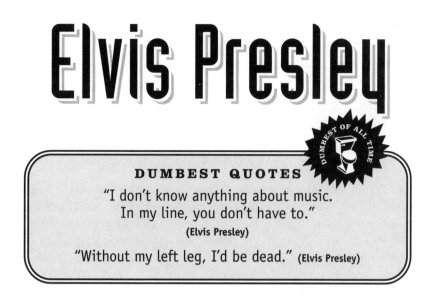

DUMBEST QUOTES

"I don't know anything about music.
In my line, you don't have to."
(Elvis Presley)

"Without my left leg, I'd be dead." (Elvis Presley)

## FACTS OF LIFE (and Death)

**ORIGIN:** Born Elvis Aron Presley, January 8, 1935, East Tupelo, Mississippi, died August 16, 1977, at home in Graceland while sitting on the toilet reading *The Scientific Search for the Face of Jesus Christ*. The Memphis, Tennessee, coroner's report listed the cause of death as "cardiac arrhythmia"—a heart attack. Hospital personnel claimed that the cause of death was a drug overdose.

**FORMATIVE YEARS:** High-school graduate.

**FAMILY PLANNING:** Met Priscilla Beaulieu when she was fourteen and he was twenty-four; Married May 1, 1967; divorced October 11, 1973; Daughter Lisa Marie Presley was born February 1, 1968.

**ROMANTIC INTERESTS:** Dozens of females, including Natalie Wood (actress), Mamie Van Doren (actress), Tempest Storm (stripper), Patti Parry (hairdresser), Ann-Margret (actress), Linda Thompson (a Tennessee beauty queen).

## SELECTED HITS (and Misses)

**SONGS:** "That's All Right Mama" (1954), "Heartbreak Hotel" (1956), "Hound Dog" (1956), "All Shook Up" (1957), "Jailhouse Rock" (1957), "Are You Lonesome Tonight?" (1960), "Return to Sender" (1962), "Do the Clam" (1965), "Queenie Wahini's Papaya" (1967), "In the Ghetto" (1969), "Burning Love" (1972), "T-R-O-U-B-L-E" (1975), "My Way" (1977), "Guitar Man" (1981).

**FILMS:** Thirty-three movies, including *Love Me Tender* (1956), *Jailhouse Rock* (1957), *King Creole* (1958), *Blue Hawaii* (1961), *Viva Las Vegas* (1964), *Frankie and Johnny* (1966), *Clambake* (1967), *The Trouble with Girls (and How to Get Into It)* (1969), *This Is Elvis* (1981).

**TV:** *Elvis* (special—1968), *Elvis: Aloha from Hawaii* (special—1973), *Elvis In Concert* (special—1977).

## QUICKIE BIO

Elvis Presley was working as a truck driver in Memphis, Tennessee, in 1954 when he decided to cut a record for his beloved mom. The kindhearted gesture led to a recording contract, an alliance with manager "Colonel" Tom Parker, 90 albums, 107 top hits, 33 films, and a drug habit that would have killed an elephant—and did kill Presley, at age forty-two. The darling of lounge singers, social scientists, and spoon collectors, Elvis—the King—became even more popular in death than in life.

## ELVIS PRESLEY DOES
## THE DUMBEST THINGS

✪ Presley was a very spiritual person. He always wore a Christian cross, a Star of David, and the Hebrew letter chi. Why? Explained Presley, "I don't want to miss out on heaven due to a technicality."

✪ Presley owned thirty-seven guns and liked to fire them. He shot at cars that wouldn't start. He shot holes in restaurants if the service was poor. He peppered his recording studio in Graceland with bullets because he didn't like the sound. He even shot at chandeliers and at his daughter's swing set.

✪ Presley also liked to shoot at TV sets whenever annoying performers appeared. He particularly enjoyed shooting at singer Robert Goulet.

✪ When Presley blasted a light switch in his Las Vegas hotel room, the bullet went through the wall and almost hit his then girlfriend Linda Thompson.

✪ Presley liked pets. He had dogs, mules, horses, peacocks, chickens, a turkey, and a mynah bird that said, "Elvis! Go to hell!"

🐶 Presley's favorite pet was a chimpanzee named Scatter. Presley and his buddies taught Scatter to drink bourbon and pinch women's butts. For a while, Scatter ate at the dinner table with a knife and fork and was

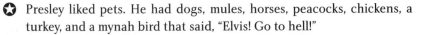

President Nixon presented Elvis Presley with an honorary Narcotics Bureau badge in 1970. Elvis was waging his own personal war on drugs at the time. He was trying to do away with them by eating as many as his doctor would give him. [photo courtesy of Archive Photos]

chauffeured around in a Rolls-Royce. Eventually, the chimp got nasty and was banished to a cage. The drunk monkey finally died of cirrhosis of the liver.

⭐ Presley liked his food as much as his animals. "I like it well done," he explained. "I ain't ordering a pet."

⭐ Before a concert in Baltimore, Presley reportedly wolfed down five sundaes for breakfast, then passed out.

⭐ Presley was a binge eater on a continual binge. Toward the end of his too-short life, Presley wore specially-made mirror glasses, so that he could eat while watching TV lying down.

⭐ Presley was not a gracious host. In 1974 Christina Crawford, the daughter of Joan Crawford, visited Presley at Graceland. At one point during their conversation, the King went ballistic, grabbed Crawford by the hair, dragged her across a marble coffee table, pushed her into another room, kicked her in the butt, and showed her the door. Perhaps he didn't appreciate her talking badly about her own Mommie Dearest.

⭐ Presley wanted to become a political activist. So he hand-delivered a letter to a guard at the White House and met with then president Richard

Nixon on December 21, 1970. Presley hugged the president, gave him a pistol, and told him he had been studying the drug culture for ten years. Nixon gifted Presley with an honorary Narcotics Bureau badge.

Presley had indeed been studying drugs for ten years. Mainly by ingesting them. Toward the end of his life, Presley chomped down about twenty-five different pills a day, prescribed by his personal physician, Dr. George Nichopoulos. When "Dr. Nick" took his pills away one day, Presley shot at him. "Elvis," said the doctor, "you're displaying some pretty bad judgment."

Shortly after Presley's burial in 1977, three men wearing bulletproof vests and armed with grenades broke into Forest Hill Cemetery. The grave-robbers claimed they didn't believe Presley was dead and wanted to inspect the body. Police felt they were going to hold the corpse for ransom. They arrested the men but eventually let them go. Long live the King!

Love him or hate him, Presley's manager "Colonel" Tom Parker knew how to make big money. Before he changed Presley into a drug-addled movie-star peacock, he made his money by painting sparrows yellow and selling them as canaries.

"Fat" Presley was worried about his weight during his 1973 *Aloha from Hawaii* concert. When he sang the song "Suspicious Minds" he crooned, *"I hope this suit don't rip up baby."* Suck it in, Elvis!

Presley was so cruel to his hair that it turned completely white by the time he turned forty.

# Public Enemy

## FACTS OF LIFE

**RINGLEADERS:** Chuck D (vocals)—born Carlton Ridenhour, August 1, 1960, Long Island, New York; Flavor Flav (vocals)—born William Drayton, March 16, 1959, Long Island, New York; Professor Griff, Minister of Information (vocals)—born Richard Griffin.

## SELECTED HITS (and Misses)

**SONGS:** "Don't Believe the Hype" (1988), "Rebel Without a Pause" (1988), "911 Is a Joke" (1990), "Welcome to the Terrordome" (1990), "How to Kill a Radio Consultant" (1991), "Hitler Day" (1994), "Give It Up" (1994), "He Got Game" (1998).

## QUICKIE BIO

For over a decade, Public Enemy was hip-hop's most political act, although at times they seemed more like cartoon characters than revolutionaries. Producer Rick Rubin, who scored big with the Beastie Boys, helped Public Enemy develop the tough street sound that emerged on the band's first album *Yo! Bum Rush the Show* (1987). The boys from suburban Long Island scored major headlines in 1989, when their Minister of Information made anti-Semitic remarks. The band ousted him and played on. However, with the rise of gangsta rap, Public Enemy lost its cutting edge. Chuck D, the most eloquent member of the group, launched a solo career that landed him a book deal, a spot on the college lecture circuit, and a gig as a news commentator for FOX TV. Chuck D even began giving poetry readings. One of his poems was titled "Male Ego Overblown Testosterone."

## PUBLIC ENEMY DOES THE DUMBEST THINGS

⭐ Some critics called Flavor Flav a cartoon. The rapper who liked to wear an enormous clock on his chest probably didn't mind. He had a Pink Panther tattoo and said that the first song he learned to play on the piano was the *Batman* TV theme. "The first record I ever bought was a Banana Splits jam that I ordered off a Corn Flakes box," admitted the hip-hop star.

⭐ In a 1988 interview, Public Enemy's Minister of Information, Professor Griff, explained the origin of the term "monkey's uncle." "It came from the Caucasian mountains because…that's who [white people] made it with in the Caucasian hills."

⭐ In 1989, Professor Griff gave an interview to a Washington newspaper in which he characterized Jews as being "wicked" and made a bunch of other anti-Semitic remarks.

⭐ After Griff made his politically incorrect remarks, Public Enemy added to the controversy by releasing "Welcome to the Terrordome." The song declared that the Jews were out to get Public Enemy just "like they got Jesus."

⭐ D fired Griff from the band, then rehired him, then fired him again. A short time later, D was on the lecture circuit, speaking in front of high-school, college, and prison groups. His message? "Get your s*** together."

⭐ D should have talked to his bandmate Flav. In 1994, Flav smoked crack, and decided that his wife was mating with a neighbor. Flav confronted the neighbor, and wound up under arrest for attempted murder. The charges were eventually dropped.

⭐ In that same year, Flav was stopped by police after a routine traffic accident. When police checked Flav's record, they discovered that his license had been suspended forty-three times! Pictures of the arrest showed Flav wearing a "Free O.J. Simpson" T-shirt.

⭐ On the college lecture circuit in 1997, D told students and faculty members that "you've got to kill some folks" in order to stop media racism. D didn't say whether "some folks" included his coworkers at the FOX television network.

# Queen

## FACTS OF LIFE (and Death)

**RINGLEADERS:** Freddie Mercury (vocals)—born Farookh Bulsara, September 5, 1986, Zanzibar, Tanzania, died November 24, 1991, London, England of AIDS-related bronchial pneumonia; Brian May (guitar)—born July 19, 1947, Surrey, England; Roger Taylor (drums)—born July 26, 1949, Norfolk, England.

## SELECTED HITS (and Misses)

**SONGS:** "Bohemian Rhapsody" (1975), "We Are the Champions" (1977), "We Will Rock You" (1977), "Crazy Little Thing Called Love" (1979), "Another One Bites the Dust" (1980), "Who Wants to Live Together?" (1986), "Bohemian Rhapsody" (1992).

## QUICKIE BIO

Queen came together in 1970 when three college-educated British scientists met a Tanzanian-born art student who called himself Freddie Mercury. The three intellectuals wanted to call the band Rich Kids. Flamboyant Mercury insisted on the name Queen and led the band into the glittering stratosphere of arena rock. The group stopped touring upon Mercury's AIDS-related death in 1991. However, in 1992, the film *Wayne's World* introduced an entire new generation to the sing-along joys of "Bohemian Rhapsody." The spirit of Mercury continued to thrive as sports promoters around the world pumped up well-endowed athletes and partying fans with Queen favorites like "We Will Rock You."

# QUEEN DOES
# THE DUMBEST THINGS

✪ On tour with his first band Ibex, Mercury landed in a north England mining town. Dressed in satin and furs, he jumped out of the van on the town's main street and ran right into a group of soot-covered miners. Freddie screamed, jumped back into the van, and pulled down the window blinds.

✪ Mercury and his London buddies enjoyed feasting on marijuana-filled brownies. One rowdy night, the police arrived to quiet the lads. Mercury offered the officers some brownies, which they gladly ate. Recalled Mercury, "I would love to have been a fly on the windscreen of their police car after about half an hour."

✪ For a while, Mercury owned a fashion stall in a London market. The stall was opposite a ladies' clothing boutique. Mercury adjusted the ladies' dressing-room mirrors and his own cash register so that he could enjoy a full view of the girls while he was making change.

✪ In the early days of Queen, Mercury hit himself so hard with his tambourine that he suffered a bruised leg.

✪ In 1973, before Queen's first appearance on film, fashionable Mercury shaved his chest.

💰 Mercury's shopping style was as flamboyant and as exasperating as his fashion sense. "Shopping with Mercury is like hitting yourself on the head repeatedly with an ice pick," recalled one friend. "It feels so good when you stop."

✪ In December 1977, Queen invited special guests onstage for a Los Angeles performance. They included a capering elf, waltzing Christmas trees, and the director of Queen's record company dressed up like a gingerbread man. An enormous Santa Claus appeared onstage carrying a huge bag. Out of the bag jumped everyone's favorite Christmas present—Freddie!

✪ In October 1978, Queen threw a royal bash at a New Orleans hotel. The band invited 400 people and flew in the press from England, South America, and Japan. Party guests were entertained by naked female mud-wrestling dwarfs, fire-eaters, Zulu dancers, and drag queens. Record executives lined up for admittance to a special back room, where a female New Orleans native spent the entire evening on her knees getting down to business.

- For his 1981 birthday bash, Mercury bought Concorde tickets for all his friends and flew them to New York. The party began at his suite in the Berkshire Hotel and ended there five days later.

- Mercury threw his 1985 party at a club in Munich, Germany. It was a black-and-white drag ball. The only man not dressed as a woman was Mercury, who was filmed diving through the fishnet stocking-clad legs of a dancing male guest. Mercury wanted to use the film as a promotional video. His record company said, "No way."

- The Queen song "Radio Gaga" was inspired by Roger's son who heard a song on the radio and called it "radio ka-ka."

- To promote the singles "Bicycle Race" and "Fat-Bottomed Girls," Queen's publicity machine hired sixty-five women to ride bicycles around a stadium in London—naked. It was a warm day, and the ladies performed well. There was only one hitch. The company that provided the bicycles refused to take back the used seats.

- Queen traveled through Latin America in 1981 with the *Gluttons for Punishment* tour. When Queen's equipment—all 110 *tons* of it—arrived by truck at the Argentina-Brazil border, one of the customs officials had a heart attack.

# The Ramones

## FACTS OF LIFE

**RINGLEADERS:** Johnny Ramone (guitar)—born John Cummings, October 8, 1951, Forest Hills, New York; Joey Ramone (vocals)—born Jeffrey Hyman, May 9, 1952, Forest Hills, New York; Tommy Ramone (drums)—born Thomas Erdelyi, January 29, 1952, Budapest, Hungary; Dee Dee Ramone (bass)—born Douglas Colvin, September 18, 1952, Fort Lee, Virginia.

## SELECTED HITS (and Misses)

**SONGS:** "Blitzkrieg Bop" (1976), "I Wanna Be Sedated" (1978), "Every Time I Eat Vegetables It Makes Me Think of You" (1983), "Bonzo Goes to Bitburg" (1985), "Cabbies on Crack" (1992), "Fascists Don't F***, They Just Screw" (unreleased).

**FILMS:** *Rock and Roll High School* (1979), *Lifestyles of the Ramones* (video—1990).

## QUICKIE BIO

Picking up where the Velvet Underground left off, this black-clad New York City quartet helped jump-start punk. Neighborhood chums Hyman and Cummings billed themselves as rock-and-roll siblings the Ramones in 1974, and began performing music that combined the simplicity of Chuck Berry with the even greater simplicity of Iggy Pop. Fans hailed them as rock's future. Critics scorned them as rock's Neanderthal past. One thing everyone agreed on was that the Ramones were consistent. For the next twenty years, the band delivered the same three-chord sound in the same two-minute sound bites. The Ramones finally called it quits in early 1996—then announced that they were reuniting for the summer 1996 Lollapalooza tour.

# THE RAMONES DO
# THE DUMBEST THINGS

⭐ As a young thug, Johnny Ramone attempted to break into a drugstore. He was caught when he broke into the wrong store—a laundromat.

⭐ At the very first Ramones performance, Dee Dee got so nervous that he stepped on his bass and broke it.

⭐ The set list for the band's debut gig included the songs "I Don't Wanna Go Down to the Basement," "I Don't Wanna Walk Around with You," "I Don't Wanna Get Involved with You," and "I Don't Like Nobody that Don't Like Me." The most positive song on the set list was "Now I Wanna Sniff Some Glue." Johnny said after the show, "We invited all of our friends down to see us and they all hated it and didn't want to be our friends anymore."

⭐ In their early years the Ramones played fast. Twenty-two songs in twenty minutes. One Rhode Island club owner called the sheriff when the band left the stage after their twenty-minute show. The Ramones defended themselves by saying they had played a full gig of music. They had just cut out all the between-song patter.

⭐ The Ramones lived like rock stars even before they started making money. Explained Dee Dee, "I was making $125 a week and I had a $100-a-day dope habit."

⭐ Joey Ramone liked to get drunk and hang around mental institutions because the girls there were "all loose." He fell in love with one girl. Every week she had electroshock therapy. "Before they took her up she was fine," said Joey. "Then she came down and she was like a zombie and didn't even know who I was."

⭐ The Ramones liked to play loud. They performed so loud while recording their first album that they destroyed several pieces of studio equipment.

⭐ At a 1977 gig in Marseilles, France, the Ramones allegedly played full volume and pulled so much power that they blacked out the entire city.

⭐ The Rivieras' 1964 hit song "California Sun" had four chords. This was one too many for the Ramones, who played the song with three chords.

⭐ The Ramones never took themselves, or anyone else, too seriously. To promote the tune "Something to Believe In," the band produced a video spoof of the Hands Across America benefit. The video featured Spinal Tap and Ted Nugent and a chorus of guys holding hands and singing while they peed into a line of urinals. The name of the Ramones' fictitious relief effort? Hands Across Your Face.

 One of the Ramones thought it would be cool to ride a Harley-Davidson motorcycle onstage during a 1992 gig in Germany. It was cool—until the Ramone crashed and broke his arm.

 The Ramones made a painful appearance at the 1995 MTV Movie Awards, when they lip-synched to their own version of a song from *The Lion King*.

 After traveling with the band for more than fifteen years, the Ramones' tour manager was philosophical. "What is the difference between a tour manager and a toilet seat?" he asked rhetorically. "A toilet seat only has to put up with one a**hole at a time."

# Red Hot Chili Peppers

## FACTS OF LIFE

**RINGLEADERS:** Anthony Kiedis (vocals)—born November 1, 1962, Grand Rapids, Michigan; Flea (bass)—born Michael Balzary, October 16, 1962, Melbourne, Australia; Chad Smith (drums)—born October 25, 1962, St. Paul, Minnesota.

## SELECTED HITS (and Misses)

**SONGS:** "Hollywood" (1985), "Party on Your P***y" (1987), "Higher Ground" (1989), "Give It Away" (1991), "Suck My Kiss" (1992), "Love Roller Coaster" (1996).

**FILMS:** *F.I.S.T.* (Anthony Kiedis—1976), *Point Blank* (Anthony Kiedis—1991), *Suburbia* (Flea—1991).

## QUICKIE BIO

The hard-partying Red Hot Chili Peppers were the first rock stars in history to prove that socks could sell records. Anthony Kiedis and Flea started their rock shenanigans at Los Angeles' Fairfax High School. They worked their red-hot stage act through the L.A. club scene in the early 1980s, and hit it big with their 1991 album *BloodSugarSexMagic*. They cooled off in the mid-1990s as a typhoon washed out a Japanese concert and two of the band members injured themselves in motorcycle accidents. (Years earlier, in 1988, the group's Israeli-born guitarist Hillel Slovak, thirty-five, had died of a drug overdose.)

# RED HOT CHILI PEPPERS
## DO THE DUMBEST THINGS

⭐ Flea (alias Mike B the Flea) and Kiedis were the class cutups in high school. They impressed their friends by climbing onto billboards, pulling out their wieners, and wiggling them at passing motorists.

⭐ Flea and Kiedis's favorite high school prank was to clamber onto the roof of a stranger's home and jump into the swimming pool. Friends and relatives warned the future Peppers that this was a dumb thing to do. But they wouldn't listen—until Kiedis misjudged a jump one day, landed on concrete, and broke his back.

⭐ Flea and Kiedis demanded more from their bandmates than solid musicianship. When John Frusciante tried out for the group in 1988, the boys asked him to strut his stuff. First, Frusciante played guitar. Then he pulled down his pants. The peppers inspected his erect equipment, and Frusciante passed the audition.

⭐ While studying at UCLA, Kiedis was disturbed by a persistent female admirer. He finally invited the girl to his room, then appeared before her wearing nothing but a tube sock over his privates. The girl was horrified and split. However, Kiedis's troupe liked the sock thing so much, they made it a regular part of their show.

⭐ Sock-suality had its ups and downs. During a 1989 show in Green Bay, Wisconsin, the Peppers' drummer lost his sock. The sight of the naked drummer inspired a roadie to jump onstage au naturel and whip his willie around like a weed whacker.

⭐ Kiedis should have kept his sock on after a 1989 performance at George Mason University in Fairfax, Virginia. Instead, the singer displayed his pecker in the face of a shocked coed. When the woman sued, the rocker declared, "I am not that type of person." The judge thought otherwise and convicted Kiedis of indecent exposure and sexual battery.

Flea kept his clothes on, but managed to get into just as much trouble during the 1990 MTV spring break party in Daytona Beach, Florida. While lip-synching to the song "Knock Me Down," Flea picked up a bikini-clad twenty-year-old, hoisted her on his shoulder, and spun her around. Flea lost his balance, dropped the girl, then asked her to indulge in what she later described as "an unnatural sex act." Flea's MTV performance cost him fines and required a letter of apology to the girl.

⭐ On tour a few months after the MTV incident, drummer Chad Smith went shopping in Amsterdam. What did he buy? The services of a woman who spanked his fanny. Bragged Smith, "My mother would be proud that I spent my money in such a good way."

⭐ In 1984, producer Andy Gill was not proud of the way the band spent their time in the recording studio. When Kiedis and Flea took a break to go to the bathroom, the British producer joked, "Don't trouble me by bringing it back, right?" A few minutes later, the boys did indeed bring it back. Gill examined the pepper turd, and pronounced it "typical."

⭐ In 1992, Kiedis decided that his life was getting way too typical. When he heard that a tattoo artist was leading an expedition into the heart of Borneo, the rock star begged to be included. After a few days in the jungle, Kiedis got extremely uncomfortable. He discovered that he was suffering from butt-sucking leeches. (No, not agents. Real live leeches.) The horrified Chili Pepper hired a helicopter to airlift him out of the wilderness.

# The Replacements

## FACTS OF LIFE (and Death)

**RINGLEADERS:** Paul Westerberg (guitar, vocals)—born December 31, 1960, Minneapolis, Minnesota; Bob Stinson (guitar)—born December 17, 1959, Mound, Minnesota, died February 18, 1995, of a drug overdose; Tommy Stinson (bass)—born October 6, 1966, San Diego California; Chris Mars (drums)—born April 26, 1961, Minneapolis, Minnesota.

## SELECTED HITS

**SONGS:** "F*** School" (1982), "Color Me Impressed" (1983), "Gary's Got a Boner" (1984), "Hold My Life" (1985), "Left of the Dial" (1985), "Alex Chilton" (1987), "Can't Hardly Wait" (1987).

## QUICKIE BIO

Middle-class Minneapolis misfits Bob Stinson and younger brother Tommy got together with Paul Westerberg in 1981 to form the Replacements. The 'Mats (as they were affectionately known by fans) didn't give performances—they hosted drunken free-for-alls. Band members frequently switched instruments mid-set (sometimes in mid-song), and performed warped cover tunes such as "Like a Rolling Pin," (a spoof of Bob Dylan's "Like a Rolling Stone"). In the early 1990s, Westerberg got sensitive. The band broke up shortly thereafter.

## THE REPLACEMENTS DO
## THE DUMBEST THINGS

⊛ Westerberg drank so much in high school that the only thing he remembered about typing class was getting out the paper.

⊛ The band started out as the Impediments. Their first gig was at a halfway house for alcoholics. The guys came to the show "pilled-up and plowed." They were promptly thrown out and told they would never play again. The next day, they changed their name to the Replacements.

🚬 At a 1984 show in Minneapolis, guitarist Bob Stinson walked onstage wearing nothing but a diaper. The "garment" kept coming undone during the show and later as the guitarist staggered around town.

⊛ When guitarist Stinson pissed onstage at a club in Cleveland, the band was thrown out of the club.

⊛ The too-hard-drinking Bob was eventually thrown out of the band, and replaced by Slim Dunlap. What was Dunlap's audition? An afternoon of drinking beer with the group.

⊛ At a Minneapolis gig, the band played so loud that the club manager shouted at Westerberg to either turn it down or get out. Westerberg shouted back, "Do we still get paid if we leave?" Westerberg then launched into the song "Shut Up" with the chorus changed to "F*** You."

⊛ The Replacements treated fans in Virginia to their "pussy set"—consisting of country tunes and tearjerking ballads. The crowd got its revenge later by trashing the Replacements' van.

⊛ One incredibly inebriated show in Ann Arbor consisted solely of the band tuning up and then falling down.

⊛ The producers of TV's *Saturday Night Live* were so worried about an appearance by the Replacements that they forced the band to sign a $20,000 agreement not to swear on the air. Westerberg managed to get away with potty-talk by mumbling the word "butt" instead of "bus" during "Kiss Me on the Bus." He later stepped back from the mike and said "F*** you." It wasn't audible so it didn't violate the agreement, but it annoyed the TV execs nonetheless.

⊛ When they got into a fight with their record company, the Replacements took things into their own hands. While one of the 'Mats kept the receptionist busy, the other band members scrounged around until they found their master tapes. The band took the tapes from the record-company offices, drove to the Mississippi River, and threw them into the muddy waters.

# Keith Richards

## FACTS OF LIFE

**ORIGIN:** Born December 18, 1943, Dartford, England.

**FORMATIVE YEARS:** Dropped out of art college.

**FAMILY PLANNING:** Had three children by Anita Pallenberg; Married Patti Hansen, December 18, 1983.

**ROMANTIC INTERESTS:** Linda Keith (model), Anita Pallenberg (actress-model), Marianne Faithfull (singer), Uschi Obermeier (Mick Jagger's former girlfriend), Lillie Wenglass Green (model).

## SELECTED HITS (and Misses)

**SONGS:** (with The Rolling Stones) "Time Is on My Side" (1964), "Get Off of My Cloud" (1965), "Play with Fire" (1965), "(I Can't Get No) Satisfaction" (1965), "Let's Spend the Night Together" (1966), "Jumpin' Jack Flash" (1968), "Honky Tonk Woman" (1969), "Angie" (1973), "Miss You" (1978), "Start Me Up" (1988), "Mixed Emotions" (1989).

**FILMS:** *Gimme Shelter* (1970), *Chuck Berry: Hail! Hail! Rock 'n' Roll* (1988).

## QUICKIE BIO

Keith Richards first met Mick Jagger in the sandbox at elementary school. According to Jagger, Richards liked to wear cowboy outfits and wanted to be like Roy Rogers and play guitar. Richards fulfilled his childhood fantasy, and many others. After learning his guitar chops with British blues bands, Richards joined the Rolling Stones in 1962 and never left. The much-busted guitarist took fame, drugs, and misfortune in stride, earning a reputation as "the world's most elegantly wasted human being." Richards wrote some of his best songs about some of the world's most horrible drugs. "Jumpin' Jack Flash" celebrated "jacks," the English term for pharmaceutical heroin. The one-time leader of the Boy Scouts' Beaver Patrol continued to hunt rock-and-roll beavers into the 1990s, declaring that he kept on playing because "the chicks still dig me."

## KEITH RICHARDS DOES
## THE DUMBEST THINGS

✪ When he got bored in art college, Richards went to the park across the street and fed speed tablets to a caged cockatoo.

✪ Early in his career, Richards wired the bathroom in his apartment for sound and taped everyone who used the facilities. "It was the funniest thing," Richards recalled. "You'd get people muttering, 'Whoa, I needed that! Ooooooh! Just made it! Larvely!'"

✪ At an early Rolling Stones press conference, Richards picked his nose and flicked it across the room. When a writer made a comment to Jagger, Jagger responded, "You're lucky it wasn't a green one. He *eats* those."

✪ Onstage in Sacramento, California, in 1965, Richards got pissed off at his microphone and smashed it with the neck of his guitar. An enormous jolt of electricity sent the rocker flying through the air. Richards landed unconscious and lay on his back. Two minutes later, he sat up. Richards later attributed his survival to the thick soles of his Hush Puppies suede boots.

✪ In 1969, Richards bought a vintage Nazi staff car and had it restored to its World War II splendor. Unfortunately, Richards nodded off at the wheel and smashed up the classic auto the first time he drove it.

✪ In 1972, Richards and his then girlfriend, Anita Pallenberg, rented a fabulous palace on the French Riviera in order to record the album *Beggars Banquet*. The household budget was $7,000 per week: $1,000 for food, $1,000 for alcohol, $2,500, for rent and $2,500 for drugs.

✪ Pallenberg made rocker Courtney Love look like Mother Goose. The actress continued to use drugs throughout her pregnancy, and convinced the teenage daughter of her French chef that heroin was cool.

She was so stoned that she set her own bed on fire, while complaining that she didn't have enough sex with Richards.

★ In 1976, Richards brought his son backstage and let him run around shooting a water gun. A friend observed that the boy was well-trained. Said the friend, "He never shot the water gun at the coke or the smack."

Richards claimed he "never had a problem with drugs." The Rolling Stone boasted, "I even learned to ski when I was a complete junkie."

★ Richards was a junkie for almost a decade. He hid his stash in a fountain pen and a shaving-cream canister, James Bond style. Sometimes he delayed concerts for an hour while promoters scurried around to get their star the drugs he required to walk out onstage.

★ Richards claimed that the corporate sponsor for the Rolling Stones' 1975 American tour was so worried about the guitarist's heroin habit that the company supplied the band with pharmaceutical heroin for the entire trek.

★ When Pallenberg and Richards moved from Switzerland, a friend cleaned up their place. The friend found fifty grams of coke, fifty grams of heroin, huge amounts of hashish, and five hundred used syringes.

★ Richards was convicted of narcotics possession in 1976 and 1977, but always resented police interference in his affairs. "I've never turned blue in someone else's bathroom," he told a reporter. "I mean, I consider that the height of bad manners."

★ The rumor is not true. Richards never had his blood "changed" to overcome his heroin addiction. He did, however, have his blood "cleaned" at a Swiss clinic in 1973. And yes, the cleansing process was part of Richards' effort to break his heroin habit.

★ In 1979, Richards toured with a band called the New Barbarians. After one gig, Richards invited everyone back to his room. "Do anything you want to do," Richards said, "just don't touch me."

★ Richards was drinking beer with guitarists Rory Buchanan, Eric Clapton, and Ronnie Wood in the 1970s. At one point, Buchanan pissed Richards off. "Go ahead, get your cock out Eric," said Richards. "We'll be pissing in that f***er's beer. He's being too pushy." Richards, Clapton, and Wood proceeded to whip them out and flavor Buchanan's brew.

# The Rolling Stones

## FACTS OF LIFE (and Death)

**RINGLEADERS:** Brian Jones (guitar)—born Lewis Brian Hopkins-Jones, February 28, 1942, Cheltenham, England, died July 2, 1969, by "drowning while under the influence of drugs and alcohol"; Bill Wyman (bass)—born William Perks, October 24, 1936, London, England; Charlie Watts (drums)—born June 2, 1941, London, England.

## SELECTED HITS (and Misses)

**SONGS:** "(I Can't Get No) Satisfaction" (1965), "Get Off of My Cloud" (1965), "Paint It Black" (1966), "Honky Tonk Women" (1969), "Brown Sugar" (1971), "Angie" (1973), "Beast of Burden" (1978), "Miss You" (1978), "Start Me Up" (1981), "Has Anybody Seen My Baby?" (1997).

**FILMS:** *Invocation of My Demon Brother* (1969), *Gimme Shelter* (1969), *One Plus One/Sympathy for the Devil* (1970), *Cocksucker Blues* (1972), *Let's Spend the Night Together* (1981).

**TV:** *The Rolling Stones' Rock 'n' Roll Circus* (special—1968, released 1996).

## QUICKIE BIO

In 1962, Brian Jones joined Mick Jagger and Keith Richards to form the Rolling Stones. Billed as "the naughty Beatles," the band lived up to the hype for the next four decades. Busted about a dozen times for everything

223

from assault to drug possession, the Rolling Stones survived the death of Jones and other associates, and presided over the most infamous concert in rock history—Altamont. Individual band members experimented with solo projects from the 1970s through the 1990s, but found that they got the most satisfaction out of performing with the Stones—except for bass player Bill Wyman, who retired to a château in France in the early 1990s. "I'm quite proud that I'm still knocking them out," said the most aged Rolling Stone, in 1997. He was talking about kids, not hits.

## THE ROLLING STONES DO THE DUMBEST THINGS

⭐ In their early days, Jagger and Richards liked to spit on the walls of their groovy bachelor pad. Then they made up names for the loogies and wrote them on the wall. Yellow Humphrey, Green Gilbert, Polka-dot Perkins.

⭐ In 1964, the Stones went into the lobby of the Astor Hotel in New York City and were besieged by fans. They tried to run away but dashed straight into a linen closet. They were trapped until police came to their rescue.

⭐ During that same trip to America, the members of the band had a difficult time getting laid. "We noticed a distinct lack of crumpet," mused Richards years later. "When you're in Omaha [Nebraska] in 1964 and you suddenly feel horny, you might as well forget it."

⭐ The crumpet count quickly improved. By 1965, Bill Wyman had screwed 278 girls, Jones 130, Jagger about 30, Richards 6 and Charlie Watts 0. At least, according to Wyman.

⭐ Jones liked to beat up girls. When one waif ran bloody and screaming from his hotel room in Florida, a Rolling Stones roadie attacked Jones and broke two of his ribs.

⭐ Jones, tripping on LSD, ran through the lobby of L.A.'s Ambassador Hotel screaming that the floor was crawling with snakes.

⭐ In the middle of a recording session, Jones rushed out of the studio, claiming that it was filled with millions of beetles. (Bugs, that is, *not* rival musicians.)

⭐ For a publicity photo, Jones dressed up like a Nazi and posed with his foot on the throat of someone pretending to be a Jew. His German girlfriend (later Keith's) Anita Pallenberg was the only one who thought the publicity shot was funny.

"I'm not working with no animal act. I worked with Elton and that was enough!" complained Keith Richards of the Rolling Stones. [photo courtesy of Photofest]

⭐ The Rolling Stones dressed up in drag for a photo shoot in New York City. Later, they had a few drinks in the back room of a bar, and started making home movies. Jones lifted up his dress, revealed that he wasn't wearing underwear, and proceeded to mate with himself while the camera rolled.

⭐ In Miami, in 1965, Jones took his girlfriend out for a ride in a motor boat. He pointed the boat out to sea and drove until he ran out of gas. The owner of the boat had to tow the stranded rock star back to shore.

⭐ Late one night in 1965, the Rolling Stones pulled into a service station in East London. Wyman asked the attendant if he could use the restroom. "Get off my forecourt!" the attendant yelled. Jones jumped out of the car and shouted, "Get off my foreskin!" Then Jagger, Wyman, and Richards peed on a nearby wall. The band was arrested for "insulting behavior" and each had to pay a fine of five pounds.

⭐ In 1967, Richards threw a party at Redlands, his English estate. Everyone who was anyone came, including the police. Investigators allegedly discovered singer Marianne Faithfull wrapped in a rug and performing sexual acrobatics with Jagger and a candy bar. They also found four speed pills in Jagger's coat and not much else. "They left a bag of heroin down the sofa," Richards later observed, "and took the incense sticks."

⭐ In 1969, the Stones hosted a West Coast Woodstock at the Altamont Speedway just outside of San Francisco. Instead of three days of peace and love, Altamont turned out to be about twelve hours of violence and murder. Total body count: four dead, dozens seriously injured, two thousand overdoses and freakouts. "We leave you to kiss each other good-bye," said Jagger at the end of the concert, just before he jumped into a waiting helicopter. "You have been so groovy. Good night."

 Onboard the Stones' jet, the *Lapping Tongue,* in the early 1970s, tongues really did get lapping. Jagger played tom-toms while roadies stripped three groupies and chased them around the plane. The tour doctor meanwhile had sex with one of the groupies in a variety of positions while the band members looked on and cheered.

⭐ Shows on the 1975 Rolling Stones tour climaxed with Mick Jagger riding a forty-foot inflatable phallus as he sang the song "Starf***er"(credited as "Star Star")

⭐ Bill Wyman met Mandy Smith when she was thirteen and he was forty-eight. Wyman paid for her education, then wed her when she turned eighteen. The marriage quickly fell apart, perhaps because Wyman's twenty-seven-year-old son Stephen was rumored to be dating his daddy's wife's mum.

⭐ Brian Jones and a number of other Rolling Stones associates passed away over the years. Explained a philosophical Mick Jagger, "A lot of my friends have died in car crashes, in plane crashes, and from drug overdoses. I've learned from that. I've always made sure I avoided driving while on a drug overdose during a plane crash."

# Diana Ross

## FACTS OF LIFE

**ORIGIN:** Born Diane Ernestine Ross (her first name was incorrectly written as Diana on her birth certificate) March 26, 1944, Detroit, Michigan.

**FORMATIVE YEARS:** Graduated from high school.

**FAMILY PLANNING:** Married Robert Silberstein (a Los Angeles public relations executive), January 20, 1971; divorced 1976; Married Arne Naess (Norwegian, mega-millionaire shipping magnate) October 23, 1985.

**ROMANTIC INTERESTS:** Warren Beatty (actor), Ryan O'Neal (actor), Gene Simmons (musician), Richard Gere (actor), Julio Iglesias (singer), Berry Gordy, Jr. (her boss at Motown Records), Michael Jackson (at least *he* thinks so).

## SELECTED HITS (and Misses)

**SONGS:** (With the Supremes) "Baby Love" (1964), "Stop! in the Name of Love" (1965), "You Keep Me Hanging On" (1966), (Solo) "Ain't No Mountain High Enough" (1970), "Touch Me in the Morning" (1973), "Love Hangover" (1976), "Endless Love" (1981), "Dirty Looks" (1986).

**FILMS:** *Lady Sings the Blues* (1972), *Mahogany* (1975), *The Wiz* (1978).

**TV:** *Out of Darkness* (telefeature—1994).

## QUICKIE BIO

Diana Ross and fellow Detroit teen dreamers Mary Wilson and Florence Ballard put together a vocal group and began hanging out at local studios. Ambition and persistence eventually paid off. In 1960, Berry Gordy, Jr., the power behind Motown Records, gave the girls some attention and material. In 1964, the Supremes got their first number-one hit with "Where Did Our Love Go?" Eventually, Ross's bandmates would ask the same question. In 1970, Ross left the group to embark on a lucrative solo career. Over the next quarter century, Ross alienated just about everyone she worked with, except for her fans. "These people wouldn't dare hurt me," said Ross of her loyal following. "I am a goddess to them." A witch, maybe. (For more of Ross on Ross, see her 1994 autobiography, *Secrets of a Sparrow*.)

## DIANA ROSS DOES
## THE DUMBEST THINGS

⭐ In town for their famous 1965 Shea Stadium gig, the Beatles were set up in the same hotel as the Supremes, and a meeting between the two groups was arranged. The Beatles couldn't wait to ask the girls how they created such a unique studio sound. The secret, according to one of the Supremes: "I think its got something to do with the knobs on the control board."

 Envious of the attention that the dogs of her fellow Supremes were receiving on tour, Ross bought herself two canines, a Maltese and a Yorkie. Ross came off the stage in New Jersey to find her precious pooches shaking and vomiting. "Call an ambulance," shouted Ross. After both dogs died (they had ingested rat poison in a dressing room), Ross canceled the remaining thirteen nights of the run.

⭐ Playing the lead in *Lady Sings the Blues*, the acclaimed 1972 film based on Billie Holiday's life, Ross broke down crying. No, not because of Holiday's sad story. Ross started crying because she thought her costumes looked so nasty. The movie crew tried to explain to the diva that the dresses were designed to look like the kinds of things the legendary blues singer would have actually worn. "But they look crappy," cried the tearful starlet. "I don't want these. I want the best." So much for cinema verité.

⭐ In 1972, a pregnant Ross was cutting a record with Marvin Gaye. Gaye lit up a joint. Ross told him to snuff the stuff. "I'm sorry, baby," said Gaye, "but I got to have my dope or I can't sing." "What kind of crap is this?" screamed Ross. She then threw some grapes at producer Berry Gordy and walked out of the session. Gaye and Ross eventually recorded their parts separately. A year later, after the album was finally released, Ross commented, "Marvin was great to work with."

⭐ When Jackie Kennedy Onassis became a book editor, Ross wanted the former first lady to get her a publishing deal. Onassis asked, "What kind of project do you have in mind?" Ross responded, "A biography but with no personal details whatsoever."

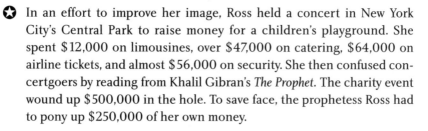 In an effort to improve her image, Ross held a concert in New York City's Central Park to raise money for a children's playground. She spent $12,000 on limousines, over $47,000 on catering, $64,000 on airline tickets, and almost $56,000 on security. She then confused concertgoers by reading from Khalil Gibran's *The Prophet*. The charity event wound up $500,000 in the hole. To save face, the prophetess Ross had to pony up $250,000 of her own money.

For a 1984 show at Caesar's Palace in Las Vegas, Ross's contract stipulated that the marquee should read "DIANA ROSS." No other words were allowed. On the day of the show, the marquee read "DIANA ROSS" all right. But on the bottom it also said "Sheena Easton Appearing in Two Weeks." As fans packed Caesar's, Ross refused to perform until the sign was altered. When Ross was told it had been done, she walked out of her dressing suite, into the crowded casino, and out through the front door to inspect the sign herself before going on. Ross's comment? "Just because I have my standards they think I'm a bitch."

In October of 1985, Ross alienated the entire population of Rome when she requested through the media that no one should be allowed to wear blue jeans to her concert. Ross urged the Romans to wear formal attire to establish the proper "mood."

At a meeting with Revlon executives to discuss the possibility of her own line of cosmetics, one company spokesperson said to Ross that he was "certain that [she] could do quite a bit for the black women's market of cosmetics." At that point Ross jumped up and left the negotiations. Several minutes later a representative from Ross's management came into the room to announce that the meeting was concluded, adding, "Miss Ross is not black. Not in her mind and not in the mind of anyone who works for her."

# RuPaul

## FACTS OF LIFE

**ORIGIN:** Born RuPaul Andre Charles, November 17, 1960, San Diego, California.

**FORMATIVE YEARS:** High-school dropout; father owned a beauty shop.

**FAMILY PLANNING:** Not likely.

**ROMANTIC INTERESTS:** "Flesh is only flesh and there's an expiration date on it."

## SELECTED HITS (and Misses)

**SONGS:** "SuperModel (You Better Work)" (1993), "House of Love" (1993), "RuPaul the Red-Nosed Drag Queen" (1997).

**FILMS:** *Starrbooty* (soundtrack—1986), *The Connie Francis Story* (19__), *Mahogany II* (19__), *American Porn Star* (19__), *PsychoBitch* (19__), *Voyeur* (19__), *Just Between Girlfriends* (19__), *Crooklyn* (1994), *To Wong Foo, Thanks for Everything! Julie Newmar* (1995), *The Brady Bunch Movie* (1995), *Wigstock: The Movie* (1995), *Blue in the Face* (1995).

**TV:** *The RuPaul Show* (1996– ).

## QUICKIE BIO

Only in America could a seven-foot cocoa-skinned, blond-wig-wearing drag queen grow up to be a rock star. Blessed with spectacularly long legs and a commanding stage presence, RuPaul followed the gender-bending trail

"Shoes are not to be taken lightly, especially when you have a pair of size 13 apple turnovers like mine," observed RuPaul.
[photo courtesy of Margaret Moser]

blazed by David Bowie, Jayne (Wayne) County, Boy George, and k.d. lang. In 1993, the stunning performer recorded the dance floor classic "SuperModel (You Better Work)." RuPaul went onto host a cable TV talk show, and unleashed a wickedly funny tell-all autobiography in 1995, *Lettin' It All Hang Out.* It was published by Disney(!)

## RuPAUL DOES THE DUMBEST THINGS

⭐ As a child, RuPaul liked to sit on her/his father's shoulders and "lick the top of his bald head because it was salty."

⭐ RuPaul starred in a very low budget spoof of blaxploitation films, *Starrbooty.* S/he snuck into a prestigious New York music industry gathering in order to do some guerrilla promotion of the flick. At the time, RuPaul

was wearing a Mohawk, football shoulder pads, and tattoos reading "F*** Off" and "A**hole."

★ RuPaul was once refused admittance to London, England at the airport because s/he lacked a return ticket and money. S/he then jumped on a flight to San Diego. However, when the flight made its scheduled stop in Dallas, its final destination was announced—Atlanta! RuPaul fled the plane and spent the night in a Dallas park before hitting the road to visit relatives in Louisiana.

★ In order to prepare for any show or appearance, RuPaul shaved his/her body from top to toe—except for the bikini area. "Once that's done," explained RuPaul, "I'm like an artist's canvas, baby."

 In the early 1990s, RuPaul worked as a "reporter" for a British TV series called *Manhattan Cable*. While doing a story on transvestite hookers, RuPaul met a very handsome "john," jumped in his car, and took a spin around the block—all on camera! RuPaul then bought breakfast with the $35 s/he'd just earned!

★ Elderly cross-dressing comic Milton Berle shared his "hands-on" experience with RuPaul at the MTV Music Awards TV show in 1993. Berle greeted RuPaul in the dressing room by grabbing his/her fake breasts. "If I had been Cindy Crawford," said RuPaul, "there would have been lawsuits flying."

★ When Uncle Miltie appeared on camera with RuPaul to present an award, he said, "You know, RuPaul, thirty years ago when I was on television, I used to wear dresses too." "That's interesting," RuPaul snapped. "You used to wear dresses. Now you wear diapers."

★ Just how does RuPaul get that "real" look? It's called "the tuck." How does s/he do it? According to RuPaul: "Take your penis (preferably your nonerect penis) and pull it back toward your butthole, pushing everything—balls and all—backward."

# The Sex Pistols

## FACTS OF LIFE (and Death)

**RINGLEADERS:** Johnny Rotten (vocals)—born John Lydon, January 31, 1956, London, England; Steve Jones (guitar)—born May 3, 1955, London, England; Paul Cook (drums)—born July 20, 1956, London, England; Sid Vicious (bass)—born John Simon Beverly, May 10, 1957, London, England, died February 2, 1979, New York City, of a heroin overdose.

## SELECTED HITS (and Misses)

**SONGS:** "Anarchy in the U.K." (1976), "Pretty Vacant" (1977), "God Save the Queen" (1977), "Holidays in the Sun" (1977).

**FILMS:** *The Great Rock 'n' Roll Swindle* (1979), *Sid and Nancy* (fictional biography—1986).

## QUICKIE BIO

The Sex Pistols were a disgusting version of the Monkees, a concept band based on the concept of hate. In 1975, guitarist Jones tried to steal clothes from SEX, a London boutique. Jones wound up with boutique owner Malcolm McClaren as his musical manager. When Lydon (later Johnny Rotten) came walking into the store wearing a torn-up Pink Floyd T-shirt with the words "I Hate" scrawled upon it, McLaren asked him to lip-synch the Alice Cooper song "School's Out." McLaren teamed frontman Lydon with

Jones and drummer Cook to create the anti-musical Sex Pistols. With the addition of former shop clerk Sid Vicious, the band set out on the great rock-and-roll swindle that soon became known as punk. The band broke up at the end of their 1978 American tour. According to McLaren, "A group that can't play is better than a group that can."

## THE SEX PISTOLS DO
## THE DUMBEST THINGS

- ✪ "I don't like your trousers," said Sid Vicious to an interviewer. Vicious then pulled out a bicycle chain and blindsided the scribe.

- ✪ Vicious told everyone, "I wanna be like Iggy Pop and die before I'm thirty." When a friend pointed out that Iggy was still alive, Sid didn't believe it.

- ✪ Vicious was so dumb he couldn't figure out how to get his hair to stand up straight. According to Rotten, "It never occurred to him to use hair-spray." Among Sid's stupid hairstyling methods: lie upside down with your head in the oven to get the desired look.

- ✪ Not long after signing to a record company for 40,000 pounds, the band appeared on a British TV program. Rotten began saying "s***" on the air, then Jones took it even further, calling the host a "dirty f***er" and a "f***ing rotter." The show was immediately cut off, and the band was banned from playing its next sixteen shows in England.

- ✪ Days later, heading for a gig in Amsterdam, the Sex Pistols barfed publicly at the airport. The record company got sick of the band's behavior and paid 50,000 pounds to persuade the Sex Pistols to leave the label.

- ✪ Another record label immediately snatched up the band with a 150,000-pound advance. On a visit to their new employers, the boys spat wine on the carpet, defecated out of the window, and mated with secretaries. Ten days later, the record company destroyed all the copies of the Sex Pistols record and paid the band another 75,000 pounds to leave that label.

- ✪ In about four months time, the record industry had paid the Sex Pistols a total of 350,000 pounds just to go away. Commented guitarist Jones, "To give away that much money for nothing—classic stupidity."

- ✪ In 1978, the Sex Pistols launched their first U.S. tour. After the premier gig in Atlanta, Rotten completed an interview. Moments later, he began receiving a blow job from a drag queen. After finishing, the queen said, "Ah, you're not so rotten after all." Rotten responded by peeing in his/her mouth.

Later on the tour, Vicious invited a girl to gobble his grapefruit. As the girl did so, Sid barfed and had an attack of diarrhea, coating his love mate.

⭐ After a show in Baton Rouge, Louisiana, fans and reporters remained in the club waiting for a promised Sex Pistols press conference. Vicious finally emerged. However, he walked right past the reporters, grabbed a woman, threw her on the bar, and jumped on top of her. Within moments, they switched positions, while photographers clicked away.

⭐ In San Francisco, Steve Jones and Paul Cook made an appearance at a local radio station. The show quickly degenerated into a Sex Pistols swearing fest. Among the gems that went out over the airwaves: Jones labeling Iggy Pop "a big tosspot." One caller claimed, "I'm eleven years old," to which Jones replied, "I'm interested." Then there was the question, "What are you guys on?" followed by, "We're on the f***ing radio! What do you think we are on?"

⭐ A 1978 performance in San Francisco turned out to be the band's final performance. At the end of the show, Rotten screamed out the song "No Fun," then laughed and said, "Ever get the feeling you've been cheated? Good night."

# Tupac Shakur

## FACTS OF LIFE (and Death)

**ORiGiN:** Born Tupac Amaru Shakur, June 16, 1971, Bronx, New York, died September 13, 1996, of wounds received in a drive-by shooting in Las Vegas six days earlier.

**FORMATIVE YEARS:** Dropped out of a Baltimore high school where he had been studying acting.

**FAMILY PLANNING:** Married Keisha Morris, May 1995, while in prison; later annulled.

**ROMANTIC INTERESTS:** Jada Pinkett (actress); fiancée at time of death was Kidada Jones, daughter of record producer Quincy Jones.

## SELECTED HITS (and Misses)

**ALBUMS:** *2Pacalypse Now* (1991), *Strictly 4 My N.I.G.G.A.Z.* (1993), *Me Against the World* (1995), *All Eyez on Me* (1995).

**FiLMS:** *Juice* (1992), *Poetic Justice* (1993), *Bullet* (1994), *Above the Rim* (1994), *Gridlock'd* (1996), *Gang Related* (1997).

## QUICKIE BIO

Named for a Peruvian revolutionary who was dismembered by horses, Tupac Shakur, also known professionally as 2 Pac, lived and died a thug's life. As a teenager, he moved from Baltimore to Marin City, California, outside of San Francisco. Tupac joined the rap group Digital Underground and worked his way up from roadie to rap star. Shakur's career took off after he played the character Bishop in the 1992 feature film *Juice*. Bishop was a nasty guy who killed his best friend to cover up his crimes. Shakur developed his

236

own nasty reputation as he became part of the violence-prone gangsta-rap scene. In 1996, Shakur was driving in Las Vegas with gangsta-rap kingpin Marlon "Suge" Knight when gunmen opened fire and killed him.

## TUPAC SHAKUR DOES THE DUMBEST THINGS

✪ Afeni Shakur, reputed to have been a Black Panther, taught her young son Tupac a party trick. When Afeni asked "What do you want to be when you grow up?" the young boy squeaked, "A revolutionary." "Here we was kickin' all this s*** about the revolution," Tupac later complained. "And we starvin'."

✈ After Tupac Shakur scored a hit with his album *2Pacalypse,* he went out and bought his dream car, a Mercedes 300. The next day he totaled it.

✪ Whenever Shakur forgot the keys to his apartment, he busted out a window and crawled in. "Aren't you worried about security?" asked a friend. "Nah," said Pac, hauling out an automatic weapon and blasting the floor. "Like rappin'," Shakur explained to his stunned pal, "You gotta practice."

✪ Although Shakur got into a lot of scrapes, he wasn't a good fighter. According to a friend, Shakur's favorite move was to lie down on his back and kick at his opponents.

✪ In 1992, L.A.-based Skakur traveled back to his old Bay Area neighborhood to attend a festival. Said Shakur, "My homies want to see me." Wrong! Shakur's homies destroyed his brand-new Jeep with baseball bats, then chased Shakur down the street. The gangsta rapper saved himself by taking refuge in the safest place he could find—underneath a police car.

✪ Shakur was feisty in the spring of 1993. First he got into a fight with a limo driver who accused him of doing drugs in the back of his car.

✪ A month later, Shakur was sentenced to ten days in jail for swinging a baseball bat at a fellow rapper.

✪ In October of 1993, Shakur was arrested in Atlanta for allegedly shooting at two police officers.

✪ When he was turned down for a part in the Hughes Brothers' 1993 film *Menace II Society,* Shakur became a menace to society and attacked the film directors with a baseball bat.

- In 1993, Shakur invited a girl up to his New York City hotel room. Pac and his date were getting it on. Then some of Pac's roadies walked in and things got ugly. Shakur was later convicted of "sexual touching without consent."

- Shakur couldn't make bail, so he went to jail at New York's Rikers Island. Marion "Suge" Knight paid the bail, and Shakur signed to Knight's company, Death Row Records. "Me and Suge," Shakur said of the 335-pound former professional football player, "we're the perfect couple."

- Knight wasn't perfect when it came to business. Shakur sold more than $60 million worth of records, but wound up owing Suge $4.9 million. Even his bail money had been charged to his account. "Me and Suge will always do business together, forever," said Shakur. Three days later he was fishing for a record contract with another label.

- In November 1994, Shakur went to a New York studio to record a rap. Instead of rapping, Shakur was shot five times by a gunman. The gunman was such a bad shot that Shakur wasn't seriously injured.

- Shakur felt that rival rap star the Notorious B.I.G. was somehow connected to the shooting. So Shakur taunted Biggie on record. On the song "Hit 'Em Up" Shakur referred to Biggie as a "fat motherf***er."

- Tupac and his buddies at Death Row Records announced that they would hand out free turkeys in South Central Los Angeles on Thanksgiving 1995. The turkeys were there on time at eleven A.M. but Tupac and the boys were several hours late. People who were waiting for their birds started chanting "Free Tupac!" The chant slowly changed to "Fuck Tupac! Free the turkeys!"

- In 1996, Shakur's girlfriend Kidada offered to pack Shakur's bulletproof vest when he drove off to see the Mike Tyson-Bruce Seldon fight in Las Vegas. Shakur told her not to pack it because "it'll be too hot." The next day he was shot to death.

# The Spice Girls

## FACTS OF LIFE

**RINGLEADERS**: Posh Spice—born Victoria Addams, April 7, 1975, Hertfordshire, England; Baby Spice—born Emma Lee Bunton, January 21, 1976, Finchley, England; Sporty Spice/Mel C—born Melanie Jayne Chisholm, January 12, 1974, Widnes, England; Scary Spice/Mel B—born Melanie Brown, May 29, 1975, Leeds, England; Sexy Spice/Ginger—born Geraldine Halliwell, August 2, 1972, Watford, England.

## SELECTED HITS (and Misses)

**SINGLES**: "Wannabe" (1996), "Say You'll Be There" (1996), "Move Over" (1997), "Spice Up Your Life" (1997).

**FILM**: *Spice World* (1998).

## QUICKIE BIO

When 1960s British supermodel Twiggy was asked about the bombing of Hiroshima, she replied, "[That] happened?" In the 1990s, the Spice Girls picked up where Twiggy left off. Like the Monkees, the Partridge Family, and Milli Vanilli, the Spice Girls were created by savvy industry packagers, in their case a British outfit called 19 Management Ltd. Recruited in 1994 and thoroughly trained before their media debut, the well-proportioned young women soared in the charts and added their spicy endorsement to everything from Pepsi to potato chips. However, by 1997, their popularity began to dip as the girls decided that they indeed had talent and fired the manager.

## THE SPICE GIRLS DO
## THE DUMBEST THINGS

✪ The record producer for the Spice Girls hired a voice and singing coach to train the girls. The coach's first assessment? "My god, there's a lot of work to be done here."

✪ When the Spice Girls walked onstage to accept their awards at the 1997 BRITS (the British version of the Grammys), Ginger Spice "accidentally" popped out of her strapless red sequin gown—twice!

✪ Ginger had experience getting naked. Before joining the Spice Girls, she posed for a series of nudie photos which appeared in numerous magazines. The photos clearly showed that Ginger was actually a brunette. Sexy Spice referred to her past nudie shots as "a lot of tired old tits."

✪ When the Spice Girls were presented to Queen Elizabeth, Ginger Spice refused to follow royal protocol and curtsy as she shook the Queen's hand. The reason? Sexy Spice was afraid her "tired old tits" would flop out of her dress if she bent over.

✪ Ginger called former prime minister Margaret Thatcher "the original Spice Girl." Yeah, Geri. But Maggie managed to keep her clothes on!

✪ Sporty Spice liked to drink. "I had to stop because I was getting a beer gut," she confessed. "I could have ended up being Fat Old Lazy Spice."

✪ The Spice Girls visited New Zealand in 1997 and performed a dance inspired by the local Maori tribe. However, instead of impressing the natives, they insulted them. The dance they performed was traditionally reserved for men only. "It is totally inappropriate," said a Maori spokesperson, "especially by girlie pop stars from another culture."

✪ A Hawaiian promoter went crazy for the Spice Girls. He sold a thousand tickets to a Spice Girls concert that was never even scheduled. After his arrest, the Spice con man explained he needed the money "for a sex change and a nose job." Maybe he wanted to become Drag Spice.

✪ After hitting the big time, the Spice Girls began to rub, er, um, shoulders with other celebrities. After a London concert in 1997, Ginger showed her appreciation for Prince Charles by grabbing him by the butt. "I'm a professional bun-pincher," she giggled.

"A cow farts enough per week to fill a hot-air balloon. Not many people know that." (Sexy Spice) [photo courtesy of Archive Photos]

⭐ When Mel B. met the male lead for their 1997 film *Spice World*, she asked, "Give us a feel of yer bum?" After a good squeeze, Scary Spice said, "You'll do."

⭐ Scary Spice liked to play with bums a lot. When one of her boyfriends complained that he was "worn out by her six-times-a-night lovemaking demands," Scary Spice snapped, "More like ten, matey!"

⭐ Baby Spice wasn't satisfied with her bum, she had her name tattooed on it—"Baby" on the left cheek, "Spice" on the right.

⭐ Sporty became philosophical when she heard Liam Gallagher claim that his band Oasis was bigger than god. "What does that make us?" she asked. "Bigger than Buddha? Because we're a darn sight bigger than Oasis."

⭐ Gallagher refused to attend an awards ceremony with the foxy fivesome. He said that if he did, he would "probably chin [punch] the Spice Girls." "I'd like to see him try," said Sporty Spice.

⭐ Beatle George Harrison appreciated the true talent of the Spice Girls. "The good thing about them," Harrison said, "is that you can look at them with the sound turned down."

⭐ Others were even more violently opposed to the group. Spice Girl hate-pages thrived on the Internet. The most popular one featured a game called "Slap a Spice Girl," which encouraged players to, well, smack the cheeky little confections.

# Spinal Tap

## FACTS OF LIFE

RINGLEADERS: David St. Hubbins (guitar, vocals)—born Michael McKean, October 17, 1947, New York City; Nigel Tufnel (guitar, vocals)—born Christopher Guest, February 5, 1948, New York City; Derek Smalls (bass)—born Harry Shearer, December 23, 1943, Los Angeles, California.

## SELECTED HITS (and Misses)

SONGS: "Listen (What the Flower People Say)" (1967), "Big Bottom" (1977), "Living in a Hellhole" (1982), "Tonight I'm Gonna Rock You" (1984), "Break Like the Wind" (1992), "Bitch School" (1992).

FILM: *This Is Spinal Tap* (1984).

TV: *Spinal Tap Reunion* (special—1992).

## QUICKIE BIO

Originally known as the Originals, Tufnel and St. Hubbins emerged from the dust of British invasion to lead a series of near-legendary bands. From 1960s folk-pop ditties to 1980s heavy metal anthems, their songs reflected the spirit of their times—and their enormous lack of talent. Briefly confined to the "Where Are They Now" bin, Spinal Tap came roaring back with a 1982 American tour, captured on film by rockumentarian Martin DiBergi (also known as Rob Reiner). More than a joke (but less than a band) Tap inspired a generation of rockers. *Smell the Glove?* Yes, indeed!

## SPINAL TAP DOES
## THE DUMBEST THINGS

⭐ Drumming for Spinal Tap was one of the deadliest jobs in rock. The band's first percussionist was John "Stumpy" Pepys, "a great tall blond geek" who died in a gardening accident. He was followed by Eric "Stumpy Joe" Childs, who choked to death on vomit (not his own, someone else's). Drummer Peter "James" Bond (literally) exploded during a concert on the Isle of Lucy. Mick Shrimpton spontaneously combusted and was replaced briefly by the stoogey Joe "Mama" Besser. Finally, Shrimpton's younger twin brother Richard "Ric" Shrimpton pounded the Tap skins for their triumphant 1992 reunion. (For other drummer deaths, see: Led Zeppelin, Keith Moon.)

⭐ Spinal Tap's 1984 album *Smell the Glove* was banned by large retail chains because of its offensive cover, which featured a naked, greased woman on all fours with a glove being forced under her nose. It was eventually released with a solid black cover. Commented Tufnel, "How much more black could this be? The answer is none. None more black." (For equally black album covers, see: Ice-T, Metallica.)

⭐ On tour to promote *Smell the Glove* in America, the band appeared onstage encased in translucent, womblike shells which were set to open on cue at the first note of "Rock and Roll Creation." Poor Derek Smalls! His shell didn't open one night. Roadies using blowtorches and hammers finally freed the trapped, sweating bass player—at the moment the song ended! (For a similar on-stage disaster, see: Boy George, U2.)

⭐ The infamous "Stonehenge" set made its first (and only appearance) at a gig in Austin, Texas. Drawn to Tufnel's specifications, the eighteen-inch-high monument was lowered to the stage and surrounded by dancing dwarves. The audience laughed. Criticized for the show, an indignant St. Hubbins said, "I do not for one think that the band was down. I think that the problem may have been that there was a Stonehenge monument on the stage that was in danger of being crushed by a dwarf." (For other controversial production ideas, see: Fleetwood Mac, Elton John, Pink Floyd.)

⭐ "We've got armadillos in our trousers," explained Nigel Tufnel, "It's really quite frightening." This statement did not apply to Derek Smalls. Passing through airport security on the 1982 American tour, Smalls set off metal-detector alarms. After emptying his pockets and taking off his jewelry, Smalls revealed the source of the problem: a tin foil–covered zucchini that he had stuffed in his pants to make himself look, well, less

small. (For other claims of size, see: David Bowie, Billy Joel, Elton John, Queen.)

 The band was once served miniature bread on a backstage cold-cut platter. Tufnel tried to fold the cold cuts to fit the bread, but gave up saying, "It's a complete catastrophe." (For other catering catastrophes, see: Aerosmith, Van Halen.)

 When the three band members met at their manager's funeral in 1992, they decided to get the band back together. Said Smalls, "It was destiny and also because none of us were making a great deal of money." (For similar reunion efforts, see: Aerosmith, The Allman Brothers, The Eagles, Fleetwood Mac, KISS, The Monkees, Ozzy Osbourne, The Rolling Stones, The Who.)

 The dumbest thing Spinal Tap ever did was to take themselves seriously. To promote their 1992 album *Break Like the Wind*, St. Hubbins appeared on a TV talk show and actually jammed with legendary guitarist Les Paul. St. Hubbins sounded, well, just like Spinal Tap. A confused Les Paul didn't get the joke. Neither did anyone else.

# Ringo Starr

## FACTS OF LIFE

**ORIGIN:** Born Richard Starkey, Jr., July 7, 1940, Liverpool, England.

**FORMATIVE YEARS:** Dropped out of school at age fifteen.

**FAMILY PLANNING:** Married Maureen Cox (model), February 11, 1965; divorced July 17, 1975; Married Barbara Bach (actress), April 27, 1981.

**ROMANTIC INTERESTS:** Lynsey de Paul (ex-girlfriend of actor James Coburn), Nancy Andrews (a Hollywood woman of ill repute).

## SELECTED HITS (and Misses)

**SONGS:** (Singing with the Beatles) "Act Naturally" (1965), "Yellow Submarine" (1966), "A Little Help from My Friends" (1967); (Solo) "It Don't Come Easy" (1971), "Back Off Boogaloo" (1972), "No No Song" (1975), "A Dose of Rock 'n' Roll" (1976), "Wrack My Brain" (1981), "I Was Walking" (1998).

**FILMS:** *Candy* (1968), *The Magic Christian* (1969), *200 Motels* (1971), *Tommy* (1972), *That'll Be the Day* (1973), *Lisztomania* (1975), *Sextette* (1978), *Caveman* (1981), *Give My Regards to Broad Street* (1984); (Plus his movie collaborations with the other Beatles) *A Hard Day's Night* (1964), *Help!* (1965), *The Magical Mystery Tour* (1967), *Yellow Submarine* (animated—1968), *Let It Be* (1970), *The Compleat Beatles* (1982).

**TV:** *Thomas the Tank Engine and Friends* (premiered 1984).

## QUICKIE BIO

When John Lennon hired Ringo Starr in 1962 to be a Beatle, he told the affable drummer to shave his beard. Starr took Lennon's lead and kept on taking his lead from the other Beatles until the band broke up in 1970. Starr wagged his head from Beatlemania to the Hollywood party circuit. He released a series of moderately successful records, appeared in feature films, married one of his costars—Barbara Bach—and basically lived well as a former Beatle. Starr partied too hearty in the 1980s, then cleaned up his act for some reunion touring and a starring role in the children's TV series *Thomas the Tank Engine and Friends*. Starr bragged that it was his granddaughter's favorite show.

## RINGO DOES
## THE DUMBEST THINGS

- ✪ Skiffle drummer Richard Starkey was given his stage name by band leader Rory Storm. He first called his drummer Rings, because he wore so many of them. Then Storm changed the nickname to Ringo, because it sounded cowboy.

- ✪ After Starr joined the Beatles, his bandmates treated him as "a faithful spaniel." Lennon in particular didn't think too much of Starr's mental abilities. "If anything goes wrong, we can all blame Ringo," said Lennon. "That's what he's here for."

- ✪ Lennon once joked, "Ringo doesn't know the meaning of fear, or any other word of more than three letters."

- ✪ Starr went along with the joke. When asked to read a cue card during an early TV appearance, Starr said, "I can't read."

- ✪ Starr's dumb demeanor helped liven up contentious Beatles press conferences. When asked, "Have you any brothers?" Starr replied, "My brother was an only child."

- ✪ Starr also took a lot of ribbing about his oversized nose. Jewish groups contacted the Beatles to find out if Starr was one of the chosen. In the film *A Hard Day's Night*, Starr explained that when people made cracks about his nose, "it goes up one nostril and down the other."

- ✪ Starr was the Beatle least affected by the band's plunge into Eastern mysticism. "At the moment I meditate every day," replied Starr after cutting short his 1968 trip to India. "Well, I might skip the odd day if I get up late or arrive in town late or something."

- ✪ Starr was equally detached from the Beatles' business affairs. Commented Ringo, "If there's a decision to blow up the building, I'll go along and raise my hand and say, 'Aye.'"

- Starr's screen career took off (kind of) after he split from the Beatles. In *The Magic Christian,* Starr costarred with movie star Peter Sellers. The film climaxed with Starr and Sellers inviting folks to collect money from the bottom of a tank filled with blood and feces.

- Starr portrayed Larry the Dwarf and Frank Zappa in the Zappa film *200 Motels.*

- In the Ken Russell movie *Lisztomania,* Starr played Pope Urban IV.

- Starr enjoyed hanging out with Lennon's Los Angeles partying pal Harry Nilsson. When Starr and Nilsson hit the Playboy club one night, the Beatle drummer tried to impress the girls by sticking cigarettes up his nose.

- To promote his 1976 album *Ringo's Rotogravure,* the drummer informed reporters that his vocals had "the range of a fly, but a large fly."

- A few years later, the self-described singing fly shaved his entire head, including his eyebrows.

- When the L.A. lifestyle got to Starr, he decided to stick to wine. Unfortunately, he stuck to sixteen bottles of wine *per day.*

- In 1989, a clean and sober Starr sued to halt the release of an album that he had recorded during his drinking period. Starr claimed that he sounded too drunk on the album. The court agreed, and the disc was buried.

- In 1995, Starr cut a Pizza Hut commercial in which he appeared as the drummer for the Monkees. Oh, how times change.

**Ringo** [photo courtesy of Photofest]

# Rod Stewart

## FACTS OF LIFE

**ORIGIN:** Born January 10, 1945, London, England.

**FORMATIVE YEARS:** Tried to break into professional soccer, but realized "a musician's life is a lot easier than all these things, and I can also get drunk."

**FAMILY PLANNING:** Married Alana Hamilton (actress, ex-wife of actor George Hamilton), April 6, 1979; divorced, 198_; Had a daughter by girlfriend Kelly Emberg 1979; Married Rachel Hunter (model) December 15, 1990. (At the time of his wedding to Hunter, Stewart promised, "I won't be putting my banana in anyone's fruit bowl from now on.")

**ROMANTIC INTERESTS:** Britt Ekland (model), Bebe Buell (see: Aerosmith, David Bowie), Kelly LeBrock (actress), Joanna Lumley (actress), Dee Harrington (secretary).

## SELECTED HITS (and Misses)

**SONGS:** "Maggie May" (1971), "You Wear It Well" (1972), "Tonight's the Night" (1976), "You're in My Heart" (1977), "Do Ya Think I'm Sexy?" (1978), "Ain't Love a Bitch" (1979), "Infatuation" (1984), "Have I Told You Lately" (1993), "Having a Party" (1994).

# QUICKIE BIO

From his 1967 debut as singer for the Jeff Beck Group, through the mid-1970s with the Faces, and as a solo perfomer, Rod Stewart cut a rooster-crowned swath through the rock world. His partying was almost as notorious as his voracious appetite for women, particularly of the leggy, blond variety. Certainly, Stewart's first career as a gravedigger had little effect on the musical path his life would take. Stewart's edge dulled in the 1980s, and his later offerings included a lame reworking of the old chestnut "Sometimes When We Touch." Ouch!

## ROD STEWART DOES
## THE DUMBEST THINGS

⭐ Stewart had a running feud with Mick Jagger. Stewart claimed, "I can sing the pants off of Mick Jagger."

⭐ Stewart had enough trouble with his own pants. His actress-girlfriend Britt Ekland confessed that Stewart "very often chose to wear my cotton panties onstage." The reason? Stewart had to combat visible panty lines. Ekland explained that Stewart "used to take [my] knickers and pull them up real tight and stick the teeny weeny part up his bum, so that all [that] was covered were the parts he wanted covered."

⭐ Of the woman who inspired the song "Maggie May," Stewart noted, "She was one of the first if not the first woman I ever loved." The woman didn't leave much of an impression on the rock star. Said Stewart, "I forget what her name was."

⭐ On tour in San Francisco in 1970, Stewart and his bandmates in the Faces climbed on top of their rented station wagon and began to jump up and down. By the time the police arrived, the rockers had crushed the vehicle.

⭐ As a youth, Stewart suffered from curvature of the spine. But it was a good thing. According to Ekland, "The one advantage of his curvature was that his rear end protruded, and no one wiggled it quite like Rod."

⭐ Stewart's father had no tolerance for such behavior. Big Daddy Stewart berated his son for acting the poof, for wearing a T-shirt with the f-word on it, and for telling the press he liked "dirty pictures." "You're a man for Christ's sake," clucked the elder Stewart, "you should bloody well behave like one."

⭐ Sometimes Stewart behaved too much like a man. During the last days of his marriage to first wife Alana Hamilton, Hamilton pinned a note

"Sometimes a woman can really persuade you to make an a\*\*hole of yourself." (Rod Stewart)
[photo courtesy of Photofest]

inside the closet of their Malibu home. The note read, "Attention all sluts. Hands off my clothes." She signed the love note, "Soon-to-be ex-mistress of this house."

★ Stewart's gal pal Ekland was a little more direct. She once told Rod, "If you screw another woman while you're with me, I'll chop your balls off."

★ Like the Gallagher brothers from Oasis, Stewart was a major fan of the Manchester United football (soccer) team. In 1973, Stewart had the chance to meet soccer superstar Denis Law. After the meeting, Stewart announced to his bandmates, "I saw Denis Law's cock in the locker-room!"

★ This statement may have given rise to a rock rumor as disgusting as the one about Stevie Nicks' cocaine application procedures. What was the rumor? That Stewart had to have his stomach pumped after a romantic encounter with the members of a sports club.

★ When Stewart split up with Ekland, she sued him for $12.5 million. Stewart, a notorious tightwad, responded, "There isn't that much money in the world." When Stewart split with his girlfriend Kelly Emberg, the world had changed. She demanded $25 million.

★ Stewart claimed that the world's greatest pick-up line was: "Hello, darling, what have you got in the basket?"

# 2 Live Crew

## FACTS OF LIFE

**RINGLEADER:** Luther "Luke Skyywalker" Campbell—born December 22, 1960, Miami Beach, Florida.

## SELECTED HITS (and Misses)

**SONGS:** "Throw the D" (1986), "Me So Horny" (1987), "S&M" (1988), "Put Her in the Buck" (1988), "C'mon Babe" (1988), "Banned in the U.S.A." (1990).

**ALBUMS:** *2 Live Is What We Are* (1987), *Move Somethin'* (1988), *As Nasty As We Wanna Be* (1989).

**TV:** *Luke's Peep Show* (Luther Campbell as host—1997).

## QUICKIE BIO

When California rapper Chris Wong-Won came to Miami in the mid-1980s, he inspired local musician Luther Campbell to become the Rodney Dangerfield of rap. Known as 2 Live Crew, Campbell and his homeboys produced a series of absolutely disgusting comedy-rap records—and a commercial for Miami politico Janet Reno. Busted on charges of obscenity and copyright infringement, 2 Live Crew made it all the way to the U.S. Supreme Court in 1993. The enormous publicity turned Campbell into a "raunch-made millionaire." In 1997, the golf-loving Campbell decided he didn't want to be so nasty. He announced the release of a PG-rated album titled *Changin' the Game*. That's for sure.

# 2 LIVE CREW DOES
# THE DUMBEST THINGS

⭐ When he was a young DJ, Campbell took the nickname Luke Skyywalker, from a character in the George Lucas movie *Star Wars*. When 2 Live Crew started getting national attention for their nasty lyrics, George Lucas, the producer of *Star Wars*, took legal action to prevent Luther from using the nickname. Said Luther, "George Lucas showed me his dark side."

⭐ Jack Thompson, a conservative Florida lawyer, waged a campaign against 2 Live Crew. In 1990, Thompson and his supporters convinced a federal district judge to declare that the song "As Nasty As We Wanna Be" was obscene. 2 Live Crew performed the outlawed song anyway and were promptly arrested. They knew it would be great publicity.

 At the 2 Live Crew obscenity trial, Duke University professor Henry Louis Gates testified on the rappers' behalf. The prosecutor asked Gates about the literary merits of references to licking an ass until the tongue turns "doodoo brown." The scholarly Gates maintained that such lyrics were to be understood on the "figurative or metaphorical" level, and referred to the band as "literary geniuses." As the prosecutors read 2 Live Crew's lyrics into the court record, the jurors asked the judge if they were allowed to laugh. The judge granted his permission.

⭐ With Gates' help, Campbell beat the obscenity rap. However, he was later arrested for aggravated assault. He allegedly pointed a gun at his girlfriend Tina Barnett and said, "I swear I will kill you and dump you in a lake somewhere." Barnett eventually dropped all charges.

⭐ In 1996, Campbell succeeded in picking up another woman during a concert in Lafayette, Louisiana. Campbell not only picked up the woman, he threw her from the stage into the crowd. The woman was knocked unconscious and later filed charges against the nasty rapper.

⭐ "Do you think that all women are whores?" asked a lady reporter at a 2 Live Crew press conference in Phoenix. Responded Campbell, "If the shoe fits, wear it."

 After the press conference, Campbell was watching a football game. His bodyguard brought a groupie into his hotel room. Campbell was bored with the game, so he talked the groupie into mating with a golf club. "You want this?" asked Campbell holding up the club. "It's a Ping!"

## FACTS OF LIFE

**RINGLEADERS:** Bono (vocals)—born Paul Hewson, May 10, 1962, Dublin, Ireland; The Edge (guitar)—born David Evans, August 8, 1961, Barking, Wales; Adam Clayton (bass)—born March 13, 1960, Chinnor, England; Larry Mullen, Jr.—born October 31, 1961, Dublin, Ireland.

## SELECTED HITS (and Misses)

**SONGS:** "I Will Follow" (1980), "Gloria" (1981), "Sunday Bloody Sunday" (1983), "Where the Streets Have No Name" (1987), "Desire" (1988), "The Fly" (1990), "Mysterious Ways" (1991), "Even Better Than the Real Thing" (1992), "One" (1992), "Discotheque" (1997).

**FILMS:** *Rattle and Hum* (1988), *Batman Forever* (soundtrack song "Hold Me, Thrill Me, Kiss Me, Kill Me"—1994).

## QUICKIE BIO

Once members of rival Dublin high school bands, the musicians of U2 came together in 1978. Led by Bono (who took his nickname from a Dublin hearing aid store) the band worked its way up to the top of the Irish rock pile with an earnest, anthemic sound that sprang in part from their shared born-again Christianity. As the 1980s gave way to the 1990s, U2 traded Christianity for crass commercialism. The group became so commercial that it kicked off a 1997 tour at a K-Mart store. Said the born-again Bono, whose stage persona had changed from the sublime to the ridiculous, "I'm starting to see the value of being irresponsible."

## U2 DOES THE DUMBEST THINGS

⭐ In 1977, Bono was driving with school chums looking for a friend named Georgie Higgins. When they stopped at a light, Bono jumped out of the car and mooned his fellow motorists. Two elderly female pedestrians pointed at Bono's privates and exclaimed, "Jaysus, look at the size of it." Bono swung over to the women and asked, "Excuse me, can you tell me where Georgie Higgins lives?"

⭐ During an early U2 gig, two girls were dancing in front of the concert stage. Bono thrust his microphone in one of the girl's face and asked, "What's your name?" "F*** off, dickhead," replied the girl. "Get on with the bleeding music, who do you think you are, David Bowie?"

⭐ Bono had a bad habit of losing things. He lost keys, money, checks, socks, and underwear. Just before U2 went into the studio to record the album *October,* Bono lost all the lyrics to the songs. The band went ahead anyway and cut the album. "I didn't really know what I was saying most of the time," said Bono of the recording experience.

⭐ On the first leg of their *October* tour, the drummer's snare drum broke onstage. Bono was furious. He kicked over the drum set and chased the drummer across the stage, until The Edge grabbed Bono by the hair and stopped him. The audience cheered. They thought U2 was pulling a Who.

⭐ In 1990, Bono and U2 inducted The Who into the Rock and Roll Hall of Fame. "It's written in rock and roll that all you need is love," said Bono. "But you also need a great nose."

⭐ At the beginning of the *October* tour, Bono marched out into the audience waving a white flag. One time, he stepped off a balcony into thin air. His roadie caught him by the belt. The roadie managed to pull the wriggling rock star back up onto the balcony. After that, Bono stopped the flag routine.

⭐ In 1988, U2 held a free noontime "Save the Yuppie" concert in San Francisco.

On tour in 1993, Bono appeared as a globe-eyed character called The Fly, after a song on the album *Achtung Baby*. Bono later morphed from The Fly to the "mirror-ball man," a cowboy evangelist preacher. Then Bono created the character MacPhisto. Bono described MacPhisto as The Fly "when he's fat and playing Las Vegas."

As part of the 1997 *Pop Mart* tour, a giant, lemon-shaped pod opened onstage during the encore, revealing the band members of U2. In Norway, the pod jammed shut, trapping the band in front of thousands of fans. According to one magazine, "Such a Spinal Tap incident couldn't have been scripted any better."

 Salman Rushdie, the novelist who has made a career out of hiding from Islamic terrorists, appeared onstage with U2 in front of 72,000 fans in London. "Afterwards I suggested that perhaps we could rename the band U2 + 1? ME2?" said Rushdie, "but I don't think they were for it."

 At the second MTV European Awards ceremony in Paris in 1995, Bono commented to the French people, "What a city. What a night…what a wanker you have for *President*."

# Van Halen

## FACTS OF LIFE

**RINGLEADERS:** Alex Van Halen (guitar)—born May 8, 1955, Nijmegen, Holland; Edward Van Halen (drums)—born January 26, 1957, Nijmegen, Holland; David Lee Roth (vocals)—born October 10, 1955, Bloomington, Indiana; Sammy Hagar (vocals)—born October 13, 1947, Monterey, California.

## SELECTED HITS (and Misses)

**SONGS:** "Ice Cream Man" (1978), "Runnin' with the Devil" (1978), "You Really Got Me" (1978), "Dance the Night Away" (1979), "(Oh) Pretty Woman" (1982), "Jump" (1984), "Panama" (1984), "When It's Love" (1988).

## QUICKIE BIO

Born to an Indonesian mother and a Dutch pianist father, brothers Eddie and Alex Van Halen moved with their folks to Southern California in the 1960s, grew their hair long and started playing rock. The Van Halen boys teamed up with fellow Pasadena City College student David Lee Roth in 1974. By the late 1970s, Van Halen had risen from the L.A. glam cesspool to multi-platinum rock star status. By the mid-1980s, Roth's flamboyant style and wide-open mouth had alienated the quiet Van Halen brothers. They fired Diamond Dave and hired Sammy Hagar, who spent a decade with the band until he also was fired in the mid-1990s. A brief but fiery reunion with Roth ended when the band hired Gary Cherone (from the band Extreme) as their new singer. By that time, Alex Van Halen was in a neck brace, Edward Van Halen was ready for hip-replacement surgery, David Lee Roth was modeling for album covers with his naked butt hanging out of a pair of leather chaps, and Sammy Hagar was mixing margaritas onstage and threatening to throw tomatoes at his former bandmates.

# VAN HALEN DOES
## THE DUMBEST THINGS

⭐ Alex claimed that he lost his virginity after a gig—when he was only nine years old.

⭐ When the band performed the song "Ice Cream Man," Dave played the "Davesickle," a guitar built in the shape of a Creamsicle.

⭐ For shows in the early 1980s, Dave donned an enormous cowboy hat, jumped onto a huge inflatable microphone, and rode it straight into the crotch of a pair of enormous inflatable legs.

⭐ Dave spent tens of thousands of dollars designing enormous inflatable statues of the devil that could pee Jack Daniel's whiskey a distance of fifteen feet out over the audience. He then filled the statues with cheap bourbon to save money.

💧 Before hitting the stage in Pueblo, Colorado, Van Halen went backstage for a snack. Looking around, Roth noticed some brown M&M's on the buffet table. According to Roth, brown M&M's were specifically forbidden in the band's contract. Roth shouted "What is this before me?" Then he turned over the buffet table, trashed the backstage area, and kicked a hole in the wall. Roth later commented on the cost of the M&M's-inspired damage: "I'm prepared to pay that to have a good time."

⭐ In the late 1970s, Roth accompanied a pal to a famous New York City bondage bar. Roth went into the dimly lit bathroom. He noticed that the urinal was a bathtub and he began to take a leak. Immediately a voice suggested, "A little more to the left." Roth realized that the voice was coming from the bathtub. Roth finished his pee and thought to himself, "Do I tip this guy?"

💰 After Van Halen concerts, Roth sat in the doorway of his tour bus and had his road manager pour Perrier on his feet.

⭐ While recording an Italian TV special in 1980, Roth took a flying leap onstage and smashed head-first into a mirror ball. Roth broke his nose in the collision.

⭐ In 1993, seven years after leaving Van Halen, a down-on-his-luck Roth got arrested in New York City for allegedly buying a $10 bag of pot. After the bust, Howard Stern phoned Roth and asked, "So, Dave, you lookin' for publicity?" "Howard, this is a thirty-five-dollar pot bust," explained Roth. "If I was looking for publicity I would have pooped on the sidewalk."

★ During a two-and-a-half hour set, Roth's replacement Sammy Hagar said "f***" or "s***" more than forty-two times.

★ Van Halen titled their 1991 album *For Unlawful Carnal Knowledge.* Hagar insisted that the title was a political statement.

★ Onstage during rehearsals, Hagar liked to play with a plastic dog turd. Explained Hagar, "I'm not very mental at all, believe me."

★ In 1992, Eddie Van Halen said on MTV that playing guitar wasn't as difficult as brain surgery. A few days later, Eddie got a letter from a brain surgeon who offered to swap surgery lessons for guitar lessons.

★ After Roth left Van Halen, there were some hard feelings. Edward Van Halen warned Roth, "I run into you, you better wear a cup. I'm going to kick you in your nuts." According to Hagar, "I was told to kick Roth in the balls if I ever saw him."

★ After he was fired from the band, Sammy Hagar told a TV talk show audience that if elected president, the first thing he would do would be to order a secret CIA hit on Van Halen.

# Vanilla Ice

## FACTS OF LIFE

**ORIGIN:** Born Robert Van Winkle, October 31, 1968, Miami Lakes, Florida.

**FORMATIVE YEARS:** High-school graduate.

**FAMILY PLANNING:** None.

**ROMANTIC INTERESTS:** Madonna (briefly).

## SELECTED HITS (and Misses)

**SONGS:** "Ice Ice Baby" (1990), "Play That Funky Music" (1990).

**FILMS:** *Cool as Ice* (1991), *Teenage Mutant Ninja Turtles 2: The Secret of the Ooze* (1991).

## QUICKIE BIO

The first rap song to hit number one on the *Billboard* pop charts was performed by a suburban white kid named Robert Van Winkle. "Ice Ice Baby" took Winkle to the top in 1990, but left him stranded with nowhere to go. The one-hit wonder tried several times to come back, but failed. "Elvis had his time," he bragged at the height of his popularity. "I'm Vanilla Ice, and it's my turn now." Too bad your turn was so short, Ice, Ice, baby.

## VANILLA ICE DOES
## THE DUMBEST THINGS

⭐ In order to improve his credibility, Vanilla Ice manufactured a rapper's childhood. "The projects were a block away from my house, and that's where my friends were from," Ice told reporters, "I grew up on the streets." Ice may have grown up on the streets, but they were the streets of a nice neighborhood in Dallas, Texas.

★ Teenage Robbie Van Winkle spent most of his free time break-dancing in a mall where he was discovered by rap producer Tommy Quon.

★ Another rap heavy was impressed by Van Winkle's dancing. Said Public Enemy's Chuck D, "A white boy dancing like that? I was like, yo!" Unfortunately, when the righteous rapper tried to get a record deal for the white talent, everyone said no.

★ Madonna also thought Vanilla Ice was cool. The material girl met the Vanilla rapper while he was filming the movie *Cool as Ice*. Madonna and Ice started going out together. She even convinced him to appear naked in her photo book *Sex*. "It kind of cheeses me out, makes me look like I'm like all the other people in there, a bunch of freaks," Vanilla Ice observed about the experience. "I'm no freak."

 The Madonna-Vanilla Ice thing went on for about eight months. Ice claimed that Madonna was jealous and called him up at all hours to ask "Are you in bed with another girl?" "I'm f***ing sleeping!" screamed Vanilla Ice, "All alone!"

★ The couple finally broke up when, in the words of Vanilla Ice, things got "too serious."

★ One showbiz personality in particular was annoyed by Vanilla Ice. Marion "Suge" Knight, the founder of Death Row Records, once threatened to throw the white rapper from a fifteenth-floor balcony.

★ When the rap thing went sour, Vanilla Ice grew dreadlocks and released the 1994 album *Mind Blowin'*. It bombed. A bummed-out Vanilla Ice then tried to blow his own mind with drugs. He passed out, received medical attention, and avoided choking on his own vomit.

★ Vanilla Ice then turned to the Lord. "I've been checking out churches, Catholic, Baptist," explained Ice. "I haven't decided on any religion yet. But definitely, God is in my life." To signal his new way of life, Vanilla Ice had a drawing of a leaf tattooed on his stomach.

★ In 1997, Vanilla Ice failed to show up for his own sold-out comeback show in Austin, Texas.

# The Who

## FACTS OF LIFE

**RINGLEADERS:** Pete Townshend (vocals, guitar)—born Peter Dennis Bland-ford Townshend, May 19, 1945, London, England; John Alec Entwistle (bass)—born October 9, 1944, London, England; Roger Daltrey (vocals)—born Roger Harry Daltrey, March 1, 1944, London, England; Keith Moon (see: Keith Moon).

## SELECTED HITS (and Misses)

**SONGS:** "I Can't Explain" (1965), "My Generation" (1965), "Substitute" (1966), "Boris the Spider" (1966), "Happy Jack" (1966), "Odorono" (1967), "I Can See for Miles" (1967), "See Me, Feel Me" (1970), "Who Are You" (1978), "Athena" (1982).

**ALBUMS:** *Tommy* (1969), *Quadrophenia* (1973).

**FILMS:** *Lifehouse* (1971), *Tommy* (1975), *Lisztomania* (Roger Daltrey—1975), *The Legacy* (Roger Daltrey—1975), *Quadrophenia* (1979), *The Kids Are Alright* (The Who—1979 documentary), *McVicar* (Roger Daltrey—1980), *Murder: Ultimate Grounds for Divorce* (Roger Daltrey—1985), *Pete Townshend: White City* (Pete Townshend—1985), *Mack the Knife* (Roger Daltrey—1989), *Cold Justice* (Roger Daltrey—1989), *Forgotten Prisoners* (Roger Daltrey—1990), *If Looks Could Kill* (Roger Daltrey—1991), *Buddy's Song* (Roger Daltrey—1991), *Lightning Jack* (Roger Daltrey—1994).

# QUICKIE BIO

Grammar-school chums Pete Townshend and John Entwistle teamed up with Roger Daltrey and drummer Keith Moon to form The Who in 1964. The Who started out as an English fashion band, copping a sharply dressed look. "The Who were grooved to the mod revolution," recalled Townshend, "whatever that means." Audiences liked it best when the band stopped playing their instruments and smashed them up. The constantly bickering (and constantly drunk) band members hit it big in 1969 with the release of their incomprehensible rock opera *Tommy.* After the death of drummer Keith Moon in 1978, the band spent their time backbiting—and reprising their hits in a series of farewell concerts. Looking back on his career, Townshend observed, "I was bitter, cynical, and angry most of the time. But most of all I was stupid."

## THE WHO DOES THE DUMBEST THINGS

⭐ In 1965, The Who was performing at a London pub. Near the end of the show, Townshend whirled his guitar around and smacked it against the low roof. When he realized that he had broken the neck of his guitar, Townshend smashed the instrument against the ground and rammed it into the amps. The crowd went wild. Townshend later explained, "I smash guitars because I like them."

⭐ The Who made instrument-smashing a part of every show. The band destroyed about 700 pounds of equipment per night—and earned only about 500 pounds. Screamed bass player Entwistle, "We'd come out ahead just by not showing up!"

 "Roger is not a very good singer at all in my opinion," said Townshend. Daltrey called Townshend "a nose on a stick," and punched that nose many times during rehearsals.

⭐ When mod fashion went out of fashion, The Who tried to bill themselves as a pop-art band. "We stand for pop-art clothes, pop-art music, and pop-art behavior," proclaimed Townshend. Asked a confused Roger Daltrey, "What is pop-art?"

⭐ At the end of a live TV program in Paris, The Who ran into the streets, lined up against a wall, and peed. The communal urination was broadcast to viewers in England and France.

⭐ The stuttering on "My Generation" was not meant to mock the speaking-impaired. It was meant to mimic the talk of Who fans, who stuttered when they ate speed tablets. "Drugs don't harm you," Townshend later told the press. "I know. I take them."

"Drugs don't harm you. I know. I take them," claimed Pete Townshend (second from the left) of The Who. [photo courtesy of Photofest]

⭐ Townshend was furious when he heard that Jimi Hendrix was going to smash his guitar and light it on fire at the Monterey International Pop Festival in 1967. The British rocker marched into Hendrix's dressing room and accused Hendrix of stealing The Who's act. Hendrix ignored Townshend and ignited his guitar just as planned.

⭐ During a New York City performance in 1969, a cop ran onstage while The Who was performing. Townshend kicked the policeman off the stage. As it turned out, the cop was not interested in arresting The Who. He was trying to clear the auditorium because the building next door was on fire.

⭐ At Woodstock in 1969, radical student leader Abbie Hoffman joined The Who onstage and tried to address the crowd. Townshend kicked him in the butt and knocked him into the crowd. Townshend later bragged that booting Hoffman was "the most political thing I ever did."

⭐ Before he started working on the rock opera *Tommy*, Townshend planned to write an opera about a big white rabbit that ruled the world.

⭐ Townshend claimed that he decided to call his opera *Tommy* because "the middle syllable was *om*." It wasn't.

⭐ When the London Symphony Orchestra performed Tommy in 1970, Townshend was supposed to play the narrator. First Townshend insulted

the audience. Then he insulted the orchestra. Then he wiped his butt with the libretto and walked offstage.

 Another Who rock opera was titled *Quadrophenia*. The title referred to quadraphonic stereo, which Townshend believed was a revolutionary new media system. Unfortunately, the new medium died so fast that the record *Quadrophenia* wasn't even released in quadraphonic sound.

 When the punk-rock scene broke in 1977, Townshend saw members of the Sex Pistols in a pub. He went over to a Sex Pistol, grabbed him by the collar and said, "Look, Johnny—" "No, no," said the Pistol, "I'm Paul Cook [the band's drummer]." Townshend put the drummer down, ranted for a few minutes, tore up some checks, and spat on them. Cook observed the punk behavior and cautiously asked, "Uh, Pete...The Who aren't going to break up, are they?"

 The Who's last performance with Moon occurred in 1978. At the end of the gig, Townshend tried to smash his guitar. But it wouldn't break. Then Moon tried to knock over his drum set. But it was nailed to the floor and wouldn't budge.

 The Who hosted the worst rock catastrophe in history. In 1979 the band was booked at the Riverfront Stadium in Cincinnati, Ohio. Before the show started, the crowd rushed the venue and eleven fans were crushed to death. "I watched Roger Daltrey cry his eyes out after the show," recalled a surly Townshend. "I didn't, but he did....I think when people are dead they're dead." Townshend later called his dumb comments "unfortunate."

# Wendy O. Williams

## FACTS OF LIFE and Death

**ORIGIN:** Born Wendy Orlean Williams, 1949, Rochester, New York, died April 6, 1998 in Storrs, Connecticut, of a self-inflicted gunshot wound to the head.

**FORMATIVE YEARS:** Dropped out of high school.

**FAMILY PLANNING:** Mating rituals unknown.

**ROMANTIC INTERESTS:** Broke into show business by acting as a dominatrix in a New York City sex show.

## SELECTED HITS (and Misses)

**SONGS:** "Butcher Baby" (1978), "Tight Black Pants" (1980), "Monkey Suit" (1980), "Bump and Grind / F*** 'n' Roll" (1985), "Sledgehammer" (1988).

**FILMS:** *Candy Goes to Hollywood* (1979), *Reform School Girls* (1986), *Pucker Up and Bark Like a Dog* (1989).

## QUICKIE BIO

Wendy O. Williams, with her hard-edged voice and muscular look, front-ed what is arguably the worst rock-and-roll band ever formed—the Plasmatics. A sex industry impresario known as Rod "Captain Kink" Swenson plucked Williams from a live-sex act to lead the punk/metal band in 1978. The Plasmatics built their show around staged chaos—and very little music. After the Plasmatics died out in the 1980s, Williams arose as a heavy-metal goddess before riding into the leather-and-latex sunset.

## WENDY O. WILLIAMS DOES
## THE DUMBEST THINGS

⭐ Plasmatics press releases credited Williams with playing "sax, chainsaw, and sledgehammer." She liked to use her sledgehammer to destroy cars onstage.

⭐ On Tom Snyder's TV show *Tomorrow* in March 1981, Wendy threw a cou-ple of sticks of dynamite into a Chevy Nova and blew it up. Snyder was so happy with the stunt that he hugged his producer.

⭐ Though the Plasmatics were peaking in 1979, Williams had time to star in a porno flick, *Candy Goes to Hollywood*. In the film, Wendy revealed herself to be a fan of Ping-Pong—balls, that is. The combination of Williams' dominatrix mating muscles and the featherweight balls made for an eye-popping scene.

⭐ In the 1980s, Williams played a character named "Butch" in the film *Pucker Up and Bark Like a Dog*.

⭐ Williams appeared on TV with evangelist Rex Humbard. The leather-clad dominatrix went up to the suited preacher and said, "Rex, you are loved." Humbard said, "You are loved too, Wendy. I think what you're doing is great." Humbard gave Wendy a "You Are Loved" pin, then looked at her outfit and said, "I don't know where you're going to put it!"

⭐ Williams was actually wearing quite a bit when she met Humbard. Sometimes onstage she wore little more than black electrical tape and clothes-pins on her nipples.

⭐ Williams was busted for her lewd stage show in Milwaukee, Wisconsin in 1981. Things got even lewder outside. According to Wendy, "One of them [the cops] grabbed my tits. Another one grabbed my rear. So I smacked them. Then they threw me down and handcuffed me hog-style in the snow while one of them beat me. I'd have gone along peacefully, but I was outraged intellectually." The charges against Williams were dropped.

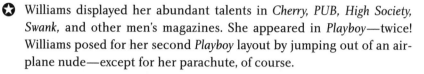 Wendy was later busted in Cleveland, Ohio, on obscenity charges involving Wendy's suggestive movements with a microphone and a sledgehammer. "We had two local lawyers defending us who made Abbott and Costello look like wizards," explained Wendy. But the prosecutors were even worse, and Wendy escaped without a conviction.

Williams displayed her abundant talents in *Cherry, PUB, High Society, Swank,* and other men's magazines. She appeared in *Playboy*—twice! Williams posed for her second *Playboy* layout by jumping out of an airplane nude—except for her parachute, of course.

In the mid-1990s, Williams gave up the stage for work at a natural-foods store in New England. The former dominatrix and sledgehammer-wielding metal goddess used her position to promote her favorite cause—vegetarianism.

# Neil Young

## FACTS OF LIFE

**ORIGIN:** Born November 12, 1945, Toronto, Ontario, Canada.

**FORMATIVE YEARS:** Young was kicked out of his first band because he couldn't play the guitar. He then practiced so much that he flunked out of high school, but received his diploma belatedly in 1992.

**FAMILY PLANNING:** Married Susan Acevedo 1968; divorced, 1970; Married Pegi Morton, 1978.

**ROMANTIC INTERESTS:** Carrie Snodgrass (actress), Robin Lane (musician).

## SELECTED HITS (and Misses)

**SONGS:** "Ohio" (with Crosby, Stills, Nash and Young—1970), "Cinnamon Girl" (1970), "After the Gold Rush" (1970), "Heart of Gold" (1972), "Hey, Hey, My, My (Out of the Blue)" (1979), "This Note's for You" (1989), "Harvest Moon" (1992).

**FILMS:** *Journey Through the Past* (1973), *Human Highway* (1982), *Year of the Horse* (1997).

## QUICKIE BIO

After working the Canadian folk circuit and playing for a time with Rick James, Neil Young threw his belongings in a hearse and headed for Los Angeles in 1965. Young's buddy Stephen Stills recognized his lumbering vehicle on the street and flagged the Canadian down. The two worked their way up to rock stardom with the Buffalo Springfield and Crosby, Stills, Nash and Young. In addition to recording with CSNY on and off for two decades, the ornery Young followed an eccentric solo path. From rockabilly to feedback to jams with Pearl Jam, the godfather of grunge continues to make music well into the 1990s—at least when he isn't playing with his model trains.

## NEIL YOUNG DOES
## THE DUMBEST THINGS

⭐ Young arrived at the Woodstock festival with fellow musician Jimi Hendrix. When the two realized that they had to travel several miles from the helicopter pad to the stage area, they stole a pickup truck and took off. Young called this car theft in 1969 "one of the high points of my life."

⭐ As a groover on the late 1960s L.A. scene, Young hung out with Charles Manson. Young found the antihero to be "mysteriously compelling." According to Young, Manson "would sing a song and just make it up as he went along…and it all made perfect sense and it shook you up to listen to it."

 Soon after scoring major hits with Crosby, Stills, Nash and Young, Young invested in an experimental sound system. To show it off, he rowed out to the middle of a private lake with bandmate Graham Nash. Then Young raised his arms. One of his songs came booming out across the lake from huge speakers hidden in a house and a barn. Young wasn't completely satisfied with the experiment. He rowed back to shore and told his techies, "More barn."

⭐ While touring with Crosby, Stills, Nash and Young, Young took advantage of all the perks of superstardom including hookers that were kept on the payroll and a twenty-four-hour party suite complete with champagne, iced shrimp, and capsules of cocaine.

⭐ In 1975, Young quit a recording session with Crosby, Stills and Nash after a furious argument with Stephen Stills—over a single harmony note.

✪ In 1983, Young signed with a new record company. He then delivered a techno-pop album (*Trans*) and a rockabilly album (*Everybody's Rockin'*). Young's fans were confused by the releases, and so were the executives at his new label. The company sued Young for not making Neil Young records.

✪ Young's politics in the 1980s were as confusing as his records. The former leader of the Woodstock generation declared himself "a true capitalist pig" who supported former president Ronald Reagan and nuclear energy. Young scoffed at benefit concerts, declaring that he wouldn't sell himself "to the world for nothing." Then he played at *Live Aid* in 1985—for nothing.

✪ For the *Rust Never Sleeps* tour, Young's stage crew wore hooded cowl-like garments with flashing red eyes. Young called them "Road-Eyes."

✪ The video for the song "This Note's for You" lampooned corporate rock sponsorship. The music video featured a faux Michael Jackson with his hair on fire, a reference to an accident that actually occurred while Jackson was filming a Pepsi commercial. A stunned MTV immediately banned the clip, then declared it Best Video of the Year at the 1989 Video Music Awards.

✪ Young had to cancel a 1997 European tour when he sliced his hand open while cutting a ham sandwich. Sighed Young, "It's macaroni and cheese from now on."

# Frank Zappa

## FACTS OF LIFE (and Death)

**ORIGIN:** Born Frances Vincent Zappa, December 21, 1940, Baltimore, Maryland, died December 4, 1993, of prostate cancer.

**FORMATIVE YEARS:** Attended junior college "for the express purpose of meeting girls."

**FAMILY PLANNING:** Married Kay Sherman (student) 1960; divorced 1963; Married Adelaide Gail Sloatman (secretary) September 1967.

**ROMANTIC INTERESTS:** "It's not ordinary and it's not mundane, but it does not involve golden showers and appliances," said Zappa about his sex life.

## SELECTED HITS (and Misses)

**SONGS:** "Memories of El Monte" (1962), "Freak Out!" (1965), "Brown Shoes Don't Make It" (1965), "Prelude to the Afternoon of a Sexually Aroused Gas Mask" (1970), "Don't Eat the Yellow Snow" (1974), "Dancin' Fool" (1979) "Sheik Yerbouti" (1979), "Valley Girl"(1982).

**FILMS:** *Head* (1968), *Uncle Meat* (1969), *200 Motels* (1970), *Baby Snakes: The Complete Version* (1979).

## QUICKIE BIO

Influenced equally by 1950s doo-wop and avant-garde classical music, Frank Zappa created the Mothers of Invention in 1965 and launched his career as an intellectual rocker who sang dumb songs. A clean-living dad, Zappa delighted in creating songs, stage shows, and films that were filled with naughty nonsense. By the end of his life, Zappa had changed from a failed porno producer to a trade representative for Czechoslovakia and an eloquent defender of potty-talk.

## FRANK ZAPPA DOES
## THE DUMBEST THINGS

★ In 1963 Zappa started a porno-movie production business. One of his first clients was an undercover investigator for the San Bernardino County Sheriff's Office. Zappa was jailed for sexual perversion. He might have been in business longer if he hadn't opened his porno-production office right across the street from the Cucamonga, California, courthouse.

★ Less controversial was Zappa's relationship with the "soft giraffe." During concert performances in the 1960s, Zappa's bandmates put on frog hand puppets, stroked an enormous stuffed giraffe, and squirted whipped cream from its butt out to the audience.

★ In 1966 a record company hired Zappa and his band, the Mothers of Invention, to cut a record with Burt Ward, who played Robin on the original *Batman* TV series. The result of the collaboration? A single titled "Boy Wonder, I Love You."

★ The Zappa song "A Pound for a Brown on the Bus" referred to the act of "browning out" (West Coast slang) or "mooning" (East Coast slang.) "If you brown out against a wire screen it's called 'the Chipped Beef,'" Zappa later explained. "And if you do it against a plate-glass window at the delicatessen it's 'The Pressed Ham.'"

★ Zappa's album covers were often as nasty as his lyrics. *Overnight Sensation*, released in 1973, featured the image of a grapefruit covered with a slimy ooze. Dubbed "roadie's delight," the picture referred to the sexual enjoyment of citrus fruits.

★ Zappa made an experimental film in 1965 by tying a camera to a string and swinging it around his head. The name of the offering: *Motion*. Commented Zappa, "Pretty stupid, eh?"

★ Zappa's film *Uncle Meat* was not about food. It was about a group of musicians who enjoy getting beaten with toilet brushes. No, it *wasn't* a documentary.

"The closest thing to s*** I ever ate was the Beef Wellington from the buffet at a...[restaurant] in Newark, New Jersey," confessed Frank Zappa

[photo courtesy of Photofest]

⭐ The Zappa movie *200 Motels* featured music by the Royal Philharmonic Orchestra and starred Ringo Starr as a Zappa look-alike named Larry the Dwarf.

⭐ Zappa booked London's Royal Philharmonic Orchestra to play a concert of his music at the Royal Albert Hall. The concert was canceled due to "lyrical obscenity." Zappa sued the Hall, but lost his court case. He could not convince the British judiciary that songs like "Shove It Right In" were not obscene.

In 1984 Zappa tried to crack Broadway with a musical titled *Thing-Fish*. It explored the adventures of a woman who made love with a briefcase and a man who made love with a miniature rubber doll.

⭐ Like Billy Joel, Zappa considered himself a composer of classical music. Sneered Frank, "The typical rock fan isn't smart enough to know when he's being dumped on." Zappa referred to his own classical work as "orchestral stupidities."

⭐ "If you look at millionaires, you'll find they all have one thing in common," observed the very wealthy Zappa. "They're all ugly people."

# ZZ Top

## FACTS OF LIFE

**RINGLEADERS:** Billy Gibbons (guitars, vocals)—born December 16, 1949, Houston, Texas; Dusty Hill (bass, vocals)—born May 19, 1949, Dallas, Texas; Frank Beard (drums)—born June 11, 1949, Frankston, Texas.

## SELECTED HITS (and Misses)

**SONGS:** "L.A. Grange" (1974), "Tush" (1975), "Cheap Sunglasses" (1979), "Tube Snake Boogie" (1981), "Sharp Dressed Man" (1983), "Legs" (1983), "Sleeping Bag" (1985), "Velcro Fly" (1986).

## QUICKIE BIO

ZZ Top worked their way up from the muddy waters of the Rio Grande to the top of MTV. In 1970, Frank Beard, Dusty Hill, and Billy Gibbons formed the Little Ol' Band from Texas. Sporting glittering cowboy suits, the group honed their Texas boogie sound until they were bad and nationwide. After a multiyear break in the late 1970s, ZZ Top retired their cowboy shtick and released synthesizer-driven rock tunes complete with stylish videos that won the bearded rockers a new generation of fans. By the 1990s, ZZ Top was working on its third wind. Behind airtight management and cheap sunglasses, the aging Reverend Willie G. and his bandmates Hill and Beard maintained an aura of outlaw mystery and continued to draw crowds of fans who were lookin' for nothing but a good time—and maybe just a little tush.

# ZZ TOP DOES
# THE DUMBEST THINGS

⭐ Hill and a friend set out for the Mexican border. On the way, they picked up a calf and stuck it in the backseat of their car. After the calf kicked out the rear window, the Texans let it go.

⭐ Gibbons met Ike Turner (Tina's ex-husband) backstage after a concert. Ike admired Gibbons' guitar and gave him a few fashion tips. Gibbons took Turner's advice and a few days later showed up onstage wearing skintight shorts, black pantyhose, knee boots, and a turtleneck.

⭐ For another gig, Gibson wore Mickey Mouse ears, black leotards, a black pleated skirt, and a mouse tail.

⭐ When he wasn't wearing hot pants or mouse ears, Gibbons sometimes liked to don reptiles. During a 1972 show in Colorado, the guitarist played from behind a stack of speakers wearing nothing but a rubber snake.

⭐ Beard was called "the Merry Frankster" because he was so fond of practical jokes. Beard once visited a friend who was very fond of his cat. When the friend was out of the house, Beard took a dump in the kitty-litter box. After seeing the enormous turd, the distraught friend was ready to rush the cat to the vet. Then Beard finally 'fessed up.

⭐ During the early days of playing "Just Got Paid," audience members threw change at the stage. The band liked the money, but hated getting hit with flying bits of metal. "We had to make the decision whether the fifty dollars or so we'd pick up in spare change a night was worth it," said Gibbons. When the band started making good money, the song was retired.

⭐ The band never retired the song "Pearl Necklace," even though the lyrics allegedly referred to decorations left on a woman's neck by a boob-inspired male orgasm.

⭐ In 1976 ZZ Top launched their *Worldwide Tour of Texas*. During the tour, the three musicians were joined onstage by a longhorn steer, a black buffalo, two turkey vultures, two black vultures, four rattlesnakes, and a timber wolf.

🐶 The tour was tough on the rock stars, but even tougher on the critters. At one point, the stage lights were so hot that they caused a vulture's wings to start smoking.

★ In 1980, ZZ Top wrote to NASA and formally requested that the band be booked as the lounge act on the space shuttle. NASA responded saying that their request would "receive all due consideration." ZZ Top never got the gig.

★ Four years later, Dusty Hill was grounded by a bullet. ZZ Top's press people claimed that Hill accidentally discharged his handgun while his girlfriend was helping him out of his boots. One of the band's roadies later suggested that the wound, which was near Dusty Hill's crotch, might have been inflicted by the girlfriend.

# EXTRA SPECIAL SUPERDELUXE EXTRA APPENDIX: ROCK STARS DO THE DUMBEST THINGS DUMBEST HITS

**Look under** each entry to find the DUMBEST HITS episode marked with an icon.

### Rock Stars Do the Dumbest Things in Planes, Trains, and Automobiles

1. Keith Moon for downshifting disasters

2. Led Zeppelin for first-class evacuation

3. Aerosmith for upsidedown stewardesses

4. George Harrison for mantra maps

5. Guns N' Roses for Whizzy

6. The Mamas and the Papas for parking

7. Tupac Shakur for his dream car

8. Neil Diamond for the pressed ham

9. Ozzy Osbourne for his deadly flying friends

10. The Rolling Stones for the *Lapping Tongue*

### Rock Stars Do the Dumbest Things on Camera

1. Chuck Berry for his home videos

2. RuPaul for investigative reporting

3. Pink Floyd for not lip-synching

4. Red Hot Chili Peppers for MTV naughtiness with coeds

5. Sinéad O'Connor for blasting the Pope

6. Björk for her pregnant appearance

7. Courtney Love for MTV naughtiness with Madonna

8. John Lennon for art films

9. Nine Inch Nails for attracting the FBI

10. Bob Dylan for his Live Aid disaster

##  Rock Stars Do the Dumbest Things with Girlfriends/Boyfriends

1. Led Zeppelin for the mudshark, the octopus…

2. Boy George for his love spats

3. Gregg Allman for Cher

4. Mötley Crüe for Pamela, mud-wrestling, and so much more

5. David Bowie for his chit-chat

6. Jayne (Wayne) County for David Bowie

7. 2 Live Crew for the golf club

8. Keith Moon for his appetite in Indian restaurants

9. Vanilla Ice for Madonna

10. The Sex Pistols for a great, mushy mess

## 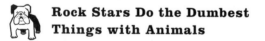 Rock Stars Do the Dumbest Things with Animals

1. Michael Jackson for his chimp, Bubbles

2. Elvis Presley for his chimp, Scatter

3. Ozzy Osbourne for the bat

4. Alice Cooper for his chicken

5. k.d. Lang for Meat Stinks

6. Linda McCartney for her sheep

7. Madonna for her psycho chihuahua

8. ZZ Top for their wildlife tour

9. Diana Ross for her pooches

10. Biggie Smalls (The Notorious B.I.G.) for Tupac

### Rock Stars Do the Dumbest Things with Money

1. John Denver for the Hunger Project

2. Michael Jackson for making confetti

3. Queen for Freddie's shopping

4. Van Halen for David Lee Roth's foot bath

5. Neil Young for more bass

6. Elton John for his wardrobe

7. Janet Jackson for her coffee enema

8. The Beach Boys for investing in Charles Manson

9. The Bee Gees for buying their own records

10. Fleetwood Mac for their cocaine tab

### Rock Stars Do the Dumbest Things to Each Other

1. The Kinks for Ray and Dave

2. Oasis for Noel and Liam

3. Mick Jagger for Keith

4. The Who for Pete and Roger

5. The Carpenters for Karen and Richard

6. Fleetwood Mac for Lindsey and Stevie

7. Pink Floyd for Roger and David

8. Courtney Love for Kurt

9. John Lennon for Yoko

10. Guns N' Roses for Axl

## Rock Stars Do the Dumbest Things to Get Arrested

1. James Brown for shooting stuff

2. Chuck Berry for his peek-a-boo potty

3. The Mamas and the Papas for frequent drugstore visits

4. Bobby Brown for his temper

5. Ozzy Osbourne for remembering the Alamo

6. Little Richard for the men's room

7. The Eagles for entertaining the young

8. Rick James for romantic evenings

9. Ted Nugent for flaming arrows

10 David Crosby for his luggage

## Rock Stars Do the Dumbest Things with Lyrics

1. 2 Live Crew for being nasty

2. Linda McCartney for nonsense

3. Bob Geldof for celebrating mass murder

4. Chuck Berry for his greatest hit

5. Elvis Presley for his Hawaiian improvisation

6. Tupac Shakur for annoying Biggie (The Notorious B.I.G.)

7. Milli Vanilli for faking it

8. Frank Zappa for Thing-Fish

9. Ice-T for annoying the police

10. Björk for her faux Icelandic

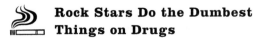

## Rock Stars Do the Dumbest Things on Drugs

1. Keith Richards for skiing

2. The Butthole Surfers for suggestive interviews

3. The Allman Brothers Band for their courtroom testimony

4. Aerosmith for their cosmetics

5. The Beach Boys for staying in bed

6. Elvis Presley for bad judgment

7. Fleetwood Mac for fiddling with the piano

8. The Replacements for the diaper

9. David Crosby for the spaghetti incident

10. Mötley Crüe for coming back from the dead

## Rock Stars Do the Dumbest Things, Just Like Spinal Tap

1. Metallica for the *Black Album*

2. Boy George for being trapped onstage

3. Aerosmith for the backstage food

4. Van Halen for the backstage food

5. U2 for the pod disaster

6. Elton John for bragging about his size

7. KISS for lifting from "Big Bottom"

8. Pink Floyd for their touring extravaganzas

9. Depeche Mode for their touring extravaganzas

10. Kurt Cobain for his video viewing habits

## Rock Fans Do the Dumbest Things

1. Björk for the fan-mail bomber
2. Oasis for the pill-retrievers
3. The Allman Brothers Band for the parachutist
4. Elvis for the grave robbers
5. Bob Dylan for the garbage sifter
6. G.G. Allin for the folks at the funeral
7. The Grateful Dead for the Spinners
8. Marilyn Manson for the felt-tip-pen-lover
9. Alice Cooper for getting hung up
10. David Bowie for kissing the boot

## The Dumbest Rock Stars of All Time

1. Michael Jackson
2. Led Zeppelin
3. Elvis Presley
4. Keith Moon
5. Mötley Crüe
6. Courtney Love
7. Ozzy Osbourne
8. John Lennon
9. The Beach Boys
10. James Brown

# BiBLiOGRAPHY

**Following is a list** of the main sources used in compiling all the dumb stuff included in this book.

## PERIODICALS

The Austin American Statesman
The Austin Chronicle
CAKE
Cosmopolitan
Creem
Esquire
Hit Parader
Movie Mirror
Musician
The National Enquirer

The New York Times
People
Rolling Stone
The Source
Spin
Vanity Fair
Vibe
The Village Voice
Yahoo Internet Life

## WEB REFERENCE SITES

(Please note that Internet Web sites frequently change their URL addresses.)

**Addicted to Noise**
http://www.addict.com

**Cybersleaze**
http://metaverse.com/vibe/sleaze/index.html

**E! Online News**
http://www.eonline.com

**Excite**
http://www.excite.com

**Imusic**
http://imusic.interserv.com

**JAM! Showbiz**
http://www.canoe.ca/search/jamsearch.html

**Mr. Showbiz**
http://www.mrshowbiz.com

**MTV Online**
http://www.mtv.com

**People Online**
http://www.people.com

**Ultimate Band List**
http://www.ubl.com

**Wall of Sound**
http://www.wallofsound.com

## REFERENCE BOOKS

Bogdanov, Vladimar, Michael Erlewine, and Chris Woodstra, eds. *All Music Guide to Rock.* San Francisco: Miller Freeman, 1995.

Heatley, Michael, ed. *The Ultimate Encyclopedia of Rock.* New York: HarperPerennial, 1993.

Krebs, Gary. *Rock and Roll Reader's Guide.* New York: Billboard Books, 1997.

Hale, Mark. *Headbangers: The Worldwide MegaBook of Heavy Metal Bands.* Ann Arbor: Popular Culture Ink, 1993.

Lazell, Barry, ed. *Rock Movers and Shakers: The A To Z of the People Who Made Rock Happen*. New York: Billboard Books, 1989.

Marsh, David, and James Bernard. *The New Book of Rock Lists*. New York: Simon and Schuster, 1994.

Rees, Dafydd, and Luke Crampton. *The Encyclopedia of Rock Stars*. New York: DK Publishing, 1996.

Romanowski, Patricia, and Holly George-Warren, eds. *The New Rolling Stone Encyclopedia of Rock and Roll*. New York: Fireside Books, 1995.

## OTHER BOOKS

Amende, Coral. *Hollywood Confidential: An Insider's Look at the Public Careers and Private Lives of Hollywood's Rich and Famous*. New York: Plume/Penguin, 1997.

Andersen, Christopher. *Jagger: Unauthorized*. New York: Delacorte Press, 1993.

———. *Michael Jackson Unauthorized*. New York: Pocket Books, 1995.

Aykroyd, Lucas. *1984: The Ultimate Van Halen Trivia Book*. Victoria, Canada: Trafford, 1997.

Azerad, Michael. *Come As You Are: The Story of Nirvana*. New York: Doubleday, 1993.

Baker, Glenn A. *Monkeemania: The True Story of the Monkees*. New York: St. Martin's Press, 1986.

Balfour, Victoria. *Rock Wives: The Hard Lives and Good Times of the Wives, Girlfriends, and Groupies of Rock and Roll*. New York: William Morrow, 1986.

Bennahum, David. *k.d. lang: In Her Own Words*. London: Omnibus Press, 1995.

Bessman, Jim. *The Ramones: An American Band*. New York: St. Martin's Press, 1993.

Blayney, David. *Keith Richards: The Biography*. New York: Poseidon Press, 1992.

———. *Sharp-Dressed Men*. New York: Hyperion, 1995.

Boy George, with Spencer Bright. *Take It Like a Man: The Autobiography of Boy George*. New York: HarperCollins, 1995.

Brown, James, with Bruce Tucker. *James Brown: The Godfather of Soul*. New York: Macmillan, 1986.

Butler, Dougal. *Full Moon: The Amazing Rock and Roll Life of Keith Moon, Late of the Who, Late of the Earth*. New York: William Morrow, 1981.

Cader, Michael. *Famous Mugs: Arresting Photos and Felonious Facts for Hundreds of Stars Behind Bars*. Kansas City: Andrews and McMeel, 1996.

Campbell, Luther, and John R. Miller. *As Nasty As They Wanna Be: The Uncensored Story of Luther Campbell of the 2 Live Crew*. New York: Barricade Books, 1992.

Cassidy, David, with Chip Deffaa. *C'mon Get Happy*. New York: Warner Books, 1994.

Clayson, Alan. *Ringo Starr: Straight Man or Joker*. New York: Paragon House, 1991.

Coffey, Frank. *The Complete Idiot's Guide to Elvis*. New York: Alpha Books, 1997.

Cole, Richard. *Stairway to Heaven: Led Zeppelin Uncensored*. New York: HarperCollins, 1992.

Coleman, Ray. *The Carpenters: The Untold Story*. New York: HarperCollins, 1994.

Considine, J.D. *Van Halen*. New York: Quill, 1985.

Cooper, Alice, with Steven Gaines. *Me, Alice: The Autobiography of Alice Cooper*. New York: G.P. Putnam's Sons, 1976.

County, Jayne, with Rupert Smith. *Man Enough to Be A Woman*. London: Serpent's Tail, 1995.

Crosby, David, and Carl Gottlieb. *Long Time Gone: The Autobiography of David Crosby*. New York: Doubleday, 1988.

Dalton, David. *El Sid: Saint Vicious*. New York: St. Martin's Press, 1997.

Davies, Dave. *Kink: The Outrageous Story of My Wild Years as the Founder and Lead Guitarist of the Kinks*. New York: Hyperion, 1996.

Davis, Stephen. *Walk This Way: The Autobiography of Aerosmith*. New York: Avon Books, 1997.

Denver, John, with Arthur Tobier. *Take Me Home: An Autobiography*. New York: Harmony Books, 1994.

Des Barres, Pamela. *Rock Bottom: Dark Moments in Music Babylon*. New York: St. Martin's Press, 1996.

Dineen, Catherine. *In His Own Words: Michael Jackson*. London: Omnibus Press, 1993.

Dolenz, Mickey, and Mark Bego. *I'm a Believer: My Life of Monkees, Music, and Madness*. New York: Hyperion, 1993.

Dome, Malcolm, ed. *AC/DC: The* KERRANG! *Files* London: Virgin Books, 1995.

Downing, David. *A Dreamer of Pictures: Neil Young, The Man and His Music*. New York: Da Capo Press, 1994.

Draper, Robert. *ZZ Top*. New York: Ballantine Books, 1984.

Dunphy, Eamon. *Unforgettable Fire: Past, Present, and Future—The Definitive Biography of U2*. New York: Warner Books, 1987.

*Duran Duran: In Their Own Words*. London: Omnibus Press, 1983.

Fein, Art. *Rhino Presents the Greatest Rock and Roll Stories: The Most Outrageous, Magical and Scandalous Events in the History of Rock and Roll!* Los Angeles: General Publishing Group, 1996.

Fleetwood, Mick, with Stephen Davis. *Fleetwood: My Life and Adventures in Fleetwood Mac*. New York: William Morrow, 1990.

Frankel, Jennie Louise, ed. *You'll Never Make Love in This Town Again*. Los Angeles: Dove Books, 1995.

Freeman, Scott. *Midnight Riders: The Story of the Allman Brothers Band*. Boston: Little, Brown, 1995.

Frost, Deborah. *ZZ Top: Bad and Worldwide*. New York: Collier Books, 1985.

Gaines, Steven. *Heroes and Villains: The True Story of the Beach Boys*. New York: Signet, 1986.

Gans, David. *Conversations with the Dead*. New York: Citadel Underground, 1991.

———. *Talking Heads: The Band and Their Music*. New York: Avon, 1985.

Geldof, Bob, with Paul Vallely. *Is That It?* New York: Weidenfeld and Nicolson, 1986.

Geller, Debbie, and Tom Hibbert. *Billy Joel: An Illustrated Biography*. New York: McGraw-Hill, 1985.

Gibb, Barry, Robin Gibb, and Maurice Gibb, as told to David Leaf. *Bee Gees: The Authorized Biography*. New York: Delilah/Delta Special, 1979.

Giuliano, Geoffrey. *Dark Horse: The Private Life of George Harrison*. New York: Dutton, 1990.

Golden, Anna Louise. *The Spice Girls: The Uncensored Story Behind Pop's Biggest Phenomenon*. London: Ballantine Books, 1997.

Goldman, Albert. *The Lives of John Lennon*. New York: William Morrow, 1988.

Goldstein, Toby. *Duran Duran*. New York: Ballantine Books, 1985.

Green, Joey. *The Partridge Family Album: The Official Get Happy Guide to America's Grooviest Television Family*. New York: HarperPerennial, 1994.

Guiliano, Geoffrey. *Blackbird: The Life and Times of Paul McCartney*. New York: Dutton, 1991.

———. *Rod Stewart: Vagabond Heart*. New York: Carrol and Graf, 1993.

Gunn, Jacky, and Jim Jenkins. *Queen: As It Began*. New York: Hyperion, 1992.

Herman, Gary. *Rock 'N Roll Babylon*. New York: Pedigree Books, 1982.

Hewitt, Paolo. *Getting High: The Adventures of Oasis*. New York: Hyperion, 1997.

Heyland, Clinton. *Dylan: Behind the Shades*. New York: Viking, 1991.

Hopkins, Jerry, and Danny Sugerman. *No One Here Gets Out Alive*. New York: Warner Books, 1995.

Hubner, John and Lindsey Gruson. *Monkey on a Stick: Murder, Madness and the Hare Krishnas*. New York: Penguin, 1988.

Huxley, Martin. *Aerosmith: The Fall and Rise of Rock's Greatest Band*. New York: St. Martin's Press, 1995.

———. *Nine Inch Nails*. New York: St. Martin's/Griffin, 1997.

Ice-T, as told to Heidi Siegmund. *Ice Opinion: Who Gives a F***?* New York: St. Martin's Press, 1994

Jackson, LaToya, with Patricia Romanowski. *LaToya: Growing Up in the Jackson Family*. New York: Signet, 1992.

Jagger, Mick. *Mick Jagger in His Own Words*. New York: Delilah/Putnam, 1982.

Krugman, Michael. *Oasis: Supersonic Supernova*. New York: St. Martin's/Griffin, 1997.

Lefcowitz, Eric. *The Monkee's Tale*. San Francisco: Last Gasp, 1989.

Lennon, Nigey. *Being Frank: My Time with Frank Zappa*. Los Angeles: Classic Books, 1995.

Malloy, Merrit. *The Great Rock 'N Roll Quote Book*. New York: St. Martin's/Griffin, 1995.

Manson, Marilyn, with Neil Strauss. *The Long Hard Road Out of Hell*. New York: HarperCollins, 1998.

Marsh, Dave. *Before I Get Old: The Story of The Who*. New York: St. Martin's, 1983.

McKeon, Elizabeth, and Linda Everett. *The Quotable King*. Nashville: Cumberland House, 1997.

McNeil, Legs, and Gillian McCain. *Please Kill Me: The Uncensored Oral History of Punk*. New York: Penguin, 1997.

Mendelssohn, John. *The Kinks Kronikles*. New York: Quill, 1985.

Miles, Barry. *Frank Zappa: In His Own Words*. London: Omnibus Press, 1993.

———. *John Lennon: In His Own Words*. London: Omnibus Press, 1994.

———. *Paul McCartney: Many Years from Now*. New York: Henry Holt, 1997.

Monk, Noel E., and Jimmy Guterman. *12 Days on the Road: The Sex Pistols' U.S.A. Tour*. London: Sidgwick and Jackson, 1990.

Mylett, Howard. *Jimmy Page: Tangents within a Framework*. London: Omnibus Press, 1983.

Nash, Bruce, and Allan Zullo. *Amazing But True Elvis Facts*. Kansas City: Andrews and McMeel, 1995.

Nelson, George. *Cool it Now: The Authorized Biography of New Edition*. Chicago: Contemporary Books, 1986.

Nickson, Chris. *Mariah Carey: Her Story*. New York: St. Martin's/Griffin, 1995.

Norman, Philip. *Elton John*. New York: Harmony Books, 1991.

———. *SHOUT! The Beatles in Their Generation*. New York: Fireside Books, 1996.

Obstfeld, Raymond, and Patricia Fitzgerald. *Jabberrock: The Ultimate Book of Rock 'N' Roll Quotations*. New York: Henry Holt, 1997.

Phillips, John, with Jim Jerome. *Papa John: A Music Legend's Shattering Journey Through Sex, Drugs, and Rock 'n' Roll*. New York: Dolphin Books, 1986.

Pop, Iggy. *I Need More*. Los Angeles: 2.13.61 Publications, 1997.

Rettenmund, Matthew. *Encyclopedia Madonnica*. New York: St. Martin's Press, 1995.

Editors of *Rolling Stone*. *Garcia*. Boston: Little, Brown, 1995.

————. *U2: The Ultimate Compendium of Interviews, Articles, Facts and Opinions.* New York: Rolling Stone Press, 1994.

Rossi, Melissa. *Courtney Love: Queen of Noise—A Most Unauthorized Biography.* New York: Pocket Books, 1996.

Roth, David Lee. *Crazy From the Heat.* New York: Hyperion, 1997.

RuPaul. *Lettin' It All Hang Out.* New York: Hyperion, 1995.

St. Michael, Mick. *Madonna: In Her Own Words.* London: Omnibus Press, 1990.

————. *Queen: In Their Own Words.* London: Omnibus Press, 1992.

Sandford, Christopher. *Bowie: Loving the Alien.* London: Little, Brown, 1996.

Schaffner, Nicholas. *Saucerful of Secrets: The Pink Floyd Odyssey.* New York: Harmony Books, 1991.

Seminara, George. *Mug Shots: Celebrities Under Arrest.* New York: St. Martin's/Griffin, 1996.

Sexton, Adam. *Rap On Rap: Straight-Up Talk on Hip-Hop Culture.* New York: Delta, 1995.

Shapiro, Marc. *The Long Run: The Story of The Eagles.* London: Omnibus Press, 1995.

Shenk, David, and Steve Silverman. *Skeleton Key: A Dictionary for Deadheads.* New York: Doubleday, 1994.

Stallings, Penny. *Rock 'N' Roll Confidential.* Boston: Little, Brown, 1984.

Starr, Victoria. *k.d. lang: All You Get Is Me.* New York: St. Martin's Press, 1994.

Stern, Howard. *Private Parts.* New York: Simon and Schuster, 1993.

Taraborrelli, J. Randy. *Call Her Miss Ross.* New York: Birch Lane Press, 1989.

————. *Michael Jackson: The Magic and The Madness.* New York: Birch Lane Press, 1991.

Thompson, Dave. *Depeche Mode: Some Great Reward.* New York: St. Martin's Press, 1994.

————. *Never Fade Away: The Kurt Cobain Story.* New York: St. Martin's Press, 1994.

————. *Perry Farrell: The Saga of a Hypester.* New York: St. Martin's Press/Griffin, 1995.

Troy, Sandy. *Captain Trips: A Biography of Jerry Garcia.* New York: Thunder's Mouth Press, 1994.

Walley, David. *No Commercial Potential: The Saga of Frank Zappa.* New York: Da Capo Press, 1996.

Ward, Burt. *Boy Wonder: My Life in Tights.* Los Angeles: Logical Figments Books, 1995.

Watson, Ben. *Zappa: The Negative Dialectics of Poodle Play.* New York: St. Martin's Press, 1993.

White, Armond. *Rebel for the Hell of It: The Life of Tupac Shakur.* New York: Thunder's Mouth Press, 1997.

White, Charles. *The Life and Times of Little Richard: The Quazar of Rock.* New York: Harmony Books, 1984.

*The Who: In Their Own Words.* New York: Quick Fox, 1979.

Wise, Nick. *The Beach Boys: In Their Own Words.* London: Omnibus Press, 1995.

Williams, Christian. *Bob Dylan: In His Own Words.* London: Omnibus Press, 1993.

Wiseman, Rich. *Neil Diamond: Solitary Star.* New York: Dodd, Mead and Co., 1987.

Wood, Ron, with Bill German. *Ron Wood: The Works.* New York: Harper and Row, 1987

Wyman, Bill, with Ray Coleman. *Stone Alone: The Story of a Rock 'n' Roll Band.* New York: Viking, 1990.

Zimmer, Dave. *Crosby, Stills and Nash.* New York: St. Martin's Press, 1985.

# INDEX

INDEX

# ABOUT THE AUTHORS

**Margaret Moser** has been writing about rock and roll for alternative newspapers since 1976. She is the daughter of Seattle psychologist Phyllis Jackson Stegall (author of *Boomerang Kids*), and sister of designer Stephen MacMillan Moser. Margaret Moser has edited tourist magazines in Hawaii, performed on MTV's *The Cutting Edge* with Dino Lee and His White Trash Revue, and directs the annual Austin Music Awards show for the South by Southwest Music and Media Conference. Moser has written for such publications as the *Austin Sun*, the *Austin American-Statesman*, *Performance* magazine, *Pop Culture Press*, the *Rocky Mountain Musical Express*, and is an annual contributor to the *Village Voice's* "Pazz and Jop Critics' Poll." She has appeared in films such as *Roadie* (starring Meat Loaf and Alice Cooper) and *Outlaw Blues* (with Peter Fonda and Susan St. James), was featured in wrestling entrepreneur Jimmy Hart's "We Hate School" video, as well as being location manager for Talking Heads' "This Must Be the Place" video.

Moser has been interviewed for, quoted in, contributed to, or been referenced in such books as *Stevie Ray Vaughan: Caught in the Crossfire* by Joe Nick Patoski and Bill Crawford; *Stevie Ray Vaughan: Soul to Soul* by Keri Leigh; *Rolling Stone's Rock of Ages* by Ed Ward, Ken Tucker, and Geoffrey Stokes; *Texas Rhythm Texas Rhyme* by Larry Willoughby; *Michael Bloomfield: The Rise and Fall of a Guitar Star* by Ed Ward; *Dissonant Identities: The Rock and Roll Scene in Austin, Texas* by Barry Shank; and *Generation Eccch!* by Jason Cohen and Michael Krugman. Moser also regularly appears on panels at the South by Southwest Music and Media Conference, including "scenemakers" with Art Fein and SubPop's Jonathan Poneman; "Women Rock Critics" with Karen Schoemer and Gina Arnold; and "Groupies" with Ann Powers and Pamela Des Barres. Moser has also written liner notes and band biographies for musicians like Candy Kane and the Johnny Depp-Gibby Haynes aggregation "P" as well as cohosting *Check This Action* for the Austin Music Network.

Margaret Moser is currently a senior editor at the *Austin Chronicle*, where she writes about multimedia, television, books, and—what else?—rock and roll.

**Bill Crawford** started writing plays at prep school in Massachusetts and hasn't stopped writing since. Crawford studied religion at Harvard University and spent a year in south India working with a traveling religious theater troupe. Putting up with foul language, drinking, smoking, and all-night performances in India was excellent preparation for writing about rock and roll.

Crawford came to Texas and worked at a beautiful music station in Midland before moving to Austin. He got an MBA from the University of Texas at Austin while writing for *Third Coast,* a city magazine. Crawford enjoyed writing much more than business. He has written pieces for *Texas Monthly,* the *Austin Chronicle, Runner's World, American Way,* and a number of other magazines. Crawford is the coauthor of three previous books: *Border Radio: Quacks, Yodelers, Pitchmen, Psychics and Other Amazing Broadcasters of the American Airwaves* (Texas Monthly Press, 1987); *Cerealizing America: The Unsweetened Story of American Breakfast Cereal* (Faber and Faber, 1995); and *Stevie Ray Vaughan: Caught in the Crossfire* (Little, Brown, 1993), which is currently under motion-picture option.

In addition to writing books and articles, Crawford has written extensively for radio, television, and multimedia. In the early 1980s, he produced a series of reports on the Austin music scene for MTV Music News as well as music videos including "Gomer Pyle is God." For seven years, he wrote and hosted the syndicated public radio program *Asian Communiqué.* He is currently the writer and host for *The Dad Show,* a talk radio program "for dads and anyone who's ever had a dad," aired each week on KAZI in Austin, Texas. Crawford has written award-winning local cable programs including a comedy show called *The International Fishing Show* and a kid's show called *The Joe Show.* Crawford wrote the award-winning CD-Rom *Nile: Passage to Egypt,* published by the Discovery Channel. He has contributed to Discovery Online and a number of other online services.

Crawford is married to a brilliant and successful attorney, which is how he can afford to have so much fun. He has two children and lives in Austin, Texas.

★　★　★　★

### Also available from Renaissance Books:

*Movie Stars Do the Dumbest Things*
by Margaret Moser, Michael Bertin, and Bill Crawford
ISBN: 1-58063-107-X • $ 14.95

*Republicans Do the Dumbest Things*
by Bill Crawford
ISBN: 1-58063-111-8 • $9.95

*Democrats Do the Dumbest Things*
by Bill Crawford
ISBN: 1-58063-112-6 • $9.95

And visit www.dumbest.com

**TO ORDER PLEASE CALL**
1-800-452-5589